THE TOPOGRAPHIC MAP MYSTERY

Geology's Unrecognized Paradigm Problem

Revised Edition

Eric Clausen

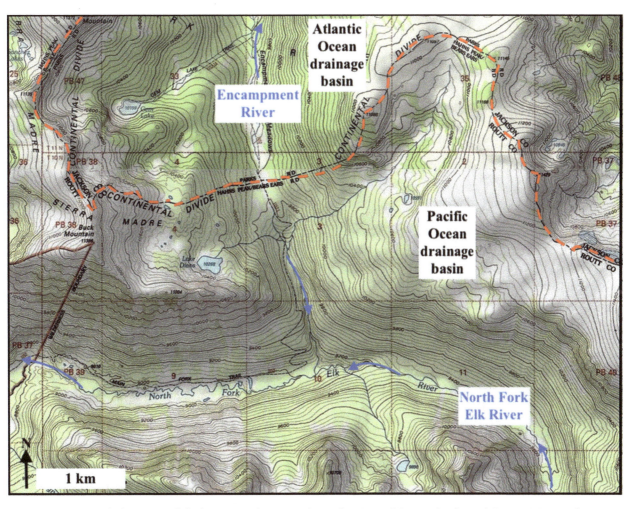

Front cover and above: Modified topographic map from the United States Geological Survey National Map website showing a northcentral Colorado mountain pass that the accepted geology and glacial history paradigm does not satisfactorily explain. The contour interval is 40 feet (about 12 meters). Top left corner: 40° 53' 21.645" N, 106° 44' 59.352" W.

Author's Tranquility Press

ATLANTA, GEORGIA

Eric Clausen / Author's Tranquility Press
3900 N Commerce Dr. Suite 300 #1255
Atlanta, GA 30344
www.authorstranquilitypress.com

Ordering Information:
Quantity sales. Special discounts are available on quantity purchases by corporations, associations, and others. For details, contact the "Special Sales Department" at the address above.

The topographic Map Mystery / Eric Clausen
Hardback: 978-1-964037-02-8
Paperback: 978-1-963636-96-3
eBook: 978-1-963636-97-0

TABLE OF CONTENTS

Preface to the Revised Edition

This book tells a scientific detective story. It is the story of anomalous evidence which the geology research community's accepted geology and glacial history paradigm (accepted paradigm) has never satisfactorily explained. The anomalous evidence which geologists typically ignore includes most drainage system and erosional landform features which blanket almost all continental areas and which are best seen on detailed topographic maps. The book's first edition was written as a red flag to warn geologists that they cannot ignore what the topographic map drainage system and erosional landform evidence has to say. The geology research community cannot properly understand Cenozoic geology and glacial history unless the well-mapped, but ignored drainage system and erosional landform evidence is also understood.

The first edition and this revised edition illustrate dozens of examples of large-scale drainage system and erosional landform features found throughout the continental United States which the accepted paradigm has never satisfactorily explained. Descriptions of those illustrated landform features in chapters 2-9 in this edition have been revised to better explain how a new and fundamentally different geology and glacial history paradigm (new paradigm) explains what the accepted paradigm has never explained. Chapters 10 and 11 describe how by trying to explain a North Dakota erosional escarpment's origin one set of anomalous evidence kept leading to other sets of anomalous evidence before the new paradigm finally emerged.

The reference section now includes a list of all of my publications including abstracts which document major steps taken as one hypothesis after another was considered during what became a multiple decade search for a topographic map mystery solution. Chapters 10-15 also provide information about my interactions with the larger geology research community (which are still on-going). Those interactions suggest the vast majority of today's geologists are completely unaware that most of the topographic map drainage system and erosional landform evidence has never been satisfactorily explained and that the geology research community has no clue as to what the well-mapped topographic map evidence has to say.

Eric Clausen

Jenkintown, PA

Chapter 1: Introduction

I arrived in 1961 as a naive freshman student on the Columbia University campus without well-thought-out future plans. My required and elective freshman year classes were not exciting and one night I decided to study the college catalog looking for more interesting classes. The resulting short list ended up with a few of what looked like really appealing classes. Two of those classes were graduate level geology courses but which were open to undergraduate geology majors, and then only with the instructor's permission. One of those intriguing classes was "Topographic Map Interpretation." United States Geological Survey (USGS) topographic maps had always fascinated me. My father, who taught Botany at Cornell University, used USGS topographic maps when planning field studies and as a Boy Scout I had used topographic maps on hiking and camping trips. The idea of spending an entire semester taking an advanced graduate-level course that taught how to interpret geologic information on the USGS published topographic maps was tempting and something I wanted to do.

After switching majors and three years later I was a Columbia College senior majoring in geology and finally able to enroll in Arthur Strahler's graduate level "Topographic Map Interpretation" class. At that time the class was required for many of the Columbia University Geology Department graduate students and other than three undergraduate geology majors including myself all of my 30 or so classmates were graduate students. I found the class fascinating as we learned how geologic features could be interpreted from topographic map evidence. Soon I was explaining topographic map features to several of my graduate student classmates (which seemed odd because some of those same class members served as teaching assistants in undergraduate geology classes which I was still taking). I considered the course to be one of the best classes I took at Columbia University, however many of my classmates probably considered the topographic map interpretation class to be a waste of their time.

That same academic year I along with an almost identical set of classmates enrolled in Arthur Strahler's graduate level "Geomorphology" class, which at that time was another requirement for many of the Columbia University Geology Department graduate students. Strahler used the then newly published (1965) *Regional Geomorphology of the United States* by W. D. Thornbury as the class textbook. What impressed me most about that class were the large number of unsolved drainage history and erosional landform origin problems found in almost every United States region. It seemed as though both Strahler and the textbook were directly and indirectly posing intriguing but yet to be answered questions about many of what I considered to be the most obvious large-scale United States erosional landform and drainage system features. I left that class believing those unanswered questions would someday be answered, however my classmates appeared to be much more interested in completely different geologic problems.

Two years after obtaining my undergraduate degree Arthur Strahler left Columbia University to become a fulltime academic author and the Geology Department discontinued the topographic map interpretation and geomorphology classes. At the time I was pursuing graduate studies at the University of Wyoming where my adviser Brainerd Mears, Jr. (who in the late 1940s had been one of Strahler's graduate students) assigned several of Strahler's published research papers through which I learned for the first time that in the late 1940s Strahler had transitioned from being a historical qualitative geomorphologist to being what he called a quantitative-dynamic geomorphologist. By making his transition, Strahler helped to change geomorphology's direction. I was surprised to learn about Strahler's transition (see Strahler 1952) after having recently taken courses in which Strahler presented himself as a historical qualitative geomorphologist and had posed numerous unanswered questions that only historical qualitative geomorphology research techniques such as topographic map interpretation could answer.

Also, I learned for the first time that an inability to explain Appalachian region drainage development in his PhD thesis project (see Strahler 1945) led Strahler to transition from historical qualitative geomorphology research to quantitative-dynamic geomorphology and that Strahler's transition had contributed to historical qualitative geomorphology's demise. Yet, at no time during the two classes I took from him did Strahler give any indication of having made such a transition. I was puzzled. The unanswered drainage history and erosional landform origin questions Strahler had raised were questions any serious geologist should want to see answered. Information needed to answer those questions was available on the USGS detailed topographic maps, and the topographic map interpretation methods Strahler taught were logical and made sense. Yet, for some reason, the topographic map evidence did not provide satisfactory answers. And to make the situation even more puzzling, Strahler, later in his life, claimed that trying to find answers to those types of research questions was largely a waste of time.

Strahler was a skilled topographic map interpreter and if anyone should have been able to answer the historical qualitative geomorphology type drainage system and erosional landform origin questions it would have been Strahler. Unlike many geomorphologists Strahler's office was located just down the hall from Columbia University's large collection of USGS topographic maps so he had no problem when wanting to access maps of any region. The problem was, no matter how hard Strahler tried he could not use topographic map interpretation methods to satisfactorily answer his drainage system and erosional landform questions. The problem which Strahler never recognized was that he kept trying to answer those questions in ways that were consistent with the geologic and glacial history which glacial geologists, vertebrate paleontologists, stratigraphers, and other geologists had developed.

Strahler's inability to answer the many unanswered drainage system and erosional landform questions was not unique. Early in the 20th century historical qualitative geomorphology in which topographic map interpretation was an important research tool had been a promising research field and the USGS was engaged in a long-term project to provide detailed topographic map coverage for all United States regions. Geomorphologists at that time expected USGS detailed topographic maps to provide the information needed to answer many of their drainage history and erosional landform origin questions. Yet, by the mid-20th-century, in spite of expanding topographic map coverage and improving map quality, almost all geomorphologists had turned away from or were turning away from historical qualitative geomorphology research methods (such as topographic map interpretation) and had left or were leaving their drainage system and erosional landform origin questions unanswered.

I was well into my career teaching geology at North Dakota's Minot State University before realizing the inability of geomorphologists to use detailed topographic map evidence to answer the unanswered historical geomorphology type drainage system and erosional landform origin questions meant the geology research community had never determined how most of the large-scale drainage systems and erosional landforms had originated and appeared to have no interest in trying to correct that knowledge deficiency. Up until that time I had honestly believed the geologic literature would eventually answer many of the unanswered historical geomorphology type landform origin questions, but my observations of the geologic literature showed no one appeared to be trying to find answers for the many still unanswered historical qualitative geomorphology type drainage history and erosional landform questions.

My long-held belief that somewhere somebody in the geology research community would answer at least some of the unanswered historical geomorphology type landform origin questions caused me to spend countless hours over a period of many years repeatedly searching the Minot State library and the libraries of more than a dozen major research universities for research reports in which unanswered historical geomorphology type drainage system and erosional landform origin questions were being addressed. I kept looking unsuccessfully for research reports describing how features such as specific drainage systems, drainage divides, mountain passes, water gaps, through valleys (valleys crossing a drainage divide), canyons cut across mountain ranges, erosional escarpments, and abrupt river and stream direction changes had been formed.

North Dakota's Missouri Escarpment which can be seen from the Minot State campus illustrates an excellent example of what I kept finding. According to Thornbury (1965, p. 290) the Missouri Escarpment "represents a rise of 300 to 600 feet [or 92 to 184 meters] from the level of the Central Lowlands to the surface of the Missouri Plateau: The origin of this escarpment is uncertain: it apparently is not the product of a particular resistant formation; more likely it marks the boundary between two topographic levels of erosion in the Central Lowlands and the Great Plains." The Missouri Escarpment extends for more than 1000 kilometers from eastern Alberta in a southeast direction across southern Saskatchewan and northwest North Dakota to central North Dakota where it turns in a south direction to eventually reach southcentral South Dakota.

Something formed the Missouri Escarpment, but my search did not find answers. The escarpment is sometimes mentioned and described with the suggestion being made or at least implied that one or more continental icesheets modified a preglacial escarpment (which left the escarpment origin question unanswered). My own observations showed a relationship between the escarpment and the continental icesheet(s), but also the continental icesheet(s) should have destroyed any preglacial escarpment formed on North Dakota's easily eroded surficial bedrock. At the time I was confused—here was a large-scale landform which extended for more than 1000 kilometers and the geology research community had no clue as to what it was. The Missouri Escarpment was evidence of something, but the geology research community did not know or even seem to care what that something was.

Like with the unanswered Missouri Escarpment origin question my search to determine how other large-scale erosional landforms had been formed sometimes encountered literature in which features such as East-West Continental Divide were mentioned and even described. But almost always the origin question was not addressed or was addressed in unsatisfactory and controversial ways. Often my search did not find any published geologic literature at all mentioning, much less explaining the specific large-scale drainage system and erosional landform features for which I sought explanations. Eventually after many years of searching I finally recognized that without ever publicly surrendering, the geology research community had simply given up on trying to answer the unanswered historical qualitative geomorphology type research questions and now is just ignoring the topographic map drainage system and erosional landform evidence.

What happened, although no one in the geology research community has officially said so, is historical qualitative geomorphologists, when trying to interpret topographic map drainage systems and erosional landform evidence, ran into a solid wall of what Thomas Kuhn, in his (1970) book *The Structure of Scientific Revolutions*, refers to as anomalous evidence or evidence an accepted scientific paradigm cannot satisfactorily explain. According to Kuhn, scientific paradigms determine how a scientific research discipline governs its research and are chosen because the paradigm rules and assumptions enable researchers to communicate with each other as they try to explain observed evidence. Kuhn argues scientific paradigms are essential and enable scientists to build on each other's work which is what enables each scientific discipline to advance.

Kuhn also notes every scientific discipline, from time to time, encounters anomalous evidence their accepted paradigm cannot satisfactorily explain. Such anomalous evidence, according to Kuhn, is dealt with in one of three ways. First, a way is eventually found (without significantly changing the accepted paradigm) to explain the problematic evidence, and the accepted paradigm continues without interruption. Second, the anomalous evidence is described—or mapped—and set aside for future scientists to explain, which, for all practical purposes, is what has happened with much of the topographic map drainage system and erosional landform evidence. Third, the anomalous evidence leads to development of a new paradigm which is able to explain what the accepted paradigm could not explain and to a battle over which of two competing paradigms should be used.

Publication of Thornbury's *Regional Geomorphology of the United States* (1965) might be considered to have been one of historical qualitative geomorphology's final gasps. Since that time, the geological literature has rarely included research addressing the historical qualitative geomorphology type questions which used historical qualitative geomorphology research methods such as topographic map interpretation. For all practical purposes, historical qualitative geomorphology as a research discipline has been dead for more than sixty years.

Modern-day geomorphologists may argue that newer and better research techniques have replaced historical qualitative geomorphology research techniques such as topographic map interpretation. However, the newer research techniques have not answered the drainage system and erosional landform origin type questions historical qualitative geomorphologists once asked and could not answer. Today, geomorphologists are addressing other types of research questions and show little or no interest in using topographic map interpretation methods to solve the types of research questions the historical qualitative geomorphologists left unanswered.

After historical qualitative geomorphology's premature demise, USGS topographic mapping continued unabated and each year, the USGS released hundreds of new topographic maps covering regions for which detailed topographic map coverage had been unavailable or improving previously published detailed topographic maps. Eventually, late in the twentieth century, the USGS had published detailed topographic maps covering the entire country. However, by that time, historical qualitative geomorphology research was dead and had not been done for decades, and almost no one in the geology research community was interested in studying the drainage system and erosional landform information the new and greatly improved topographic maps described.

By the beginning of the 21st-century topographic maps showed in great detail all United States drainage system and erosional landform features and were digitalized for broader distribution. Now USGS detailed topographic maps along with other map types and air photo and satellite imagery are available at the USGS National Map website and from a number of other sources. However, historical qualitative geomorphology as a research discipline for all practical purposes does not exist and the geology research community is showing no interest in using the easily available topographic map information to determine drainage system and erosional landform origins.

Geology is a science and good science requires all observable evidence to be addressed. Detailed topographic maps make drainage system and erosional landform evidence easy to observe and study, yet the geology research community has chosen, perhaps unknowingly, to omit that readily available evidence. The topographic map mystery is how long will it take for the geology research community to recognize that drainage systems and erosional landforms blanket almost all continental areas and detailed topographic maps represent one of the best ways to study how those features formed. And when the geology research community does recognize the value of the topographic map drainage system and erosional landform evidence, how will that evidence change the Cenozoic geology and glacial history story the geology research community now tells?

Chapter 2:
The Topographic Map Mystery Begins

The now accepted North American Cenozoic geology and glacial history paradigm (accepted paradigm) began with 19th century geologists interpretating what at that time was the known observable geologic evidence which included drainage patterns seen in figures 2.1 and 2.2. What those geologists, who lacked access to good maps, saw was Ohio River tributaries from the south and east were generally longer and drained larger regions than tributaries from the north and west and Missouri River tributaries from the south and west were usually longer and drained larger regions than tributaries from the north and east. Those drainage patterns were recognized at about the same time that geologists recognized continental icesheets had once covered much of North America's northern half. What those early geologists (who traveled in boats along lakes and rivers and on horseback or on foot when on land) observed was glacially transported and deposited debris was almost always located to the north and west of the Ohio River and to the north and east of the Missouri River. Further the early geologists noticed glacially deposited debris now partially filled valleys extending in north directions from where some of the long north-oriented tributaries now join what appeared to be icesheet-marginal Ohio and Missouri Rivers.

The 19th century geologists interpreted the above-described set of geologic evidence to mean the Ohio and Missouri River drainage routes developed when a continental icesheet blocked north-oriented preglacial drainage routes and forced water to flow along the icesheet margin. Evidence used in making this 19th-century interpretation was observable by anyone who took the time to look and used common sense logic, but only one interpretation was considered so no comparisons with alternate interpretations were made. That early interpretation became an accepted paradigm pillar upon which the geology research community has built and is still building its research. That 19th-century interpretation was made before the United States Geological Survey (USGS) topographic mapping project began. The USGS topographic mapping project is now complete and has introduced vast quantities of new drainage system evidence 19th-century geologists never knew existed, yet by the mid 20th century geomorphologists had given up on trying to interpret most of that yet to be explained topographic map drainage system evidence.

Figure 2.1 is a slightly modified map taken from a 1903 USGS Professional Paper (Tight, 1903) which illustrates what 19th-century geologists considered to be five preglacial north-oriented drainage basins (numbered 1, 2, 3, 7, and 8) now located in the larger Ohio River drainage basin. The figure 2.1 map was prepared when the USGS was just beginning to publish some of the region's first detailed topographic maps and Tight did not have access to the topographic map information now available. The interpretation that a continental icesheet blocked preglacial north- and northwest-oriented drainage basins so as to create today's Ohio River is a reasonable interpretation of the then known evidence, but there are other ways that same set of evidence could have been explained some of which could have led to completely different glacial history interpretations.

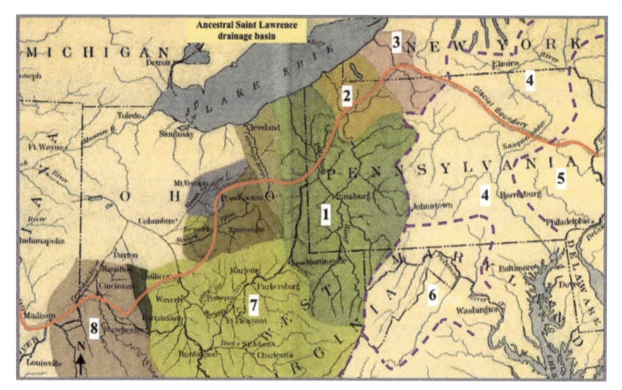

Figure 2.1: Modified map from Tight (1903, plate 1) showing "preglacial" drainage basins draining to the Ohio River identified as follows: (1) Monongahela, (2) Middle Allegheny, (3) Upper Allegheny, (7) Teays, and (8) Cincinnati. Draining to the Atlantic Ocean are the (4) Susquehanna, (5) Delaware, and (6) Potomac Rivers. The red line shows the icesheet's southern boundary.

A major implication of Tight's interpretation is that drainage basins numbered 1, 2, 3, 7, and 8 and their north- and northwest-oriented slopes predate the continental icesheet(s). A second implication is icesheet marginal lakes formed upstream from where the continental icesheet(s) had blocked each of the identified north- and northwest-oriented preglacial valleys with the lakes overflowing along the icesheet margin to form the Ohio River. A third implication is almost all, if not all, of the continental icesheet meltwater flowed down the Ohio River valley and did not flow in south directions across those north-oriented preglacial drainage basins. A fourth implication based on the abandoned valleys to the north and west of the present-day Ohio River valley is that in many places continental icesheet(s) did not deeply erode the underlying bedrock.

An alternate interpretation of the same evidence begins with a large continental icesheet occupying a deep "hole" in the North American continent. The deep "hole" was created by the icesheet's weight and by icesheet erosion. Immense south-oriented meltwater floods flowed across all regions south of the icesheet margin but were eventually reversed to flow into and across deep "hole" space which icesheet melting opened-up. At some point enough deep "hole" space was opened-up that the south-oriented meltwater floods were diverted from south to north and this diversion cooled the climate which froze the then north-oriented drainage around decaying first ice sheet remnants to create a second and much thinner icesheet. This alternate interpretation (perhaps with some tweaking) can explain all of the evidence that Tight described and would have led future geologists in a different direction from the direction the geology research community took.

Early geologists also interpreted north-oriented Missouri River headwaters and tributaries seen in figure 2.2 to have been components of what is now referred to as the preglacial north-oriented Bell River drainage system (see Jackson, 2018). Supporting this interpretation are abandoned valleys partially filled with glacially deposited debris that extend in a northward direction into and across Canada. The Missouri River in North and South Dakota roughly follows the southern and western margin of areas containing abundant fine- and coarse-grained glacially deposited debris. For this reason, most early geologists considered the Missouri River (downstream from its north-oriented headwaters) to have been formed when an icesheet margin blocked the north-oriented Missouri River headwaters and the north-oriented Yellowstone River, Little Missouri River, Cheyenne River (and other north- and northeast-oriented drainage routes not shown in the figure).

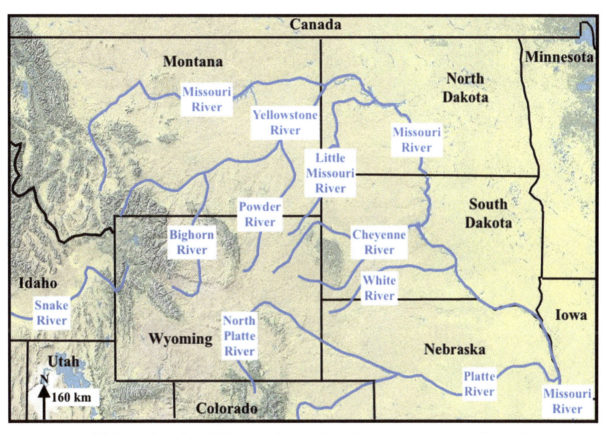

Figure 2.2: Modified map from the USGS National Map website showing major rivers in the northern Missouri River drainage basin region. Note the long north-oriented Missouri River headwaters and tributaries. The west-oriented Snake River flows to the Pacific Ocean.

However, the evidence is confusing because in the northern Missouri River drainage basin scattered coarse-grained glacial erratic material can be found as much as 50-to-100-kilometers to the south and west of the Missouri River valley. For that reason, Leonard (1912) considered some North Dakota Missouri River valley segments to be preglacial in origin and commented "The deep valley of the Missouri did not serve as a barrier to the onward movement of the ice." But he did not challenge the interpretation that the north-oriented Missouri River headwaters, Yellowstone River, Little Missouri River, and Cheyenne River (and other drainage not shown in the figure) predated the continental icesheet(s) and he and other geologists of his time did not consider the possibility that the same set of large-scale evidence could be explained in any alternate ways.

Some early geologists reported problems when trying to explain topographic map drainage system evidence. For example, Stone (1905, p. 2) who used a then newly released 1904 topographic map (scale 1:62,500) for geologic mapping purposes reported in his USGS Waynesburg [PA] Quadrangle study "A noticeable feature of this quadrangle is that besides flowing east [to the north-oriented Monongahela River], all of the main [tributary] streams have longer tributaries on the north than on the south. In other words, the streams do not lie midway between the divides, but crowd the south side of the drainage basin. …No adequate explanation of this lack of symmetry in the drainage basins has yet been found. This unsymmetrical arrangement occurs in several counties in southwestern Pennsylvania. It cannot be ascribed to the present structure of the rocks, because it disregards anticlines and synclines. …So far as the character of the rocks is concerned the tributaries on both sides of the streams should be of equal length."

Figure 2.3 illustrates long south-oriented tributaries in the asymmetric Castille Creek drainage basin on the 1904 Waynesburg, PA topographic map which Stone used. The Castille Creek drainage basin is in the larger north-oriented Monongahela River drainage basin which according to the accepted paradigm has always flowed in a north direction and which Stone recognized should have a different type of drainage pattern than what the then new topographic map showed.

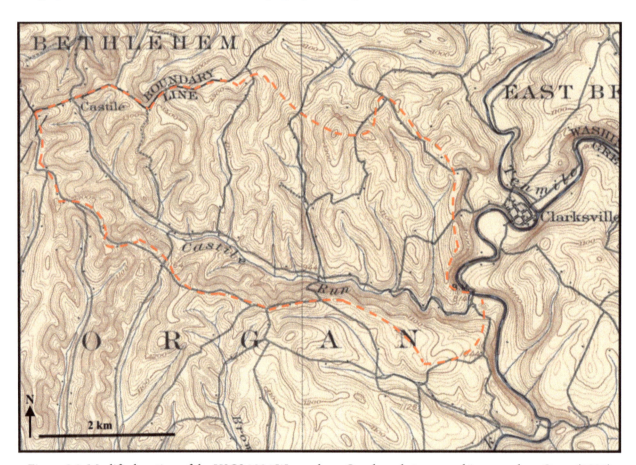

Figure 2.3: Modified section of the USGS 1904 Waynesburg Quadrangle topographic map where Stone (1905) noticed asymmetric drainage basins. Dashed red lines show drainage divides around the asymmetric Castile Run drainage basin, which drains to north-oriented South Fork Tenmile Creek, which joins south-oriented Tenmile Creek at Clarksville and then flows in an east direction to join the north-oriented Monongahela River. The contour interval is 20 feet (6 meters).

The large number of south-oriented streams found in the north-oriented Monongahela River drainage basin (such as seen in figure 2.3) fit the definition of barbed tributaries or tributaries that do not flow in the same direction as the direction of the stream or river to which they flow. Thornbury (1969, p. 120) in his geomorphology textbook, which describes several different types of drainage patterns points out what early geologists expected to see, by saying barbed drainage patterns should be of local extent and then only in drainage system headwaters areas. He then suggests barbed tributaries indicate a drainage reversal may have taken place.

Yet early geologists observed barbed tributaries throughout the large Monongahela River drainage basin. For example, Hennen and Reger (1914, p. 46) remarked tributaries to the north-oriented Cheat River in Preston County (West Virginia) "do not flow northward to correspond with the current of the parent stream, but have a contrary course toward the south." They go on to say this evidence might suggest the Cheat River (now a north-oriented Monongahela River tributary) once flowed to the south, but then reject the idea because what they regard as normal north-oriented tributaries also flow into the north-oriented Cheat River. Figure 2.4 uses a newer topographic map to illustrate some Preston County, West Virginia south-oriented tributaries that Hennen and Reger observed. To historical qualitative geomorphologists Monongahela River drainage basin asymmetric tributary drainage basin and barbed (south-oriented) tributary evidence seen on the topographic maps suggested the Monongahela River drainage system might have once flowed in a south direction, but the accepted paradigm did not provide the tools needed to challenge the previously established interpretation that the preglacial Monongahela River had always flowed in a north direction.

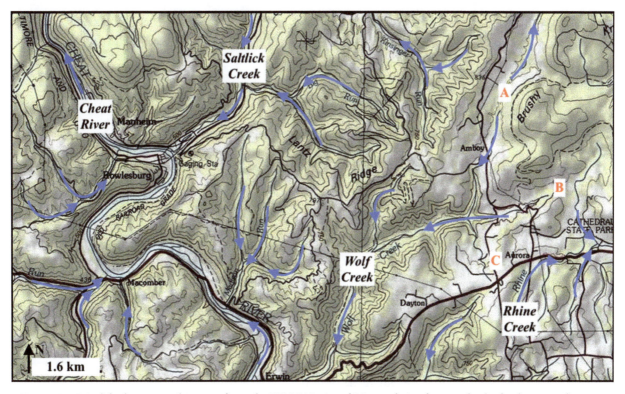

Figure 2.4: Modified topographic map from the USGS National Map website showing barbed tributaries flowing to the north-oriented Cheat River. The contour interval is 50 meters. Top left corner: 39° 22' 55.123" N, 79° 42' 53.918" W. Red letters identify text discussed locations.

In addition to numerous barbed tributaries the newly available topographic maps showed through valleys (valleys now crossed by one or more drainage divides) such as those identified in figure 2.4 by the letters A, B, and C and which chapter 7 discusses. Historical qualitative geomorphologists could determine that water flowing in one direction or the other had eroded most of those through valleys and in many cases could even determine how stream captures had diverted previous streams to flow in other directions. However, the then new topographic maps in many Monongahela River drainage basin areas, showed numerous through valleys that required much more complicated stream capture events than the accepted paradigm permits (see Bishop, 1995).

Historical qualitative geomorphologists also had difficulty explaining what was becoming an increasing amount of northern Missouri River drainage basin topographic map drainage system evidence. Figure 2.5 shows southeast-oriented barbed tributaries and northwest-oriented tributaries flowing to a northeast-oriented Powder River valley segment located about 12 kilometers to the north of the Montana-Wyoming border. This southeast-northwest tributary orientation is found throughout much of the southeast Montana and northeast Wyoming Powder River drainage basin. Further, the southeast-northwest tributary orientation is found throughout much of the Great Plains region located to the south and west of the Missouri River.

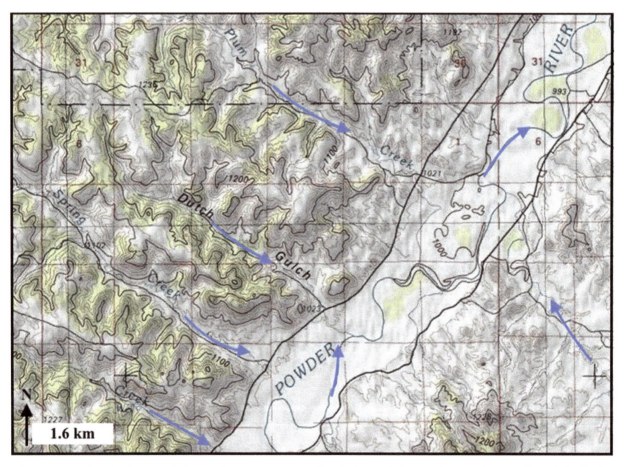

Figure 2.5: Modified topographic map from the USGS National Map website showing southeast-oriented (barbed tributaries) flowing to a northeast-oriented Powder River valley segment located about 12 kilometers to the north of the Montana-Wyoming border. The contour interval is 20 meters. Top left corner: 45° 11' 27.668" N, 105° 54' 08.689" W.

With respect to the aligned drainage Thornbury (1965, p. 306) says "The alignment can hardly be explained as a result of regional tilting, for the direction of alignment does not parallel the regional slope. Neither can it be attributed to the influence of some particular geologic formation, for the aligned streams flow on rocks ranging in age from the Cretaceous Pierre shale to the Tertiary Ogallala formation." Many aligned drainage areas are to the south and west of a continental icesheet margin and could have developed when north-oriented valleys eroded headward across southeast-oriented icesheet-marginal meltwater floods, but because the accepted paradigm considers the north-oriented drainage routes to be preglacial this hypothesis was not considered.

Instead, other hypotheses were proposed. Russell (1929) attributed the aligned drainage to longitudinal northwest-southeast oriented dunes which have since disappeared, Flint (1955) considered the dune idea possible but did not provide a specific explanation, and Crandell (1958) rejected joint control and was forced to conclude the drainage alignment in an unspecified way was somehow related to prevailing northwesterly winds. While most, but not all of these hypotheses attributed the aligned drainage and barbed tributaries to wind action there was no consensus as to how the prevailing winds could produce the southeast-northwest aligned drainage.

What the topographic map evidence clearly shows, but the geology research community has yet to recognize is that all drainage divides between north-oriented trunk streams are notched by divide crossings (low points along the drainage divide) which link the valleys of southeast-oriented tributaries draining to the north-oriented trunk stream located east of the drainage divide with valleys of northwest-oriented tributaries draining to the north-oriented trunk stream located west of the drainage divide. The geologic principle of cross cutting relationships requires the southeast-northwest drainage alignment to have been developed before the north- and northeast-oriented trunk streams, yet the geology research community has ignored this fact.

Figure 2.6 shows aligned drainage along a northwest South Dakota drainage divide between the north-oriented Little Missouri River and north-northeast oriented Shaw Creek (which joins the Little Missouri River north of the figure). The Little Missouri River and Shaw Creek meander on floors of wider north-oriented valleys suggesting larger volumes of water than now once flowed in those valleys. Southeast- and northwest-oriented tributaries drain to both Shaw Creek and the Little Missouri River and those aligned tributary valleys are linked by divide crossings (low spots along the drainage divides which are identified by red letters). Divide crossings seen along the Shaw Creek-Little Missouri River drainage divide segment are typical of divide crossings found along drainage divides between almost all northern Missouri River drainage basin north- and northeast-oriented trunk streams. This evidence was not available to geologists who first proposed the north-oriented Little Missouri River originated in preglacial time.

Figure 2.6 shows at least seven closely spaced southeast-oriented streams of water once flowed across the Shaw Creek-Little Missouri River drainage divide prior to erosion of the north-northeast oriented Shaw Creek valley. The evidence also suggests the north-northeast oriented Shaw Creek valley eroded headward across those seven southeast-oriented streams of water and had been deep enough to cause flow reversals on the northwest ends of the beheaded southeast-oriented channels so as to create what are now northwest-oriented Shaw Creek tributaries.

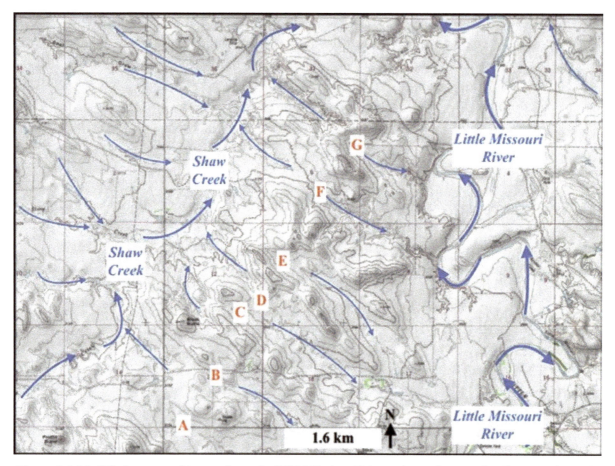

Figure 2.6: Modified topographic map from the USGS National Map website showing the Shaw Creek- Little Missouri River drainage divide in South Dakota's northwest corner. The contour interval is 20 feet (6 meters). Top left corner: 45° 50' 04.987" N, 103° 59' 05.997" W. Red letters identify divide crossings along the Shaw Creek-Little Missouri River drainage divide.

Closely spaced divide crossings found along drainage divides between the north- and northeast-oriented trunk streams such as seen in figure 2.6 suggest southeast-oriented complexes of anastomosing channels once crossed the region. If so, the north-oriented valleys eroded headward in sequence (from the southeast to the northwest) to capture huge southeast-oriented meltwater floods and diverted the floodwaters in a north direction toward the icesheet location.

In addition to not satisfactorily explaining the aligned drainage and the numerous barbed tributaries (where southeast-oriented secondary streams join larger north-oriented streams) the accepted paradigm did not explain the northern Missouri River drainage basin's asymmetric drainage basins. Detailed topographic maps are not needed to observe the asymmetric Knife, Heart, Cannonball, Grand, and Moreau River drainage basins seen in figure 2.7. The 200-kilometer-long (or longer) Knife, Heart, Cannonball, Grand, and Moreau Rivers begin in places almost on the eastern edge of the north-oriented Little Missouri River valley. Geology's principle of cross cutting relationships suggests headward erosion of the north-oriented Little Missouri River valley beheaded what were southeast-oriented drainage systems. Yet, most geologic literature which describes this region completely ignores this easy-to-observe evidence.

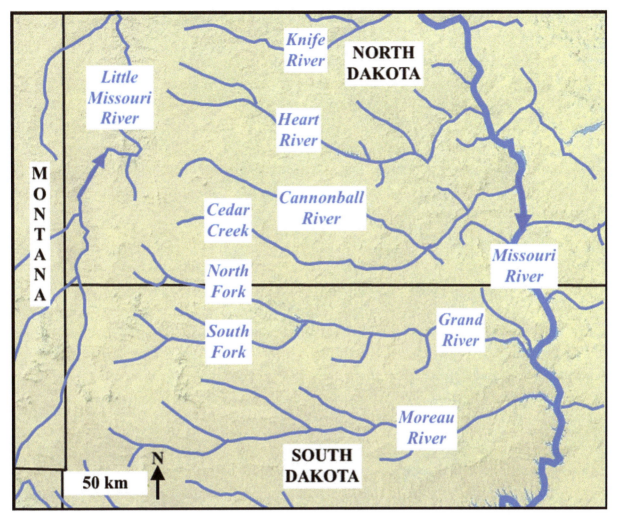

Figure 2.7: Modified map from the USGS National Map website showing asymmetric east-oriented drainage basins between the north-flowing Little Missouri River and the south-flowing Missouri River in southwest North Dakota and northwest South Dakota.

What the geologic literature does mention is the Knife, Heart, Cannonball, and Moreau Rivers flow in northeast directions to join the south-oriented Missouri River as barbed tributaries. This evidence supports the interpretation that one or more continental icesheets blocked north- and northeast-oriented "preglacial" drainage routes However, that accepted paradigm interpretation does not address why the southeast-oriented Knife, Heart, Cannonball, and Moreau River headwaters turn to flow in northeast directions before reaching the Missouri River as barbed tributaries. The turns from flowing in a southeast direction to flowing in a northeast direction are elbows of capture which indicate northeast-oriented valley headward erosion captured southeast-oriented streams.

To the north of figure 2.7 the Missouri River flows in an east and then southeast direction before turning in a south direction (as seen in figure 2.2). In both North and South Dakota icesheet deposited glacial tills and erratic materials are abundant in the region to the north and east of the Missouri River. For as much as 50 to 100 kilometers to the south and west of the Missouri River coarse-grained glacial erratic debris without any finer grained glacial till material suggests an icesheet once extended across what are now the eastern halves of the Knife, Heart, Cannonball, Grand, and Moreau River drainage basins.

Interestingly, detailed topographic maps show no convincing evidence that the icesheet which extended to the south and west of the present-day Missouri Rive valley blocked the north-oriented "preglacial" drainage routes to form an icesheet marginal river (comparable to the Missouri River). Instead, detailed topographic maps show aligned northwest-to-southeast oriented tributaries to the north- and northeast-oriented streams (such as seen in figure 2.6) dominate the region located to the south and west of the coarse-grained glacial erratic material zone. Massive southeast-oriented icesheet marginal meltwater floods can explain the southeast-oriented Knife, Heart, Cannonball, Grand, and Moreau River headwaters but, such an interpretation conflicts with the commonly accepted interpretation that the Little Missouri River and the northeast-oriented Knife, Heart, Cannonball, Grand, and Moreau River segments predate the continental icesheet(s).

If the topographic map evidence is to be trusted the north-oriented Little Missouri River valley and northeast-oriented Knife, Heart, Cannonball, Grand, and Moreau valley segments must have eroded headward from a continental icesheet location across immense southeast-oriented icesheet marginal meltwater floods. Such an interpretation which explains the aligned drainage evidence requires the continental icesheet floor to have been lower in elevation than the surrounding landscape on which the southeast-oriented icesheet marginal meltwater floods were flowing. If so, the icesheet must have created and occupied a deep "hole" by deeply eroding the underlying bedrock and perhaps by causing the uplift of surrounding regions, but that alternative was never seriously considered.

The geology research community has constructed its North American glacial history paradigm around the assumption that continental icesheets did not deeply erode the underlying bedrock and did not create and occupy a deep "hole." When White (1972) argued that continental icesheets should have deeply eroded the underlying bedrock the glacial geology research community including Sugden (1976) overwhelmingly rejected his arguments. Evidence against deep continental icesheet erosion that glacial geologists frequently cite includes the now partially buried (with glacially deposited debris) north-oriented valleys found to the north of the hypothesized icesheet marginal Missouri and Ohio Rivers. Some of these valleys are in regions where the bedrock is easily eroded which led White to suggest that the glacial geologists were defying common sense logic by implying that the icesheets "daintily tiptoed" across the landscape.

White's paper also included a description of how continental icesheets eroded the North American continent. Unfortunately, that description was not based on detailed topographic map evidence and like accepted paradigm interpretations failed to adequately explain most of the detailed topographic map drainage system and erosional landform evidence. As a result, White did not offer an interpretation that explained the drainage system and erosional landform evidence.

However, White raised a valid point when he said that glacial geologists by interpreting the north-oriented Ohio and Missouri River tributaries to be parts of a preglacial north-oriented drainage system had caused the geology research community to construct a North American glacial history in which continental icesheets "daintily tiptoed" across valleys eroded in easily eroded bedrock. With that statement he pointed out a serious, but unrecognized paradigm problem which shows up in the geology research community's inability to use the accepted paradigm to explain most of the topographic map drainage system and erosional landform evidence.

Throughout the United States the geology research community has yet to satisfactorily explain other drainage system evidence such as the southeast Oklahoma asymmetric Canadian-Red River drainage divide seen in figure 2.8. The Canadian River is the southernmost of several long east-oriented Arkansas River tributaries and begins in the Rocky Mountains near the Colorado-New Mexico border and flows in an east-southeast direction to a point just to the south of Raton Pass. From that point the river turns in a south direction and enters a deep south-oriented canyon before turning in an east direction to flow across eastern New Mexico, northern Texas, and Oklahoma. In eastern Oklahoma (east of figure 2.8) the Canadian River turns in a northeast direction to join the southeast-oriented Arkansas River (which then flows to the Mississippi River).

Muddy Boggy Creek seen in figure 2.8 is flowing in a northeast and east direction and to the east of figure 2.8 turns in a southeast direction to flow for more than 120 kilometers (as a crow would fly over its meandering route) to reach the southeast-oriented Red River which then flows to the Louisiana Mississippi River delta area. The asymmetric Canadian-Red River drainage divide seen in figure 2.8 is almost impossible to explain unless the east-oriented Canadian River valley eroded headward from the Arkansas River valley across massive south-oriented floods.

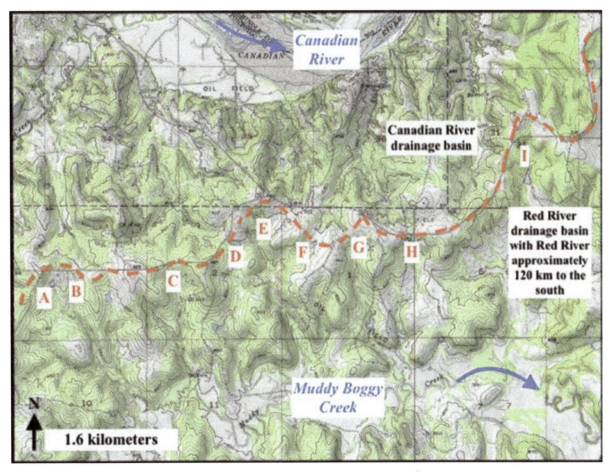

Figure 2.8: Modified topographic map from the USGS National Map website showing a segment of the asymmetric Canadian-Red River drainage divide in eastern Pontotoc County, Oklahoma. The contour interval is 10 feet (3 meters). Top left corner: 34° 52' 26.001" N, 96° 33' 51.143" W. Red letters identify divide crossings along the Canadian-Red River drainage divide.

Unexplained and ignored drainage divides are found throughout the United States. Figure 2.9 illustrates a 1902 topographic map showing a central Pennsylvania drainage divide identified by the dashed red line marked by the red numbers 1, 2, 3 and 4. That drainage divide is the Allegheny Front crest. To the east of that drainage divide east-oriented tributaries flow down the steep Allegheny Front to the Juniata River which then flows for about 200 kilometers in an east direction to join the south-oriented Susquehanna River. The red dashed line marked by numbers 3 and 4 along the Allegheny Front crest and then which continues along the line marked by the letters A-F is the Atlantic Ocean-Gulf of Mexico drainage divide. No existing geologic literature explains why the Atlantic Ocean-Gulf of Mexico drainage divide turns away from the Allegheny Front crest at this location.

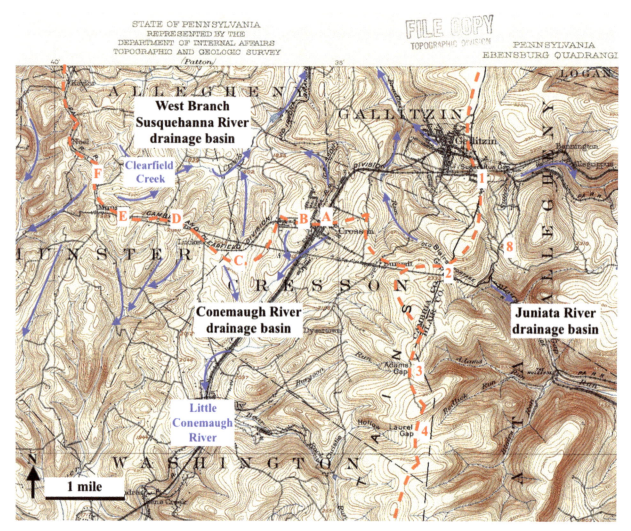

Figure 2.9: Modified section of the 1902 Ebensburg, Pennsylvania topographic map obtained from the USGS topoView website. The contour interval is 20 feet (6 meters) and the dashed red lines show major drainage divides. Blue arrows emphasize present-day drainage flow directions and red numbers and letters identify drainage divide low points or gaps.

To the east of the figure 2.9 map area is Altoona, Pennsylvania and Horseshoe Curve where the former Pennsylvania Railroad mainline began its climb up the Allegheny Front. The railroad climbed (and still does) from the Juniata River valley in the Susquehanna River drainage basin to travel through the gap marked in figure 2.9 with a number 1 and then to enter the Mississippi River drainage basin by passing through a shallower gap marked by the letter A. Prior to Pennsylvania Railroad construction travelers used canals to reach the Allegheny Portage Railroad which then climbed the Allegheny Front to reach the gap marked by the number 2.

What early 1900s geomorphologists should have reported, but never did, is the gaps at numbers 1 and 2 are on the floors of through valleys which on opposite sides of the drainage divide drain in opposing directions. East of the gaps and of figure 2.9 the two eastern valleys converge as they drain toward the east-oriented Juniata River which flows to the south-oriented Susquehanna River. West of the gaps the western valleys converge to form northwest-oriented Bradley Creek which flows to north-oriented Clearfield Creek. Clearfield Creek flows to the northeast- and east-oriented West Branch Susquehanna River which eventually turns in a south direction to join the North Branch Susquehanna River and to form the south-oriented Susquehanna River.

Early in the 1900s geomorphologists should have recognized (but never publicly said they did) that diverging and converging streams of water which once flowed between the Clearfield Creek and Juniata River drainage basins had eroded the two gaps and that something, perhaps uplift of the Allegheny Front area, reversed the flow on the west side of the gaps to create the drainage divides seen today. Based on today's topography it is probably safe to assume the gaps were eroded by diverging and converging streams of south-oriented water which were flowing from the now north-oriented Clearfield Creek drainage basin into the east-oriented Juniata River drainage basin.

Also, in figure 2.9 red letters mark somewhat shallower gaps located along the drainage divide between the north-oriented Clearfield Creek and the south-oriented Little Conemaugh River drainage basins through which multiple streams of south-oriented water must have once flowed. The figure 2.9 drainage divide and gap evidence should tell a skilled map interpreter that multiple diverging and converging streams of south-oriented water once flowed in a south-direction from the now north-oriented Clearfield Creek drainage basin, which suggests large amounts of water must have been involved. What stopped geomorphologists from publishing anything about how the figure 2.9 gaps were eroded is the accepted paradigm does not provide a water source for the large amounts of south-oriented water which must have once flowed from the now north-oriented Clearfield Creek drainage basin into the Juniata and Little Conemaugh River drainage basins.

The practice of ignoring topographic map drainage system and erosional landform evidence can be traced back to 1889 when William Morris Davis published his "A River Pirate" paper in which he described how barbed tributaries seen on a very small section of an advance copy of the 1890 Doylestown (Pennsylvania) topographic map had formed. In that paper and in a subsequent paper (Ward, 1892) which was written with obvious assistance from Davis nothing was said about the abundant and much more obvious barbed tributary evidence elsewhere on the same map. Figure 2.10 illustrates barbed tributaries flowing to east-oriented Neshaminy Creek on that same 1890 Doylestown topographic map. The same 1890 Doylestown map also shows several northeast-oriented barbed tributaries flowing to the southeast-oriented Delaware River. Nothing was said in either of the two papers about the Neshaminy Creek and the Delaware River barbed tributaries (which are much more obvious than the barbed tributaries the two papers do discuss).

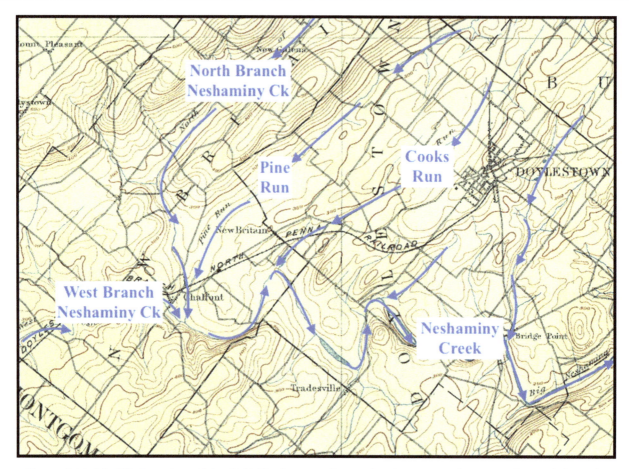

Figure 2.10: Modified section of the 1890 Doylestown, Pennsylvania topographic map obtained from the USGS topoView website. W.M. Davis in his "River Pirate" paper explained barbed tributary evidence in a small Doylestown map section located to the northwest of this figure.

Figure 2.10 illustrates southwest-oriented North Branch Neshaminy Creek, Pine Run, Cooks Run, and an unnamed stream all flowing as obvious barbed tributaries to zig-zagging and east-oriented Neshaminy Creek. The much less obvious barbed tributaries that Davis described are located in the map's northwest quadrant and are in a relatively small drainage basin which is smaller than the Cooks Run drainage basin seen in figure 2.10. The barbed tributary evidence on the Doylestown map seen in figure 2.10 suggests headward erosion of the east-oriented and zig-zagging Neshaminy Creek valley captured multiple southwest-oriented stream channels which were subsequently beheaded and reversed by the headward erosion of the southeast-oriented Delaware River valley to create the northeast-oriented barbed Delaware River tributaries (seen on the same map).

Davis focused his 1889 "A River Pirate" paper on a relatively minor drainage basin which based on barbed tributary evidence he interpreted to be capturing drainage area from an adjacent drainage basin. Had he focused his paper on the much more obvious Neshaminy Creek and Delaware River barbed tributaries (shown on the same map) Davis would have recognized the southeast-oriented Delaware River valley had eroded headward across what were probably large southwest-oriented floods (which he might have recognized as icesheet meltwater floods). However, Davis ignored the obvious map evidence and pointed the geology research community toward a Delaware River valley interpretation that does not explain the obvious topographic map evidence.

Chapter 3:
Barbed Tributaries

Shortly after publishing his "A River Pirate" paper Davis published his much longer 1889 *National Geographic Magazine* "Rivers and Valleys of Pennsylvania" article in which he described Pennsylvania's drainage history. Few Pennsylvania topographic maps were available in 1889, but in writing that second paper Davis not only ignored what drainage system evidence was available on those few topographic maps but he also ignored much of the large-scale barbed tributary evidence shown on less detailed maps which were available at that time. For example, Figure 3.1 illustrates with imagery barbed tributaries in the Johnstown, Pennsylvania area (which Davis should have been able to recognize from the less detailed maps available to him) where the north-oriented Stony Creek River is joined by the southwest-oriented Little Conemaugh River to become the north-oriented Conemaugh River (which further downstream changes direction and eventually reaches the Allegheny River seen in figure 2.1). Mill Creek, Laurel Run, and Hinckston Run also flow to the north-oriented Stony Creek-Conemaugh River as barbed tributaries and suggest a major south-oriented drainage system preceded the north-oriented drainage system which exists today.

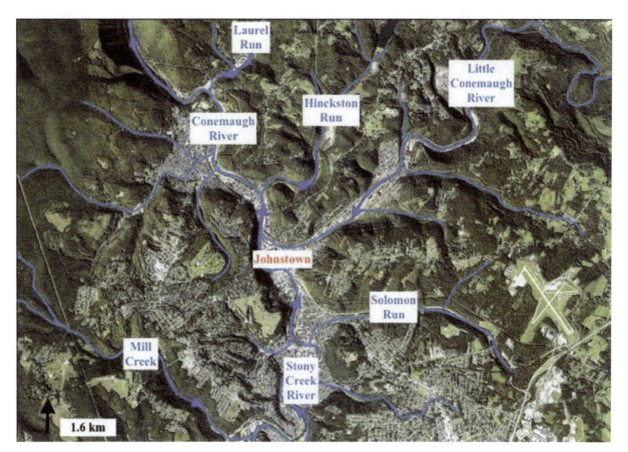

Figure 3.1: Modified imagery from the USGS National Map website showing major drainage routes and barbed tributaries near Johnstown, Pennsylvania. Arrows show present-day flow directions. Top left corner: 40° 22' 48.922" n, 79° 00' 03.967" W.

The Davis "Rivers and Valleys of Pennsylvania" paper interpretation, which was widely accepted following its publication argues a northwest-oriented drainage system preceded the present-day Pennsylvania drainage system with today's southeast-oriented river systems developing as the earlier northwest-oriented drainage system was gradually reversed. That Davis interpretation shaped how Davis and the geologists who accepted his interpretation viewed topographic map evidence as new maps became available. For example, in subsequent years new topographic maps showed south-oriented barbed tributaries in western Maryland flowing to the north-oriented Youghiogheny River (in the larger north-oriented Monongahela River drainage basin) including Little Laurel Run, Snowy Creek, and White Meadow Run seen in figure 3.2.

Even though almost every newly published topographic map in the early 1900s showed barbed tributary evidence geomorphologists of the time, including Davis, dismissed almost all of that barbed tributary evidence as unimportant because they were convinced a previous northwest-oriented Pennsylvania drainage system had been reversed to create southeast-oriented drainage systems seen today. While the Davis hypothesis is no longer widely accepted the practice of ignoring barbed tributary evidence continues and the geology research community still does not recognize the importance of the many south-oriented barbed tributaries found in West Virginia and western Pennsylvania and western Maryland. Those barbed tributaries are saying a major south-oriented drainage system eroded the entire region and has since been reversed to form today's north-oriented Monongahela River drainage system and what are today north-oriented Allegheny River tributary drainage routes. Yet in spite of the map evidence most of the geology literature still says the Monongahela River has always flowed in a north direction.

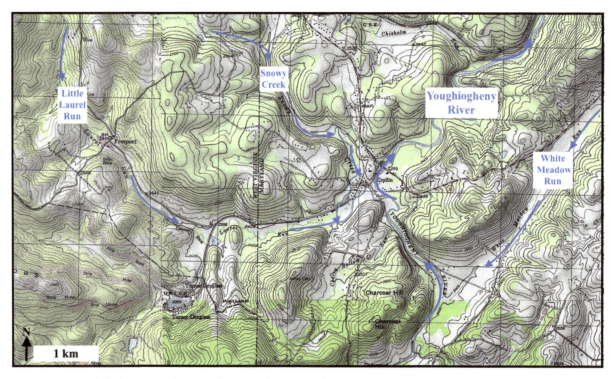

Figure 3.2: Modified topographic map from USGS National Map website showing barbed tributaries flowing to Maryland's north-oriented Youghiogheny River. The contour interval is 20 feet (6 meters). Top left corner: 39° 24' 34.695" N, 79° 31' 28.191" W.

Further to the west barbed tributaries flow to other north-oriented rivers. For example, in figure 3.3 south-oriented tributaries join the north-oriented Cumberland River which is flowing in a north direction across the Tennessee-Kentucky state line. About six kilometers to the west of the figure is the north-oriented Tennessee River with the Cumberland River and Tennessee River flowing in adjacent and parallel north-oriented valleys to reach the Ohio River (near where the Ohio River turns from flowing in a south direction to flow in a west direction). Upstream (east of the figure) the Cumberland River headwaters flow in a southwest direction before turning (much like a barbed tributary) to become the north-oriented river seen in the figure.

South-oriented barbed tributaries seen in figure 3.3 include Shelby Creek, Saline Creek and its Scott Branch, Dyers Creek, Bellwood Branch, Cub Creek, and Barrett Creek, and flow to the north-oriented Cumberland River which suggests a major south-oriented drainage system preceded today's north-oriented drainage. Yet the geology research community rarely discusses such evidence. Similar south-oriented barbed tributaries flow to the nearby and adjacent north-oriented Tennessee River suggesting an earlier south-oriented drainage system must have crossed the entire western Kentucky and Tennessee region. The drainage reversal that created the present-day north-oriented Cumberland River and Tennessee River routes must have been a significant geologic event, but the accepted paradigm geology literature does not mention the event.

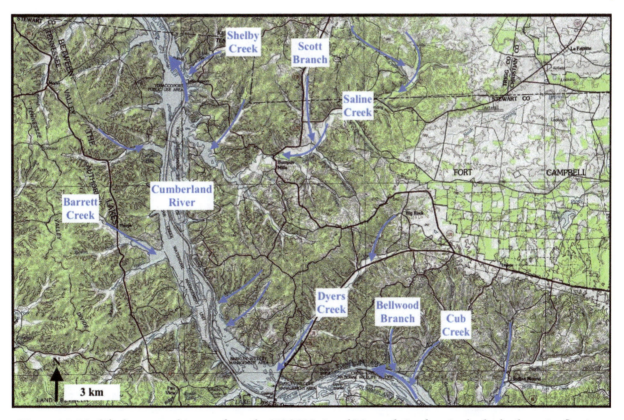

Figure 3.3: Modified topographic map from the USGS National Map website showing barbed tributaries flowing to a western Kentucky north-oriented Cumberland River segment. The contour interval is 10 meters. Top left corner: 36° 40' 30.219" N, 87° 59' 57.601" W.

Geomorphologists have always had trouble explaining the Tennessee River which in the southern Appalachian Mountains flows in a southwest direction until reaching northern Alabama where the river turns in a northwest direction to enter Tennessee and then in a north direction (with some eastward jogs) to reach the Ohio River (see figure 8.3). There is geology literature debating whether or not the Tennessee River once flowed directly across Alabama to reach the Gulf of Mexico. Recently Odom and Granger (2022) stated "The Tennessee River, a primary drainage of the southern Appalachians ...is considered to be the product of captures that rerouted the river from a more direct ...course" to the Gulf of Mexico. Usually overlooked when discussing Tennessee River captures are south-oriented barbed tributaries such as those seen in figure 3.4 which are flowing to the north-oriented Tennessee River which in the figure makes an eastward jog (about 40 kilometers to the north of Tennessee's southern border).

Like with the Cumberland River barbed tributary evidence the barbed tributaries seen in figure 3.4 suggest a major south-oriented drainage system preceded the present-day north-oriented Tennessee River route. Massive south-oriented continental icesheet meltwater floods (while uplift of what is now the Tennessee River-Gulf of Mexico drainage divide to the south was taking place) can account for the topographic map drainage system evidence and the Tennessee River U-turn. But Odom and Granger use river terrace age data to suggest that the Tennessee River captures had occurred by early Pliocene time, before the accepted paradigm's continental icesheets had formed.

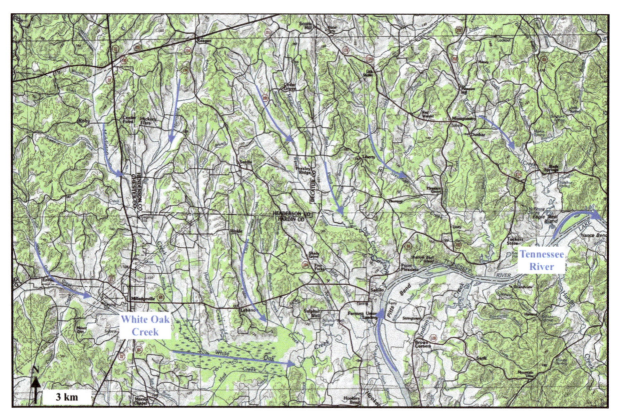

Figure 3.4: Modified topographic map from the USGS National Map website showing south-oriented barbed tributaries flowing to a north-and east-oriented Tennessee River segment. The contour interval is 20 meters. Top left corner: 35° 31' 12.254" N, 88° 26' 33.228" W.

Figure 3.5 in the state of Missouri shows southeast-oriented Pointers Creek, Owens Creek, and Swan Creek flowing to the north- and northeast-oriented Gasconade River. What makes figure 3.5 intriguing is the large abandoned entrenched meander now drained by segments of Swan Creek, Graveyard Brook, and Brush Creek. The Gasconade River, like other north- and northeast-oriented Missouri River tributaries (in Missouri) flows for much of its length in similar entrenched meanders. The entrenched meanders origin has been controversial with one hypothesis being ancestral rivers flowed on soft sediments (now completely eroded away) while other hypotheses suggest regional bedrock characteristics caused the rivers to form the entrenched meanders.

Still other hypotheses have suggested the entrenched meanders are related to the tributary valley orientations (which figure 3.5 evidence supports). Yet this unresolved discussion rarely if ever mentions the south-oriented (barbed) tributaries flowing to what is now a north-oriented river which suggests a major drainage reversal has taken place. Further, the south-oriented (barbed) tributaries are found throughout the entire region suggesting the drainage reversal probably occurred as massive amounts of south-oriented water were reversed to flow in north or northeast directions. The logical water source would be a melting continental icesheet, but at least some of the geologic literature suggests the regional drainage pattern originated as far back in geologic time as the late Paleozoic, or long before any North American continental icesheets existed.

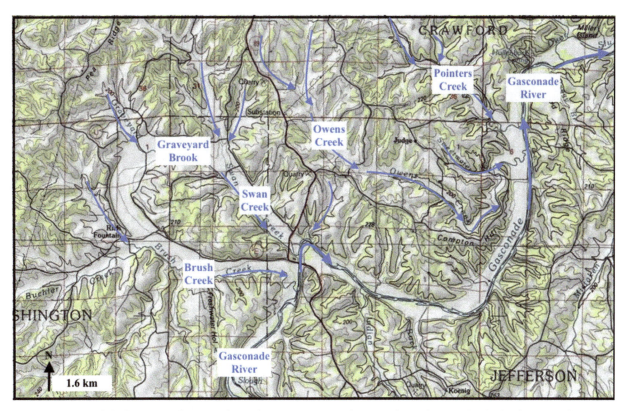

Figure 3.5: Modified topographic map from the USGS National Map website showing barbed tributaries flowing to Missouri's north-oriented Gasconade River. The contour interval is 20 meters. Top left corner: 38° 27' 13.762" N, 91° 55' 11.360" W.

Tappen Gulch (in figure 3.6) is a barbed tributary flowing to the north-oriented South Platte River (south of Denver, Colorado). An abandoned valley (number 1) links southeast-oriented Tarryall Creek with south-southeast oriented Tappen Gulch and suggests Tarryall Creek once continued in a southeast direction to the South Platte River valley. Another abandoned valley (number 2) links the northeast-oriented Tarryall Creek segment with Tappen Gulch and suggests southwest-oriented water flowing from the South Platte River valley once joined southeast-oriented water from Tarryall Creek to flow in the Tappen Gulch valley and to join south-oriented water flowing in the now north-oriented South Platte River valley.

If so, the now north-oriented South Platte River originated as a south-oriented drainage route with flow in the valley at least for a time forming two diverging and converging channels defined by the South Platte River valley and the abandoned valley at number 2 which links the northeast-oriented Tarryall Creek valley with the Tappen Gulch valley. Colorado region uplift must have been responsible for reversing flow in the South Platte River and northeast-oriented Tarryall Creek valleys which in turn enabled the reversed flow to capture the southeast-oriented upstream Tarryall Creek drainage. While evident from topographic map evidence the accepted paradigm forces geologists to reject this interpretation because the accepted paradigm offers no source for the large volumes of south-oriented water which are required to explain the map evidence.

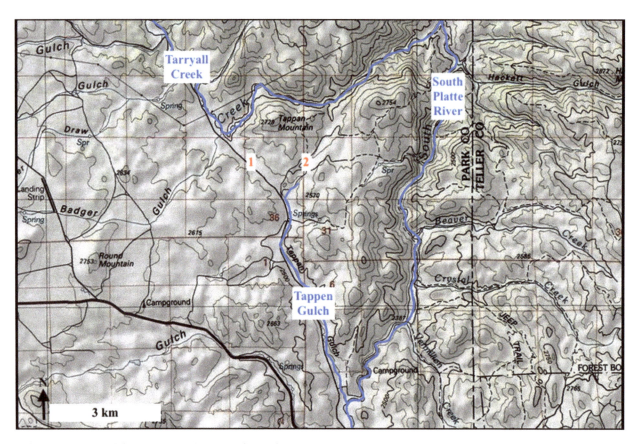

Figure 3.6: Modified topographic map from the USGS National Map website showing south-oriented Tappen Gulch flowing as a barbed tributary to a north-oriented South Platte River valley segment located to the south of Denver, Colorado. The contour interval is 50 meters. Top left corner: 39° 05' 47.980" N, 105° 28' 19.102" W.

Figure 3.7 illustrates how the southwest Montana Big Hole River flows in a north, southeast, and south direction before turning in a northeast direction to join the northeast-oriented Beaverhead River and to form the northeast-oriented Jefferson River. Staisch et al (2022) used detrital zircon sands to suggest the

Snake River may have flowed in a north direction along the Beaverhead River and the now south-oriented Big Hole River valley segments to reach Deer Lodge Pass (seen in figure 7.1) and the Clark Fork River valley. In an alternate interpretation Sears (2013) and Sears and Beranek (2022) suggested the Colorado River once turned in a north direction to enter Montana where it flowed in what are now the Beaverhead and Jefferson River valleys to eventually reach northern Canada.

What those studies fail to address is the barbed tributary evidence seen in figure 3.7. Not only does the Big Hole River flow in a south direction to join the north-oriented Beaverhead River but other south-oriented barbed tributaries are present including Grasshopper Creek and two unnamed streams. Detailed topographic maps show other south-oriented tributaries flowing to the south-oriented Big Hole River and to the north-oriented Ruby River as well as to the north-oriented Beaverhead and Jefferson Rivers (and even to the north-oriented Big Hole River headwaters). The barbed tributaries suggest that prior to formation of the present-day drainage system a south-oriented drainage system drained the entire region and regional and mountain range uplift caused a massive drainage reversal, but the accepted paradigm prevents the geology research community from seeing this rather obvious barbed tributary evidence.

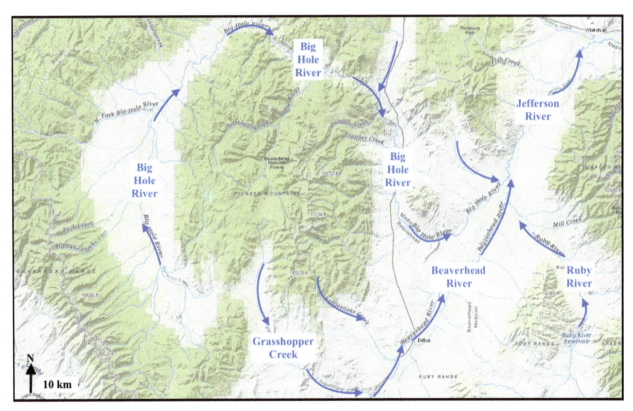

Figure 3.7: Modified map from the USGS National Map website showing how Montana's Big Hole River joins the north-oriented Beaverhead and Ruby Rivers to form the north-oriented Jefferson River. Top left corner: 45° 54' 27.568" N, 113° 53' 20.871" W.

North-oriented barbed tributaries flowing to south-oriented rivers usually are linked by through valleys with south-oriented valleys. These linked north- and south-oriented valleys form through valleys which cross a drainage divide and suggest a drainage reversal in the north-oriented valley has occurred. Prior to that reversal the through valley was eroded by a south-oriented stream that diverged from what is today the main south-oriented trunk stream or river. The diverging south-oriented channels usually also provide evidence for large south-oriented floods which the accepted paradigm prevents geologists from seeing even though detailed topographic maps show many examples of north-oriented streams and rivers flowing to south-oriented rivers.

An excellent example seen in figure 3.8 shows the confluence of the North Fork Flathead River (which begins in Canada and flows across the border to reach figure 3.8) and the Middle Fork Flathead River (which for a distance forms Montana's Glacier National Park southern boundary). The northwest-oriented Middle Fork Flathead River joins the south-oriented North Fork Flathead River as a barbed tributary to form the south-oriented Flathead River which the northwest-oriented South Fork Flathead River then joins. The northwest-oriented Middle and South Forks of the Flathead River flow in mountain valleys with Middle Fork headwaters linked at Sun River Pass (seen in figure 5.1) with south- and east-oriented Sun River drainage to the Missouri River. South Fork Flathead River headwaters are linked by an almost level through valley which crosses the drainage divide (seen in figure 3.9) between north-oriented drainage to the South Fork Flathead River and south-oriented drainage to the west-oriented Blackfoot River.

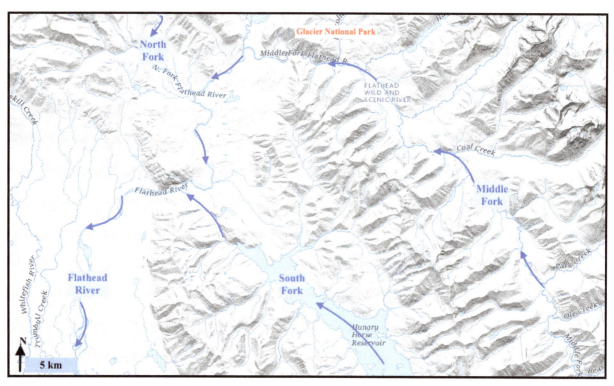

Figure 3.8: Modified map from the USGS National Map website showing how the north-oriented Middle and South Forks join the south-oriented North Fork to form northwest Montana's south-oriented Flathead River. Top left corner: 48° 32' 13.338" N, 114° 18' 54.700" W.

The simplest explanation for the Flathead River barbed tributary evidence is large floods from a continental ice sheet (which was located to the north of the figure area) diverged into three large south-oriented streams of water flowing along the south-oriented Flathead River alignment and along the now northwest-oriented Middle and South Fork alignments. Each of these three major streams eroded valleys into what was an actively rising mountainous area until uplift forced flow reversals in the Middle and

South Fork valleys while the south-oriented flow continued in the North Fork and Flathead River valleys. The red number 1 in figure 3.9 identifies the drainage divide located between north-northwest oriented Danaher Creek (flowing to the northwest-oriented South Fork Flathead River) and southeast-and south-oriented Dry Fork North Fork Blackfoot River. Note the deep through valley and the almost level through valley floor which crosses the present-day drainage divide. Large volumes of south-oriented water must have eroded the deep valley before mountain uplift forced a reversal of flow.

The south-oriented Flathead River could also be considered to be a barbed tributary flowing to the northwest-oriented Clark Fork River. The northwest-oriented Clark Fork River makes a major loop in the western Montana mountains before joining the Flathead River, although a through valley now used by a major railroad line bypasses the loop and suggests water once flowed in a southeast and south direction from the Flathead River valley to join the now northwest-oriented Clark Fork River upstream (or to the southeast) of its northwest-northeast oriented loop.

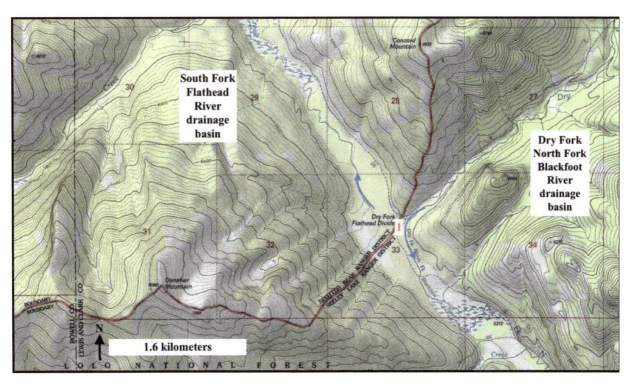

Figure 3.9: Modified map from the USGS National Map website showing an almost level through valley linking the north-oriented South Fork Flathead River valley with the south-oriented Dry Fork North Fork Blackfoot River valley (number 1). The contour interval is 40 feet (12 meters). Top left corner: 47° 17' 38.196" N, 113°04' 07.695" W.

The figure 3.9 evidence suggests south-oriented flow diverged from the south-oriented Flathead River to reach the Blackfoot River which today is a west-oriented Clark Fork River tributary. South-oriented flow in the valley seen in figure 3.9 before being captured by headward erosion of the west-oriented Blackfoot River valley may have continued in a south-direction to flow along the now north-oriented Sturgeon Creek alignment. Figure 3.10 shows how a through valley at the red letter "A" links north-oriented Sturgeon Creek with south-oriented Morris Creek, which flows to the northwest-oriented Clark Fork River as a barbed tributary. Several similar through valleys are eroded across mountain ridges now crossing the Blackfoot River-Clark Fork River drainage divide and link north-oriented Blackfoot River tributaries with south-oriented Clark Fork River barbed tributaries.

Through valleys like the one seen in figure 3.10 and the south-oriented barbed tributaries flowing from them to join the now northwest-oriented Clark Fork River suggest multiple streams of water flowed across rising mountain areas from now north-oriented Flathead River tributary valleys to join a southeast- and south-oriented drainage route on the present-day northwest-oriented Clark Fork River alignment and then to flow southward across Deer Lodge Pass and into the figure 3.7 area and then southward along the south-oriented Big Hole River and northeast-oriented Beaverhead River alignments.

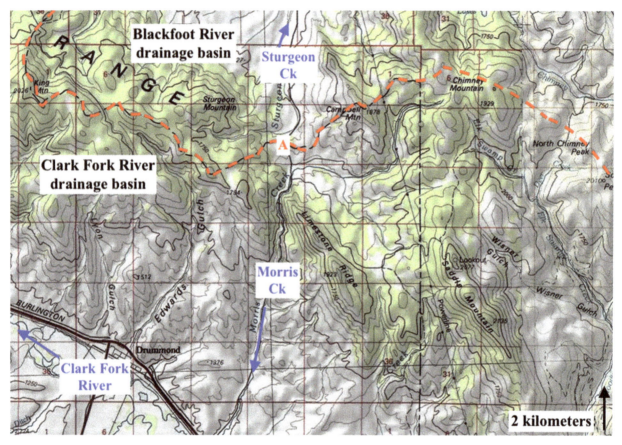

Figure 3.10: Modified section of USGS 1958 Butte, Montana 1:250,000 scale topographic map from USGS topoView website with a 200 ft (60 m) contour interval. Blue arrows indicate flow directions. The red dashed line shows the Blackfoot River-Clark Fork River drainage divide. Red letter "A" marks where the Sturgeon Creek-Morris Creek through valley crosses the drainage divide. Left corner: 46° 45' 13", 113° 10' 52".

Figure 3.11 illustrates where Green River headwaters originate in the northwest Wind River Mountains and flow in a north and northwest direction before turning to become the south-oriented Green River. The Big Bend direction change is the equivalent of a north- and northwest-oriented river joining a south-oriented river as a barbed tributary, which suggests a drainage reversal took place in the now north- and northwest-oriented Green River headwaters. If so, like in the Flathead River situation, the Green River direction change can be explained if as Wind River Mountain uplift was just beginning, prolonged and large floods of south- and/or southeast-oriented water diverged into two major channels with one channel flowing in a south direction along the present-day south-oriented Green River route and the other channel flowing in a southeast and south direction along the now north- and northwest-oriented Green River headwaters route.

North-oriented Green River headwaters are now linked by high elevation mountain passes (seen in figure 3.12) with south-oriented Pine Creek headwaters valleys. Pine Creek eventually joins the south-oriented Green River to the south of figure 3.11. Green River Pass at the number 1 in figure 3.12 has an elevation of approximately 3164 meters, the unnamed pass at the number 2 has an elevation of approximately 3425 meters, and Shannon Pass at the number 3 has an elevation of approximately 3400 meters (the somewhat higher east-west continental divide is located along the Wind River Mountains crestline about 5 kilometers to the east of figure 3.12).

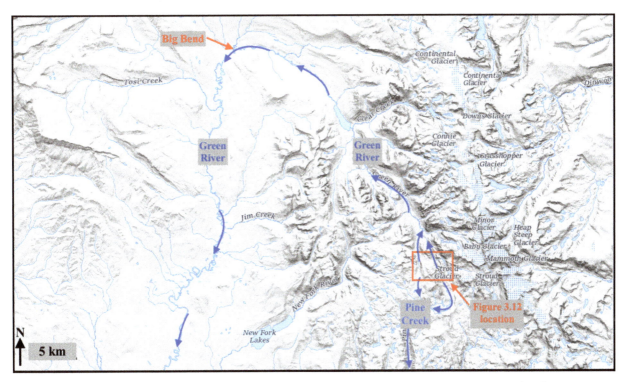

Figure 3.11: Modified map from the USGS National Map website showing the Green River headwaters area along the Wyoming Wind River Mountains' southwest flank. Top left corner: 43° 23' 52.013" N, 110° 17' 15.631" W.

The three passes seen in figure 3.12 must have been eroded by large and long-lived diverging and converging streams of south-oriented water. Elevations at Big Bend where the Green River turns to flow in a south direction are less than 2400 meters and to the south of Pinedale, Wyoming, where Pine Creek joins the New Fork of the Green River elevations are less than 2200 meters suggesting the pass erosion probably occurred as Wind River Mountains uplift was just beginning, which was probably long before any Wind River Mountains icecap would have existed. Uplift of the Wind River Mountains must have first blocked south-oriented flow across pass number 3 and second across pass number 2 with the south-oriented water then being channeled to flow through pass number 1. The pass number 1 depth suggests as much as 400 meters of mountain uplift occurred before the uplift rate exceeded the ability of the water to erode a deeper valley which would have ended south-oriented flood flow across what is now the figure 3.12 map area.

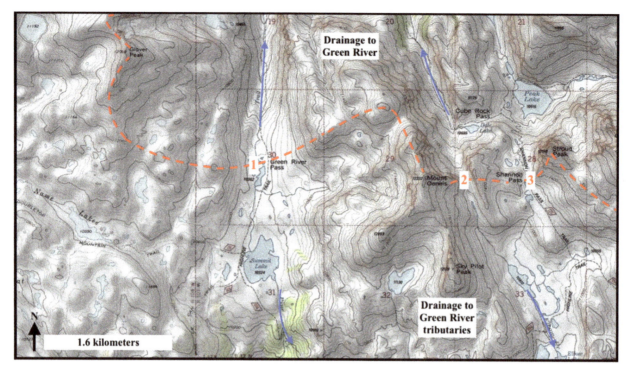

Figure 3.12: Modified map from USGS National Map website showing mountain passes linking north-oriented Green River headwaters valleys with south-oriented Green River tributary valleys. The contour interval is 40 feet (12 meters). Top left corner: 43° 09' 37.646" N, 109° 46' 43.626" W.

Chapter 4:
Large Escarpment-Surrounded Basins

Barbed tributaries are just one of many topographic map drainage system and erosional landform features that suggest massive and prolonged south-oriented continental icesheet meltwater floods once flowed across what must have been actively rising mountain regions. Also suggestive of large and prolonged floods are large escarpment-surrounded basins which can be found throughout the Great Plains and Rocky Mountain regions and at various other locations scattered across the United States. The large escarpment-surrounded basins as seen on topographic maps are usually amphitheater-shaped features which can be up to several kilometers or more in width. The basins most frequently open in a downhill direction and are often but not always bounded by steep walls which often appear to be topped by some type of erosion resistant caprock.

The geology research community knows large escarpment-surrounded basins exist and some geologic literature even proposes controversial hypotheses describing how the basins might have been formed. The controversies arise because topographic maps show no evidence of streams or rivers flowing into the now amphitheater-shaped basins, but otherwise the basins have all of the characteristics of being large water-eroded features.

W. M. Davis in the late 1800s introduced the concept of baselevel which determines how deep a river valley can be eroded. When a river's baselevel is lowered the river cuts a deeper valley headward in an upstream direction. The deeper valley head then represents what is referred to as a knickpoint. Over time knickpoints migrate upstream until the river's gradient has reached an equilibrium. Should the river cease to flow before equilibrium is reached a knickpoint might become "frozen" in the abandoned river valley. Knickpoints along some rivers, such as Niagara Falls on the Niagara River head deep steep-walled downstream gorges. In the case of Niagara Falls the Niagara River water source is obvious (it is the Lake Erie outlet) and there is little controversy. Assume for some reason Lake Erie drainage should be diverted in the opposite direction so as to drain to the Mississippi River instead of Lake Ontario, then the Niagara River would dry up leaving Niagara Falls as a "frozen" knickpoint at the head of an almost dry gorge.

Large escarpment-surrounded basins have the characteristics of "frozen" knickpoints, but with wider abandoned downstream valleys than Niagara Gorge and with no obvious evidence of an abandoned upstream river channel. Almost always an upstream river or stream valley cuts directly across the route that water flowing toward the "frozen" knickpoint and the downstream amphitheater-shaped basin would have had to have used. Controversies arise because geologists do not know where the water that eroded most large escarpment-surrounded basins came from.

The Goshen Hole escarpment-surrounded basin seen in figure 4.1 illustrates why geomorphologists have trouble when trying to determine what eroded these features. Note how the Goshen Hole escarpment-surrounded basin western end is a V-shaped notch and how the basin opens in an east and downhill direction. Most geomorphologists looking at the Goshen Hole shape for the first time probably immediately think a large east-oriented stream or river eroded a deep basin headward and that is what Rapp et al (1957) proposed. However, after looking further many geomorphologists note the lack of any east-oriented stream or river valley leading to the V-shaped notch and the north-oriented Chugwater Creek valley which is located directly to the west of the Goshen Hole basin and ask, where did the surface water to erode Goshen Hole come from?

As seen in figure 4.2 Goshen Hole is located to the east of the north-south oriented Laramie Range which further complicates the problem. The Laramie Range is now crossed by an anastomosing complex of canyons, but those canyons head in the high Laramie Basin and the accepted paradigm does not recognize a Laramie Basin water source capable of eroding the Laramie Range canyon complex, much less the Goshen Hole escarpment-surrounded basin. For these reasons the Goshen Hole escarpment-surrounded basin origin has remained an unresolved geomorphology mystery. A commonly published Goshen Hole explanation is described by Adams (1902) and Osterkamp and Higgins (1990) who suggest the escarpments surrounding Goshen Hole retreated as spring seepage undermined the escarpment walls. Spring seepage is now occurring, but even if spring seepage is contributing to Goshen Hole escarpment wall retreat spring seepage does not explain the Goshen Hole V-shape, how the anastomosing Laramie Range canyon complex developed, or how the north-oriented Chugwater Creek valley and drainage system came to be.

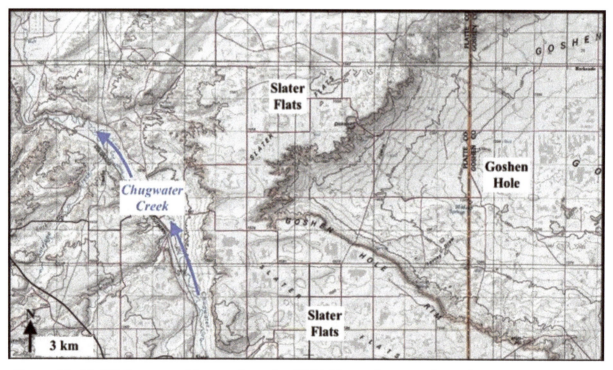

Figure 4.1: Modified topographic map from the USGS National Map website showing the Wyoming-Nebraska Goshen Hole relationship to north-oriented Chugwater Creek. The contour interval is 10 meters. Top left corner: 42° 01' 34.948" N, 104° 55' 56.788" W.

The Goshen Hole relationship to the anastomosing canyon complex which is cut across the north-to-south oriented Laramie Range (the canyons on detailed topographic maps are more numerous and complex than figure 4.2 shows) might look to a geomorphologist as though immense and prolonged floods coming from the high-elevation Laramie Basin (west and southwest of figure 4.2) and flowing to an actively eroding North Platte River valley carved the anastomosing canyons into a rising Laramie Range and then downstream from the anastomosing canyon complex the floodwaters eroded the Goshen Hole escarpment-surrounded basin in a headward direction. Goshen Hole erosion ended when headward erosion of the north-oriented Chugwater Creek valley from an actively eroding Laramie River valley (which was also eroding headward from the actively eroding North Platte River valley) captured the east-oriented flood flow. That capture left the Goshen Hole escarpment-surrounded basin as a "frozen" knickpoint on the former flood flow route.

But any such explanation from the accepted paradigm perspective is impossible for several reasons including a lack of any recognizable large Laramie Basin region floodwater source. Today the Laramie Basin is a dry intermontane basin drained by the north-oriented Laramie River. The Laramie River drains formerly glaciated mountains and geomorphologists have no problem when trying to imagine larger Laramie River flows than today, but those flows would have been in a north direction not a south direction as most barbed tributary evidence suggests. Also, the local alpine glaciers did not contain enough water to erode the anastomosing canyon complex so a much larger flood source is needed. Unable to explain the topographic map evidence, geomorphologists usually ignore the map evidence and look for other ways to explain the Goshen Basin origin (how large south-oriented floods reached the Laramie Basin will be addressed in the discussion related to figure 5.9 in the next chapter).

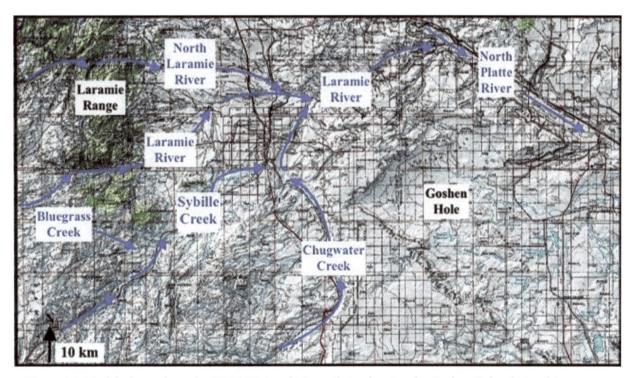

Figure 4.2: Modified map from the USGS National Map website showing the Goshen Hole relationship to some of the major canyons in the Laramie Range anastomosing canyon complex and to the North Platte River. Top left corner: 42° 14' 49.343' N, 105° 32'0.193" W.

The Jumpoff seen in figure 4.3 is another intriguing escarpment-surrounded basin located in northwest South Dakota about 25 kilometers to the south of the figure 2.6 (or in an upstream direction along the north-oriented Little Missouri River valley). The Jumpoff is surrounded in all directions with aligned drainage areas. The Jumpoff basin is not as deep as the Goshen Hole basin and is located less than five kilometers to the east of a shallow valley in which the north-oriented Little Missouri River now meanders. The escarpment rim (emphasized with a red dashed line) is today the asymmetric Little Missouri-South Fork Grand River drainage divide (see figure 2.7). Map evidence suggests a large east-oriented flood eroded a large South Fork Grand River valley knickpoint in a west direction before headward erosion of the north-oriented Little Missouri River valley captured the flow, but again the accepted paradigm provides no floodwater source.

The Jumpoff escarpment-surrounded basin is however located approximately 100 kilometers to the south and west of continental icesheet deposited erratic boulders and is a logical location for the route that large southeast-oriented icesheet marginal meltwater floods should have used. However, the accepted paradigm considers the north-oriented Little Missouri River and east-oriented Grand River to be components of a preglacial north-oriented drainage system. And, the accepted paradigm does not recognize any preglacial floods large enough to erode the South Fork Grand River valley headward and then erode the north-oriented Little Missouri River valley headward across it. The Jumpoff for that reason is rarely discussed in the geology literature as an erosional landform (although it is mentioned in the paleontology literature).

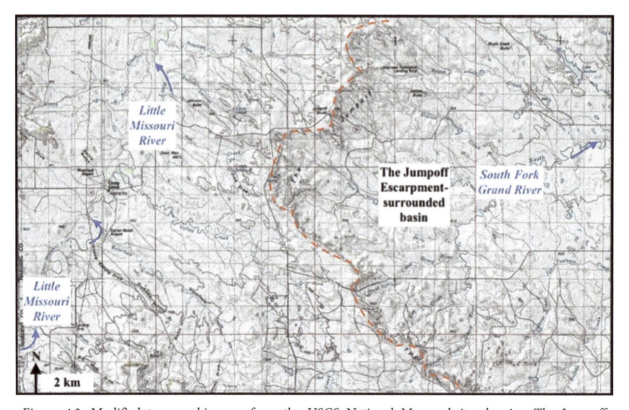

Figure 4.3: Modified topographic map from the USGS National Map website showing The Jumpoff escarpment-surrounded basin and the Little Missouri River in northwest South Dakota. The Montana- South Dakota border is located along the figure's western edge. The contour interval is 20 meters. Top left corner: 45° 38' 05.840" N, 104°02' 26.686" W.

Hoskin Basin in south central Montana is another large escarpment-surrounded basin that historical qualitative geomorphologists did not want to explain. As seen in figure 4.4 Hoskin Basin is located on the Musselshell River-Yellowstone River drainage divide southeast side (about 25 kilometers to the north of Billings, Montana) and opens in a southeast direction and appears to have been eroded headward as a giant knickpoint by large volumes of southeast-oriented water. However, to the northwest of Hoskin Basin is northeast-oriented Painted Robe Creek which flows to the east- and northeast-oriented Musselshell River which from the accepted paradigm perspective is a preglacial north-oriented drainage route and which should have captured any large southeast-oriented river/flood flowing toward the Hoskin Basin knickpoint.

Large and prolonged volumes of southeast-oriented water flowing into the deep Yellowstone River valley must have eroded Hoskin Basin. Yet the northeast-oriented Painted Robe Creek and Musselshell River valleys probably caused early geologists who conducted field work in the region (much was done before the availability of detailed topographic maps) and who described other regional landforms to omit making any mention of the Hoskin Basin escarpment-surrounded basin (e. g. Ellis and Meinzer, 1924 and Alden, 1932). Some major geologic process must have eroded the Hoskin Basin escarpment-surrounded basin headward in a northwest direction and while spring seepage is sometimes mentioned it would be remarkable if spring seepage alone could erode a feature as large as and shaped like Hoskin Basin.

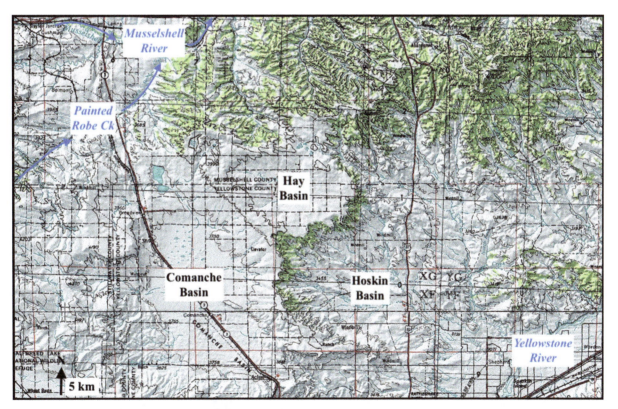

Figure 4.4. Modified map from USGS National Map website showing the Hoskin Basin escarpment-surrounded basin on the Musselshell River-Yellowstone River drainage divide. Billings, Montana is located in the Yellowstone River valley to the south of the figure. The contour interval is 200 feet (60 meters). Top left corner: 46° 18' 20.748" N, 109° 05' 17.180" W.

Somewhat similar to Hoskin Basin in shape and position is the northeast Colorado North Pawnee Creek escarpment-surrounded basin which is eroded into a Chalk Bluffs upland area (see figure 4.5) located approximately 10 kilometers to the south of where Colorado, Wyoming, and Nebraska meet. The Chalk Bluffs upland area seen in figure 4.5 is about 50 kilometers to the north of an east-oriented South Platte River segment and about 70 kilometers (as a crow flies) to the northwest of where southeast-oriented Pawnee Creek joins a northeast-oriented South Platte River segment. To the west of the Chalk Bluffs upland area is a 40-kilometer-wide valley in which Crow Creek, which after flowing in roughly an east direction from near the Laramie Range crest onto the southeast Wyoming plains turns in a south direction to join the South Platte River.

Sidney Draw is a northeast-oriented drainage route flowing to east-oriented Lodgepole Creek which also begins near the Laramie Range crest. Lodgepole Creek flows parallel to and just to the north of Crow Creek onto the southeast Wyoming plains, but unlike Crow Creek flows in an east direction into western Nebraska before turning in a southeast direction to join the northeast-oriented South Platte River. On detailed topographic maps the basin appears to have been eroded by massive southeast-oriented floods which headward erosion of the shallow northeast-oriented Sidney Draw valley captured. Headward erosion of the much deeper south-oriented Crow Creek valley subsequently captured the floods and also captured the east-oriented Crow Creek upstream segment. However, the Sidney Draw, Crow Creek, and Lodgepole Creek valley locations make it difficult to imagine how southeast-oriented floods could cross the Chalk Bluffs upland.

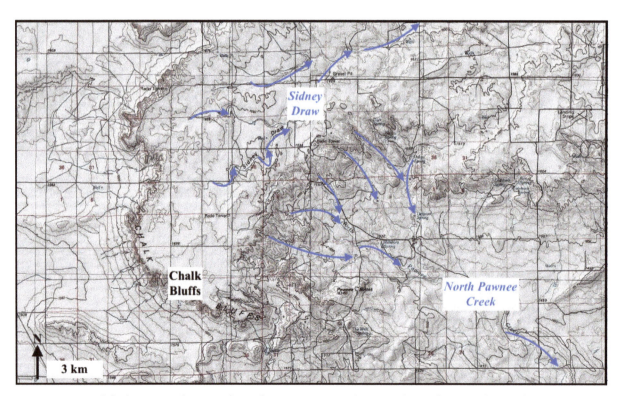

Figure 4.5: Modified topographic map from the USGS National Map website showing the northeast Colorado Chalk Bluffs area about 10 kilometers to the south of the Colorado-Wyoming-Nebraska corner. The contour interval is 10 meters. Top left corner: 40° 56' 31.944" N, 104° 10' 47.251" W.

Further to the south in east-central Colorado is a different type of large escarpment-surrounded basin. Adobe Creek originates on the Colorado Piedmont in the south-southeast oriented escarpment-surrounded basin seen in figure 4.6 and is fed by springs which emerge from the escarpment walls. Today Adobe Creek flows in a south-southeast and south direction to join the east-oriented Arkansas River and to the north of the figure is the deep east- and northeast-oriented South Platte River valley, which is approximately 400 meters lower in elevation than the surface surrounding the Adobe Creek escarpment-surrounded basin. No evidence of a south-southeast oriented valley leading to the basin is seen on detailed topographic maps although to the north of the basin both South and North Rush Creeks now flow across all routes south-oriented water would have had to have used to reach the Adobe Creek escarpment-surrounded basin.

Spring seepage is obviously occurring, but does spring seepage explain the escarpment-surrounded basin size and shape? In the case of the Adobe Creek escarpment-surrounded basin, large south-southeast oriented floods could have flowed across the Colorado Piedmont region toward a deep and actively eroding east-oriented Arkansas River valley before being captured by headward erosion of the deep (and wide) east- and northeast-oriented South Platte River valley. If so North and South Rush Creek valley headward erosion would have first ended south-oriented flow which would have left the Adobe Creek escarpment-surrounded basin as a "frozen" knickpoint. Subsequently headward erosion of the much deeper east- and northeast-oriented South Platte River valley would have captured the south-oriented floodwaters and ended all flood flow across the Colorado Piedmont region to the Arkansas River tributary valley system.

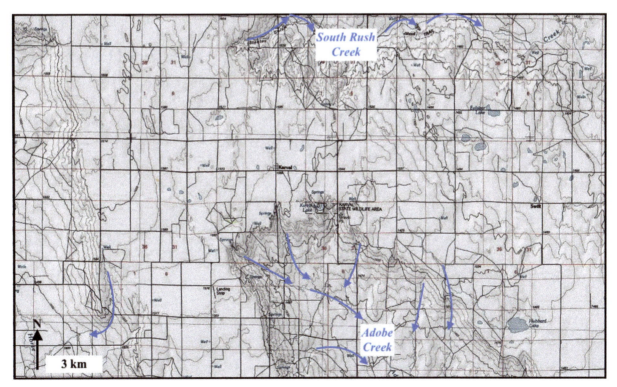

Figure 4.6: Modified map from the USGS National Map website showing the escarpment-surrounded Adobe Creek headwaters basin in east-central Colorado. The contour interval is 10 meters. Top left corner: 38° 48' 25.106" N, 103° 41' 55.668" W.

Figure 4.7 shows the South Dakota Scenic Basin which is located between the northeast-oriented Cheyenne and White Rivers. Figure 4.8 shows a larger area so as to include Sage Creek Basin which is adjacent to the Scenic Basin. Remove the northwest-oriented Spring Draw, Bear Creek, and Sage Creek valleys and the Scenic and Sage Creek Basins have the same characteristics seen in the previously discussed large escarpment-surrounded basins. However, unlike the previously discussed large escarpment-surrounded basins which drain toward the basin open end, the Scenic and Sage Creek Basins do not drain through the amphitheater basin open ends but instead drain in the opposite direction. The Scenic Basin and the adjacent Sage Creek Basin (seen in figure 4.8) and their drainage systems are pieces of a puzzle for which there must be a solution.

The walls of the northwest-oriented Spring Draw, Bear Creek, and Sage Creek valleys are similar to the escarpment walls which can be seen surrounding the Scenic and Sage Creek Basins, which strongly suggests that surface water erosion and not spring seepage was responsible for creating the Scenic and Sage Creek Basins. The Scenic and Sage Creek Basins probably became "frozen" knickpoints when headward erosion of the northeast-oriented Cheyenne River valley beheaded two roughly parallel southeast-oriented flood flow channels moving large quantities of water into what at that time was probably an actively eroding east-oriented White River valley. The northwest-oriented Spring Draw, Bear Creek, and Sage Creek valleys were probably eroded at a later time when a short-lived lake filled the White River valley and briefly spilled over the White River-Cheyenne River drainage divide into the Cheyenne River valley. The northwest-oriented spillage would have been along the drainage divide's lowest points which would have been where the two "frozen" knickpoints were located (along the two former southeast-oriented flood flow channels). The puzzle still needing to be solved is why did a temporary lake fill the White River valley?

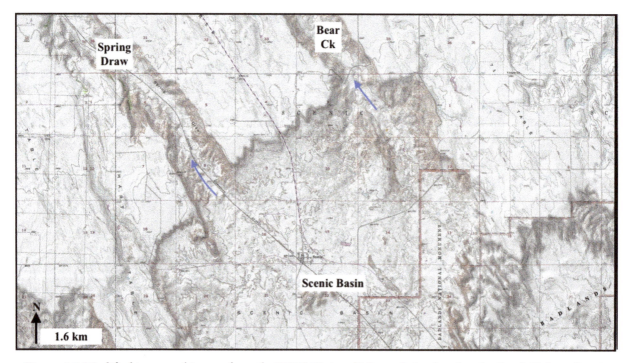

Figure 4.7: Modified topographic map from the USGS National Map website showing the South Dakota Scenic Basin escarpment-surrounded basin. The contour interval is 10 feet (3 meters). Top left corner: 43° 50' 05.630" N, 102° 38' 50.689" W.

The key to solving this complicated drainage history puzzle is to think of how immense southeast-oriented continental icesheet meltwater floods would have flowed across and then around a gradually rising Black Hills upland. The isolated Black Hills upland region is located immediately to the west of figure 4.8 and today southeast-oriented streams (like Rapid Creek) flow from high Black Hills upland areas to join the northeast-oriented Cheyenne River as barbed tributaries. These barbed tributaries provide evidence the Cheyenne River valley eroded headward across southeast-oriented floodwaters, which must have flowed across what are now high elevation Black Hills areas. Black Hills uplift must have occurred as floodwaters flowed across the region which gradually forced the southeast-oriented floodwaters to flow around the rising upland area.

Southeast-oriented floodwaters flowing across the figure 4.8 region were first captured by White River valley headward erosion and subsequently by Cheyenne River valley headward erosion (which beheaded southeast-oriented flow to the Sage Creek and Scenic Basin knickpoints). However, after those two knickpoints had been "frozen" the actively eroding White River valley was still capturing southeast-oriented flood flow that had been forced to flow around the rising Black Hills' southern end. That captured flood flow perhaps with the aid of ice jams temporarily filled the White River valley to overflowing and caused water to briefly spill across the Sage Creek and Scenic Basin rims into the newly eroded Cheyenne River valley and to carve the northwest oriented Spring Draw, Bear Creek, and Sage Creek valleys. While impossible from the accepted paradigm perspective such a scenario explains the topographic map evidence.

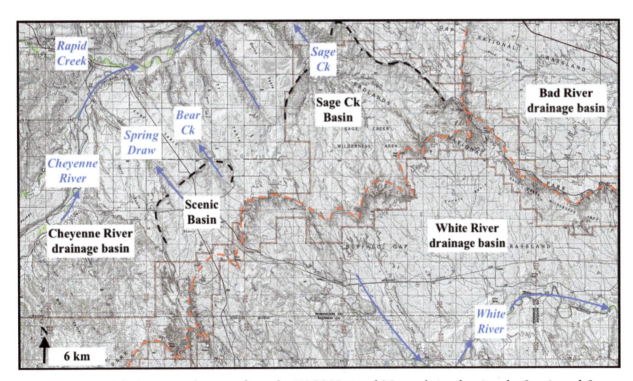

Figure 4.8: Modified topographic map from the USGS National Map website showing the Scenic and Sage Creek Basin relationship to the Cheyenne and White Rivers. Black dashed lines outline Scenic and Sage Creek Basin escarpment rim locations and the red dashed lines show major drainage divide approximate locations. The contour interval is 20 meters. Top left corner: 43° 56' 16.527" N, 102° 46' 34.020" W. For a regional map, see figure 8.1.

41

The vast majority of the Great Plains and Rocky Mountain region escarpment-surrounded basins open in southeast directions, although there are a few high elevation exceptions including the Bates Hole escarpment-surrounded basin seen in figure 4.9. Bates Hole is located in Wyoming to the north and west of the Shirley Basin and to the south and west of the northern Laramie Range. Bates Hole is drained in a northwest direction to the north- and northeast-oriented North Platte River, which after flowing around the Laramie Range northwest end turns to flow in an east and then southeast direction (see figure 2.2). The Shirley Basin drains in a south direction to the west-oriented Medicine Bow River, which joins the north- and northeast-oriented North Platte River (to the south of where northwest-oriented Bates Hole drainage enters it).

On topographic maps Bates Hole appears to have been eroded by a large northwest- or west-oriented flood, but there is no apparent water source. Further there is no barrier between the Shirley Basin and the adjacent Laramie Basin from which the previously discussed topographic map evidence suggests large north- and east-oriented floods flowed via the Laramie Range anastomosing canyon complex to the east-oriented Goshen Hole escarpment-surrounded basin. Northwest-oriented flood flow responsible for eroding Bates Hole could have occurred if as immense south-oriented floods flowed across the region the southeast-oriented North Platte River valley eroded headward around a rising Laramie Range northwest end and beheaded and reversed what had been a major south-oriented flood flow channel so as to create what today are the north-oriented North Platte River headwaters (see figure (2.2).

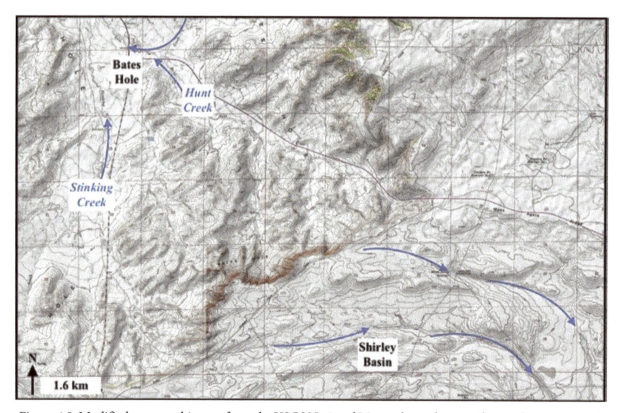

Figure 4.9: Modified topographic map from the USGS National Map website showing the northwest-oriented Bates Hole escarpment-surrounded basin. The contour interval is 20 feet (6 meters). Top left corner: 42° 25' 27.404" N, 106° 26' 00.877" W.

While not surrounded by steep-sided escarpments the Little Gravois Creek headwaters region seen in figure 4.10 (in the state of Missouri) illustrates escarpment-surrounded basin characteristics. Little Gravois Creek is a south-oriented tributary to south-oriented Gravois Creek, which in turn flows to the east- and northeast-oriented Osage River which eventually reaches the east-oriented Missouri River. To the north of the Little Gravois Creek headwaters are north-oriented tributaries flowing to the Missouri River. Large south-oriented floods appear to have eroded the Little Gravois Creek drainage basin (and other adjacent south-oriented Gravois Creek subbasins) headward in a northward direction. Continental icesheet evidence is located to the north of the "icesheet-marginal" Missouri River and suggests a logical floodwater source with headward erosion of the east-oriented Missouri River valley (aided by uplift of the region to the south of the Missouri River valley) accounting for the beheading and reversal of the south-oriented flood flow that ended headward erosion of the Little Gravois Creek drainage basin.

However, because the Missouri River in the state of Missouri is located approximately along the southern margin of the recognized glacially deposited sediments it is also considered to be an icesheet marginal river. For this reason, the accepted paradigm makes it difficult for geologists to see how what are today northeast-oriented Missouri River tributary valleys could erode headward across massive and long-lived south-oriented meltwater floods. As an alternative many geologists might attribute the Little Gravois Creek drainage basin headward erosion to climatic changes acting over extremely long periods of geologic time, although that interpretation does not explain the south-oriented tributaries to an east-oriented Missouri River tributary seen in the figure 4.10 northeast quadrant or direction changes made by some of the other Missouri River tributaries.

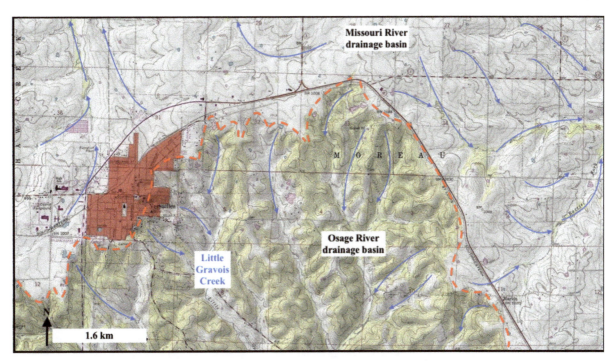

Figure 4.10: Modified topographic map from the USGS National Map website showing the Missouri-Osage River drainage divide (red dashed line) near Versailles, Missouri. The contour interval is 10 feet (3 meters). Top left corner: 38° 27' 28.824" N, 92° 51' 57.053" W.

Locations and orientations of some of the larger Great Plains and Rocky Mountain escarpment-surrounded basins are plotted on figure 4.11 (basin sizes are not drawn to scale). The North Dakota Russian Springs Escarpment western end is not illustrated in this book but is located at the head of the southeast- and northeast-oriented Knife River seen in figure 2.7 and also is near the southwest margin of continental icesheet deposited erratic material. Based on their orientations the Hoskins Basin, Russian Springs Escarpment western end, The Jumpoff, Scenic Basin, Sage Creek Basin, Chalk Bluff basin, and Adobe Creek basin can all be explained by immense southeast-oriented meltwater floods flowing between the recognized southwest margin of continental icesheet deposited debris and what are now higher elevation Rocky Mountain regions.

While located to the east of the Rocky Mountains the water that eroded the Goshen Hole basin must have flowed from the now high elevation Laramie Basin and then across the Laramie Range. Even more intriguing are the Bates Hole and Beaver Divide basins which are not only located in high Rocky Mountain basins but which are oriented in north directions. If the large escarpment-surrounded basins are "frozen" knickpoints located along former continental icesheet meltwater flood flow routes the Bates Hole, Beaver Divide, and Goshen Hole basins are evidence the meltwater floods flowed into what are now high elevation Rocky Mountain regions. Further, those three basins can only be explained if the floods reversed their flow direction, probably because the Rocky Mountain region was being uplifted as floodwaters flowed into and across the region.

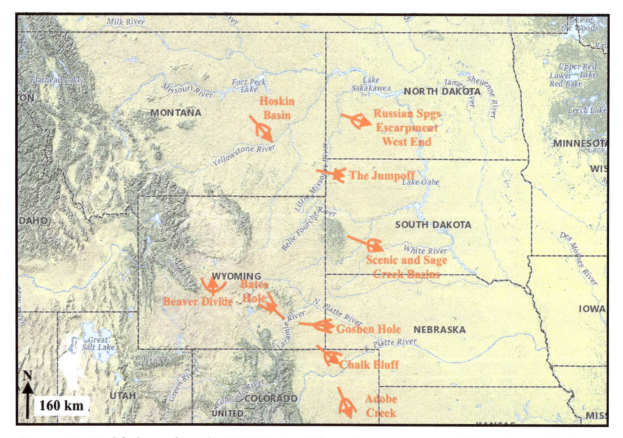

Figure 4.11: Modified map from the USGS National Map website showing probable meltwater flood flow directions determined from several of the larger Great Plains and Rocky Mountain region escarpment-surrounded basins. Basin sizes are not drawn to scale.

Chapter 5:
Mountain Passes Along the East-West Continental Divide

A skilled topographic map interpreter can quickly identify drainage divides, although less skilled map interpreters may find barbed tributaries and large escarpment-surrounded basins easier to see. Regardless of one's map interpretation skills detailed topographic maps almost always provide all of the information needed to identify drainage divides and to determine how an identified drainage divide was formed. However, the geologic literature contains few research reports in which geologists have used topographic maps when determining specific drainage divide origins. For example, I have yet to find a published research report (which I did not write) in which the origin of North America's east-west continental divide is seriously discussed.

The east-west continental divide which separates drainage to the Atlantic Ocean from drainage to the Pacific Ocean is without question North America's best-known drainage divide and, like most other North American drainage divides has a fascinating story to tell. That fascinating story is told by detailed topographic map drainage system and erosional landform evidence which the geology research community at least to date has been ignoring.

Important to the study of any drainage divide are low points along that drainage divide. Usually, but not always those low points are places where water once flowed across what is now a drainage divide. A skilled topographic map interpreter can use the map evidence to determine where the water that once flowed across a present-day drainage divide came from and where that water went. Also, the skilled topographic map interpreter can determine how that former drainage route was changed so as to create the modern-day drainage divide.

Many low points along some east-west continental divide segments are now high Rocky Mountain passes. Some Rocky Mountain passes are well-known features where major highways and railroads now cross the continental divide. Other Rocky Mountain passes are only seen when exploring back country wilderness areas. Up close the Rocky Mountain passes are large-scale landforms and their relationships with adjacent drainage systems may be difficult to visualize. However, when seen on detailed topographic maps it is easy to see on both sides of the drainage divide how a present-day Rocky Mountain pass links the valleys of modern-day drainage routes.

A stream or river flowing across what is now the east-west continental divide must have eroded each of the mountain passes seen today. In fact, mountain pass depths which can easily be determined from the topographic map evidence record how much the mountain ridge was uplifted before the uplift outpaced the valley erosion. This information should be valuable for geologists studying Rocky Mountain history, but unfortunately the geology research community has yet to recognize the importance of what the topographic maps show.

In northern Montana Sun River Pass and the unnamed pass seen in figure 5.1 both cross the east-west continental divide, which in the figure has a northeast and then southeast orientation. To the north of those passes water flows to the northwest-oriented Middle Fork Flathead River before joining the south-oriented Flathead River (see figure 3.8) which eventually joins the northwest-oriented Clark Fork River before ultimately reaching the Pacific Ocean. To the south of those passes water flows to the east-oriented Sun River which flows to the northeast-, east-, and southeast-oriented Missouri River (at about the point where in figure 2.2 northwest-oriented Missouri River headwaters turn in a northeast direction before turning to flow in an east direction) to eventually reach the Gulf of Mexico. The two passes illustrate how diverging and converging streams of south-oriented water once flowed along and across the continental divide.

Significant and prolonged streams of water probably flowing across a rising mountain region eroded the two marked passes in figure 5.1. The two adjacent passes were eroded by diverging and converging channels such as might be found in a flood formed anastomosing channel complex. What had once been stream valleys became mountain passes when uplift proceeded faster than the streams could erode the rising mountain ridge. The result was a drainage divide and water in the upstream valley was forced to reverse its flow direction until the water reached a still open south-oriented valley. North-oriented drainage from the figure area now flows toward Glacier National Park (see figure 3.8) and then turns to flow in a south direction in the Flathead River suggesting large meltwater floods eroded the passes until mountain uplift blocked the route, which diverted large quantities of south-oriented water from the now north-oriented Missouri River headwaters valley to the Flathead River valley.

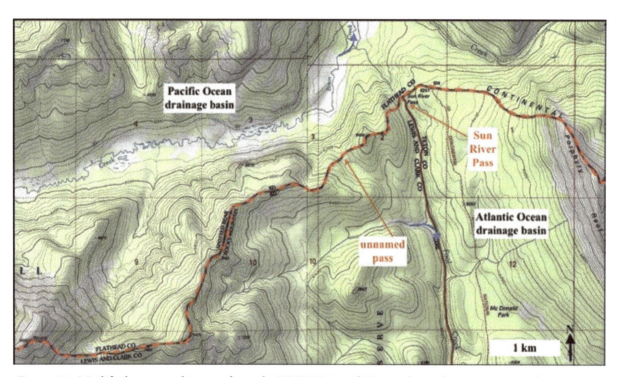

Figure 5.1: Modified topographic map from the USGS National Map website showing Montana's Sun River Pass, an unnamed pass, and the east-west continental divide (red line). The contour interval is 50 feet (15 meters). Top left corner: 47° 57' 43.598" N, 113° 03' 00.953" W.

South-oriented flow that eroded Sun River Pass at first continued in a south direction between what are today high mountain ridges to reach what is now the north-oriented South Fork Sun River valley before headward erosion of the east-oriented Sun River valley captured the flow. Clausen (2019b) describes the area and illustrates mountain passes at the south end of the north-oriented South Fork Sun River drainage system which link the Sun River with south-oriented tributaries flowing to the now north-oriented Missouri River headwaters and also with south-oriented tributaries now flowing to the west-oriented Blackfoot River on the opposite side of today's continental divide. What is remarkable about this region is detailed topographic maps suggest immense and prolonged south-oriented floods must have flowed in a large complex of diverging and converging channels which paralleled and repeatedly crossed what is now the east-west continental divide.

In the area to the south of the Sun River drainage basin figure 5.2 shows Elk Park Pass near Butte, Montana. Unlike Sun River Pass which is in a wilderness area Elk Park Pass is near a good-sized city and also is used as a major transportation route. Elk Park Pass is an excellent example of a deep mountain pass that now crosses the continental divide. The pass was eroded by one of the many diverging and converging south-oriented flood flow channels. Those south-oriented flood flow channels carved the valleys between what are now north-to-south oriented mountain ridges (including the ridges which now make up the continental divide). Flood flow that flowed through the Elk Park Pass valley flowed from what is now the Atlantic Ocean drainage basin into what is now the Pacific Ocean drainage basin.

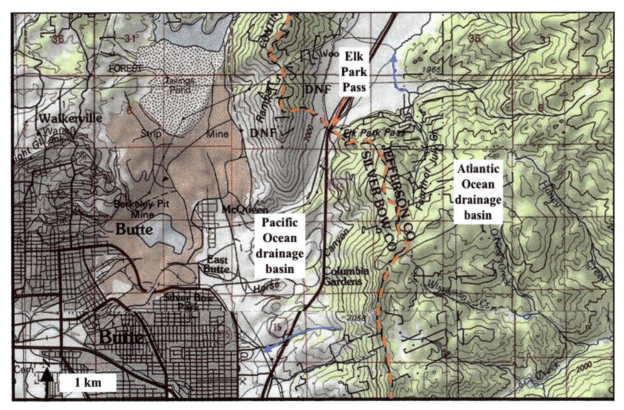

Figure 5.2: Modified topographic map from the USGS National Map website showing Elk Park Pass, which crosses the east-west continental divide (red dashed line) near Butte, Montana. The contour interval is 50 meters. Top left corner: 46°03' 31.852" N, 112°33' 08.654" W.

While frequently located along well-defined mountain ridges there are places where the east-west continental divide is located along a mountain slope as seen in figure 5.3 (located in western Montana near the Idaho border and where the continental divide now is the Beaverhead-Ravall1 County line). Note how East Fork

Camp Creek in Ravalli County flows in a deep narrow valley in a north-northeast and then north-northwest direction in the Pacific Ocean drainage basin while Trail Creek in Beaverhead County flows in a south-southeast direction in the Atlantic Ocean drainage basin on what might be considered a ledge formed along the East Fork Camp Creek valley wall. The figure 5.3 drainage routes pose an intriguing drainage history puzzle. Somehow running water eroded the region in such a way that East Fork Camp Creek was able to erode a deep north-oriented valley adjacent to the much shallower south-oriented Trail Creek valley.

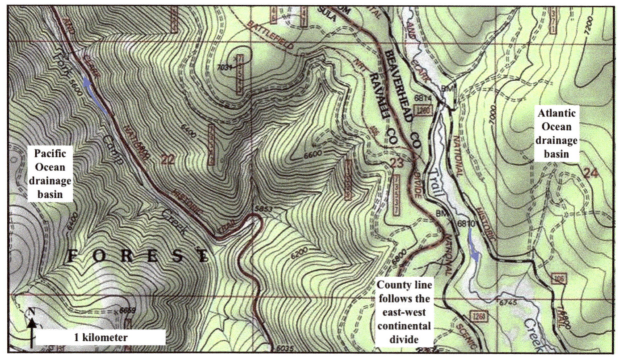

Figure 5.3: Modified topographic map from the USGS National Map website showing the Beaverhead-Ravalli County (Montana) border, which follows the east-west continental divide. The contour interval is 50 feet (15 meters). Top left corner: 45° 44' 38.083" N, 113° 56' 26.034" W.

One solution to this drainage history puzzle requires now north-oriented East Fork Camp Creek to have flowed in a south direction perhaps as one channel in what was a large flood formed south-oriented diverging and converging channel complex with now south-oriented Trail Creek being another channel in that complex. Today Trail Creek flows in a south and southeast direction to join north-oriented Big Hole River headwaters as a barbed tributary. Figure 3.7 shows how the Big Hole River now flows in a north, then east and south direction before turning in a northeast direction to join the northeast-oriented Beaverhead River and to form the northeast-oriented Jefferson River. South-oriented barbed tributaries and through valleys linking the north-oriented Big Hole River valley with the northeast-oriented Beaverhead River suggest large amounts of water in the now north-oriented Big Hole River headwaters valley once flowed in a south direction probably to join south-oriented water in the now north-oriented Beaverhead River valley. The water then flowed further to the south across what are now deep passes notched into the continental divide to reach the present-day west-oriented Snake River drainage basin.

Such a solution requires massive and prolonged south-oriented floods (probably of continental icesheet meltwater) to have flowed along what is now the east-west continental divide. Uplift of the mountains which occurred as floodwaters flowed across them and headward erosion of deep valleys from both the east and the west systematically diverted the floodwaters in new directions. In the case of the Big Hole River, headward erosion of what is now the east-oriented Big Hole River valley segment combined with tectonic uplift reversed what had been south-oriented flood flow to create the north-oriented Big Hole River headwaters segment seen today.

The south-oriented flood flow channel on the now north-oriented East Fork Camp Creek alignment diverged from the Trail Creek channel and flowed across Lost Trail Pass (letter A in figure 5.4) and was captured by headward erosion of the deep west-oriented Salmon River valley (which had a shorter route to the Pacific Ocean than water in the then south-oriented Big Hole River headwaters valley had to either the Atlantic or Pacific Ocean). Subsequently the headward erosion of deep valleys from the now northwest-oriented Clark Fork River valley beheaded and reversed flow along the East Fork Camp Creek alignment so as to create the drainage divide at Lost Trail Pass and north-oriented East Fork Camp Creek. Diverging and converging south-oriented flood flow channels prior to being captured by the headward erosion of deep valleys from the east and west probably eroded what are passes now crossing the continental divide like Chief Joseph Pass which is seen at the letter B in figure 5.4.

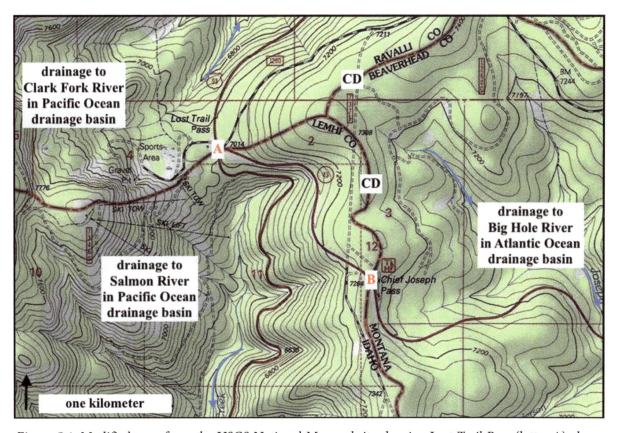

Figure 5.4: Modified map from the USGS National Map website showing Lost Trail Pass (letter A) along Clark Fork River-Salmon River drainage divide to the south of figure 5.3. Letters "CD" identify the east-west continental divide and letter B identifies Chief Joseph Pass. The contour interval is 40 feet (about 12 meters). Top left corner: 45° 42' 06.899" N, 113° 58' 02.422" W.

Raynolds Pass (seen in figure 5.5) is located a short distance to the west of Yellowstone National Park and is one of three fairly closely spaced deep passes eroded by diverging and converging streams of water that once flowed across what is now the east-west continental divide. Raynolds Pass is a through valley linking north-oriented drainage to the north-oriented Madison River in the Atlantic Ocean drainage basin with south-oriented drainage to the Snake River in the Pacific Ocean Basin. Targhee Pass and Rheas Pass are located to the southeast of figure 5.5 and link north-oriented drainage to the Madison River and north-oriented Gallatin River (further to the east) with south-oriented drainage to the Snake River. After flowing through separate and deep mountain valleys the Madison and Gallatin Rivers join with the Jefferson River at Three Forks, Montana to form the north-oriented Missouri River headwaters seen in figure 2.2.

The three passes when viewed in the context of the larger regional drainage network appear to have been eroded when large and prolonged south-oriented streams of water diverged in the Three Forks area and flowed along separate south-oriented routes to the region just to the west of Yellowstone National Park where the streams converged with the water then flowing in a south direction on what is today the Henrys Fork of the Snake River and then the Snake River alignment. The logical water source would have been a large continental icesheet, but accepted paradigm interpretations describe the north-oriented Missouri River headwaters (including the north-oriented Madison and Gallatin Rivers) as being part of a preglacial north-oriented drainage system (which one or more continental icesheets blocked to form the downstream Missouri River).

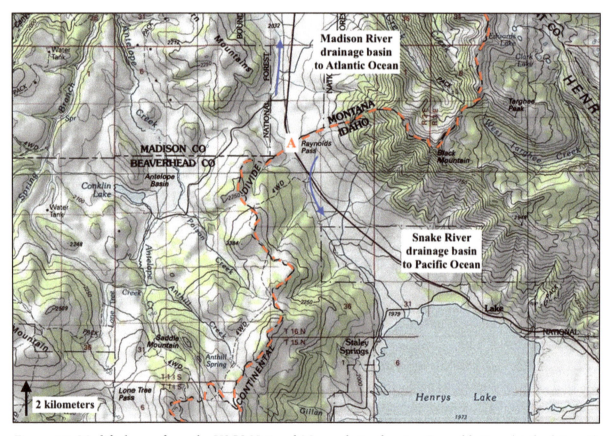

Figure 5.5: Modified map from the USGS National Map website showing Raynolds Pass (at the letter A) crossing the continental divide (red dashed line) and located west of Yellowstone National Park. The contour interval is 50 meters. Top left corner: 44° 44' 43.300' N, 111° 34' 19.165" W.

Numerous passes of varying depths are notched into the continental divide as it extends in a southeast direction across Yellowstone National Park from the figure 5.5 area to Phelps and Two Ocean Passes, which are located in a northwest Wyoming wilderness area just to the south of Yellowstone National Park and which are shown in figure 5.6. Phelps and Two Ocean Passes are deep through valleys which link north-oriented Yellowstone River headwaters (flowing to Yellowstone Lake and eventually to the Missouri River) with southwest-oriented streams flowing to the south-oriented Snake River, which, after many direction changes, eventually joins the Columbia River in Washington State. Phelps and Two Ocean Passes are in a remote and difficult-to-access region and are easy to overlook. Heavily traveled highways use several other Yellowstone National Park region mountain passes, but geologists also overlook those easily accessed mountain passes (at least in terms of determining how the passes originated).

Phelps and Two Ocean Passes can be explained if large and prolonged streams of southwest-oriented water diverged from a powerful and prolonged stream of south- and southeast-oriented water on what is now the northwest- and north-oriented Yellowstone River alignment. Mountain uplift must have eventually outpaced the ability of those streams to erode their valleys which forced a reversal of flow in the Yellowstone River valley. The reversal of flow created what is now the east-west continental divide and the north-oriented Yellowstone River headwaters. While such an interpretation explains the map evidence, it requires large and prolonged south-oriented flood flows, which from the accepted paradigm perspective did not occur, which leaves geologists with no other way to explain how water eroded the Phelps Pass and the Two Ocean Pass through valleys.

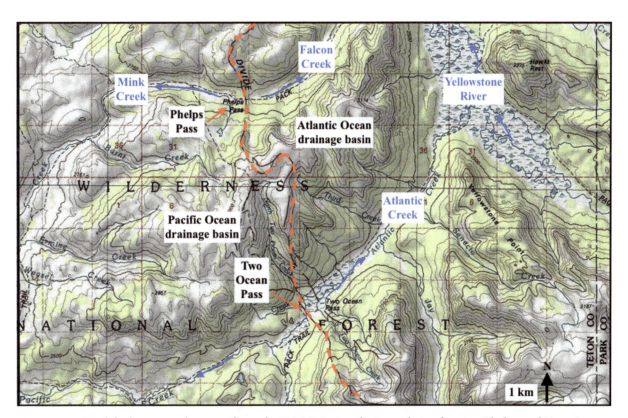

Figure 5.6: Modified topographic map from the USGS National Map website showing Phelps and Two Ocean Passes crossing the continental divide (red line) south of Yellowstone National Park. The contour interval is 50 meters. Top left corner: 44° 07' 00.587" N, 110° 17' 10.687" W.

Figure 5.7 shows another puzzling continental divide area near central Wyoming's South Pass. Today a gravity-fed surface irrigation ditch moves Sweetwater River water from the Atlantic Ocean drainage basin into the Pacific Ocean drainage basin. To the northwest of the figure, the high northwest-southeast oriented Wind River Mountains crest ridge for a considerable distance serves as the east-west continental divide, although near the crest ridge's southeast end (just before reaching Sweetwater Gap, which is seen in figure 7.4), the continental divide leaves the crest ridge and turns in a south and southeast direction and descends along the Wind River Mountains south flank and is just to the west and southwest of the Sweetwater River headwaters. The Sweetwater River begins at Sweetwater Gap and flows in a south and then southeast direction before turning in an east direction to flow almost along the east-west continental divide. Further to the east the Sweetwater River flows just to the north of Wyoming's Great Divide Basin (a large internally drained basin which straddles the east-west continental divide).

Geologists who abide by accepted paradigm rules and assumptions have a difficult time explaining why a river like the Sweetwater River flows for a considerable distance almost along the east-west continental divide and also in explaining why a large internally drained region is located along a significant section of the Wyoming east-west continental divide. The topographic map evidence can be explained if immense and prolonged south-oriented meltwater floods flowed across Wyoming at a time when the Wind River Mountains were just beginning to emerge and then continued to flow across Wyoming until blocked and reversed by regional uplift. Such an explanation requires a link between a large continental icesheet and Wyoming mountain uplift, which, as previously mentioned from the accepted paradigm perspective, is impossible because continental icesheets and Wind River Mountains emergence occurred at different times and continental icesheet meltwater floods could not have reached Wyoming.

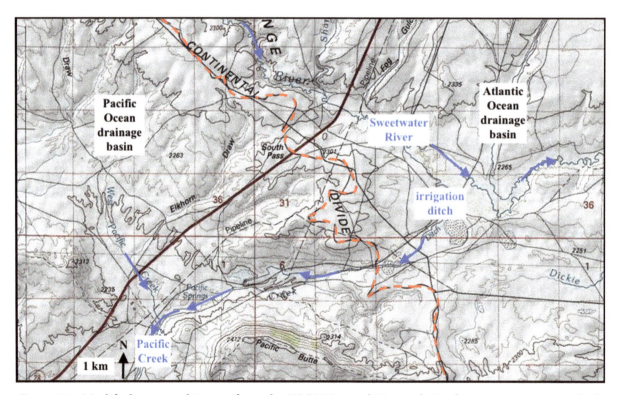

Figure 5.7: Modified topographic map from the USGS National Map website showing an irrigation ditch crossing the east-west continental divide (red dashed line) at South Pass, Wyoming. The contour interval is 20 meters. Top left corner: 42° 24' 00.372" N, 109° 00' 06.954" W

Another intriguing wilderness area mountain pass crossing the east-west continental divide can be found in northcentral Colorado and links the north-oriented Encampment River valley with the north-, west-, and southwest-oriented North Fork Elk River valley (seen in figure 5.8). The Encampment River flows in a north direction to join the north-oriented North Platte River, which, in central Wyoming, turns in a southeast direction, with its water eventually ending up in the Gulf of Mexico (see figure 2.2). The North Fork Elk River just to the west of the figure turns in a southwest direction to join the south-oriented Elk River, which then joins the north- and west-oriented Yampa River (see figure 7.5) to flow to the south-oriented Green River (with the water eventually reaching the Colorado River and the Pacific Ocean).

The deep pass seen in figure 5.8 must have been eroded by a large and long-lived south-oriented stream of water flowing across what must have been a rising mountain area to what is now the north-oriented Yampa River headwaters. A well-defined through valley (which is seen in figure 7.6) links north-oriented Yampa River headwaters with the Colorado River valley and suggests water once flowed in a south direction from the now north-oriented Yampa River valley to the Colorado River valley. Uplift of the entire region must have outpaced the ability of the south-oriented water to erode a deeper valley which forced a reversal of flow and created the drainage divide seen today.

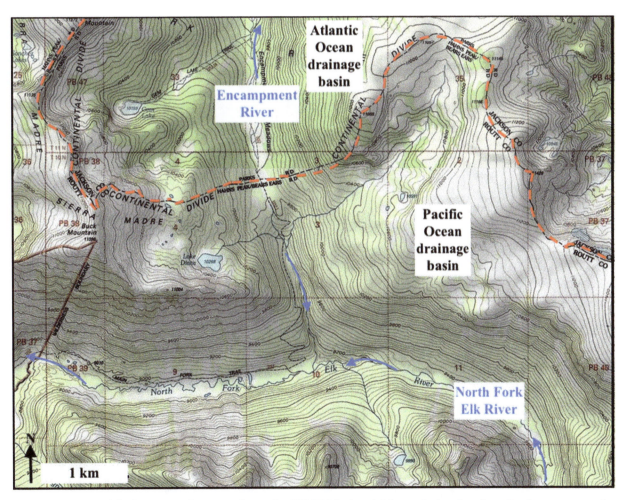

Figure 5.8: Modified topographic map from the USGS National Map website showing the deep unnamed mountain pass linking the north-oriented Encampment River valley with the north-, west-and southwest-oriented North Fork Elk River valley. The contour interval is 40 feet (12 meters). Top left corner: 40° 53' 21.645" N, 106° 44' 59.352" W.

The figure 5.9 red rectangle shows the figure 5.10 and 5.11 location with the figure 5.8 location being just a short distance to the west. To understand the regional drainage history, note how the Colorado, the Cache la Poudre, and the Laramie Rivers and a west- and northwest-oriented North Platte River tributary (the Michigan River) all begin in the red rectangle area (the Encampment River seen in figure 5.8 begins in Colorado just to the west of the North Platte River headwaters). Note also how with the exception of the Colorado River each of the rivers now flows along completely different routes to end up in the same Nebraska Platte River.

Mountain passes link North Platte (Michigan), South Plate (Cache la Poudre), Laramie, and Colorado River headwaters. Those linkages suggest South Platte-Cache la Poudre River valley headward erosion in a west direction across immense south-oriented floods beheaded and reversed what are now north-oriented South Platte River headwaters and then beheaded and reversed flow that had been moving to the south-oriented Colorado River headwaters. North Platte River valley headward erosion (in a northwest direction) probably closely followed South Platte River valley headward erosion and beheaded and reversed flow on the now north-oriented Laramie River alignment and later on the now north-oriented North Platte River headwaters alignment.

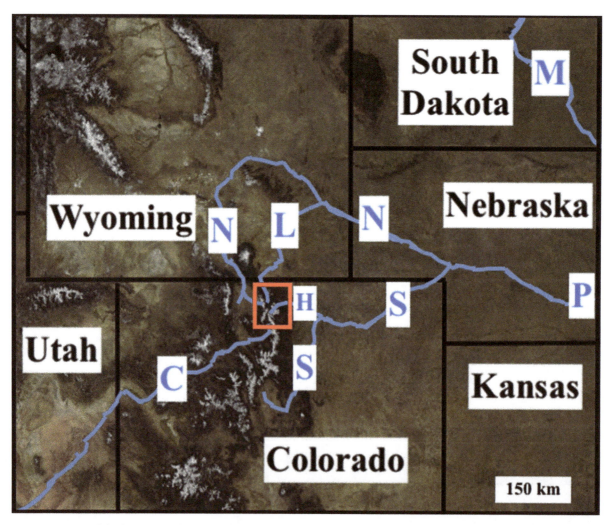

Figure 5.9: Modified imagery from USGS National Map website showing the North (N) and South (S) Platte River location relative to Colorado (C), Cache La Poudre (H), Laramie (L), Missouri (M) and Platte (P) River locations. Red square shows the figure 5.10 and 5.11 location.

La Poudre Pass (seen in figure 5.10) links northeast-oriented La Poudre Creek with south-oriented Colorado River headwaters. La Poudre Creek starts near the pass and joins the north-oriented Cache la Poudre River, which, to the north of the figure, turns in an east direction to join the South Platte River, with the water eventually reaching the Gulf of Mexico. Cameron Pass links the west-oriented Michigan River with the north- and east-oriented Cache la Poudre River and with the north-oriented Laramie River. The west-oriented Michigan River turns in a northwest direction to join the north- and southeast-oriented North Platte River, while the Laramie River after flowing through the Laramie Basin turns in an east and northeast direction so as to flow across the Laramie Mountains and to reach the southeast-oriented North Platte River (see figures 4.2 and 5.9).

La Poudre Pass can be explained if, during large and prolonged south-oriented floods and while mountain uplift was beginning, south-oriented water flowing on the now north-oriented Cache la Poudre River alignment split into diverging streams, one of which flowed in a southwest direction to erode the south-oriented Colorado River valley headward toward La Poudre Pass and the other of which flowed along what is now the Cache la Poudre River headwaters valley to Milner Pass (see figure 5.11). Mountain uplift eventually forced flow reversals that created the north-oriented Cache la Poudre River headwaters. Cameron Pass shows how mountain uplift blocked south-oriented floodwaters that were then still moving on the now north-oriented North Platte River headwaters alignment and forced the south-oriented water to flow in an east direction around the Medicine Bow Mountains southern end to reach what had become by that time the north- and east-oriented Cache la Poudre and north-oriented Laramie Rivers (today the North Platte and Laramie Rivers flow in north directions on opposite sides of the north-to-south oriented Medicine Bow Mountains).

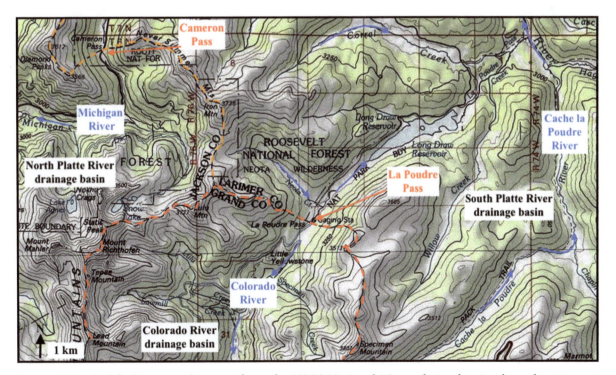

Figure 5.10: Modified topographic map from the USGS National Map website showing how the east-west continental divide (red dashed line) loops around the Colorado River headwaters and the North Platte River-South Platte River drainage divide (orange dashed line). The contour interval is 50 meters. Top left corner: 40° 31' 42.345" N, 105° 55' 07.629" W.

Milner Pass in figure 5.11 provides supporting evidence for a hypothesis that before mountain uplift forced flood flow reversals diverging streams of south-oriented water eroded what are now the north-oriented La Poudre Creek and Cache la Poudre River valleys (seen in figure 5.10) and the south-oriented Colorado River headwaters valley. The Cache la Poudre River today begins at Milner Pass and flows in a northeast and north direction from figure 5.11 into the figure 5.10 area. Milner Pass, like La Poudre Pass, is on the floor of a deep through valley linking the north-oriented Cache la Poudre River valley with the much deeper south-oriented Colorado River valley.

Water flowing in one direction or the other eroded the two through valleys, and based on the deeper Colorado River valley, the direction of flow was almost certainly in a south direction. The diverging valleys seen in figures 5.10 and 5.11 suggest large and prolonged volumes of south-oriented water must have been involved, while the through valley depths suggest the south-oriented flow continued for a significant time period. To explain how immense and long-lived floods of south-oriented water could have flowed across this region it is necessary to describe a Cenozoic geology and glacial history in which the Rocky Mountains were just beginning to be uplifted at a time when huge south-oriented meltwater floods from a large continental icesheet flowed across the region (which is fundamentally different from the Cenozoic geology and glacial history the accepted paradigm forces geologists to describe). A much more detailed discussion of the figure 5.8, 5.9, 5.10, and 5.11 drainage history is provided in Clausen (2020b and 2021a). Other papers describing North and South Platte River drainage history details include Clausen (2019g, 2020a, 2020c, 2020d, 2020c, 2021d, and 2022d)

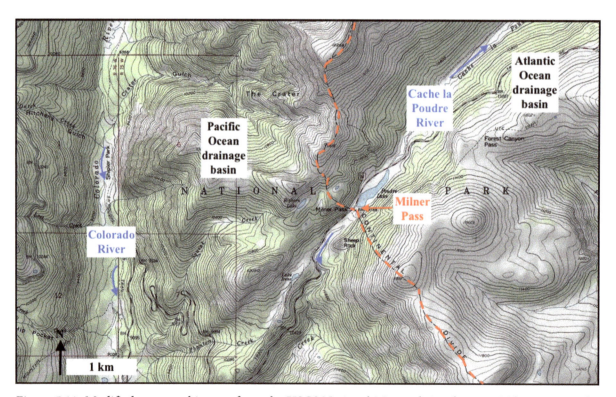

Figure 5.11: Modified topographic map from the USGS National Map website showing Milner Pass in the region to the south of figure 4.7. The contour interval is 40 feet (12 meters). Top left corner: 40° 26' 33.426" N, 105° 51' 51.575" W.

Chapter 6:
Water Gaps and Rivers Flowing Across Mountain Ranges

Water gaps are river or stream valleys which have been eroded across ridges or even high mountain ranges. Geologists have always had problems when trying to explain how rivers and streams could erode valleys across what are now ridges or mountain ranges. Geomorphology textbooks define the rivers and streams that eroded the water gaps as being either antecedent or superimposed. Antecedent rivers and streams predate the ridge or geologic structure which they now cross and were able to erode a valley as the ridge or geologic structure emerged. Superimposed rivers and streams developed their courses on a sedimentary rock cover which had buried the ridge or geologic structure and then the river or stream eroded down through the sediment cover.

The water gap origin problem became evident when geologists tried to explain Susquehanna River water gaps such as those north of Harrisburg, Pennsylvania (seen in figure 6.1). The antecedent hypothesis did not appear to be correct because the water gaps are eroded across the limbs of large synclines which the accepted paradigm sometimes interprets to have formed when Pennsylvania had northwest-oriented rivers. This interpretation caused some geomorphologists to propose the south-oriented Susquehanna River developed its course on a cover of sedimentary rocks, but no evidence of that sedimentary rock cover has ever been found.

Figure 6.1: Modified topographic map from the USGS National Map website showing water gaps to the north of Harrisburg, Pennsylvania. The contour interval is 20 meters. Top left corner: 40° 25' 58.326" N, 77° 09' 16.654" W.

In one such hypothesis Douglas Johnson (1931) proposed most Appalachian region drainage systems developed on top of Cretaceous marine sediments, which had buried the mountain ridges with the Susquehanna River and its tributaries cutting down through the underlying geologic structures as the marine sediments were removed. An alternate hypothesis suggested the water gaps had been eroded along zones of rock weakness such as fault lines. Strahler (1945), who was one of Johnson's PhD students conducted a detailed study to determine which of the various hypotheses that had been proposed (up until that time) best explained the water gap evidence. In that study Strahler was forced to reject all of the different hypothesis that he considered except for Johnson's sedimentary cover hypothesis for which he could find no supporting evidence.

The south-oriented Susquehanna River drainage basin includes hundreds of water gaps (a 2013 study by Lee counted more than 600 with most located along tributary drainage routes). Figure 6.2 illustrates one example of the confusing Susquehanna River water gap evidence. North-oriented Shamokin Creek headwaters in Pennsylvania now flow through the two deep water gaps and a third water gap is located to the north of the figure. To the north of that third water gap, Shamokin Creek turns in a west direction to flow in a valley between lower elevation west-to-east oriented ridges before eventually joining the south-oriented Susquehanna River. The Shamokin Creek water gaps and direction changes can be explained by immense and prolonged south-oriented continental icesheet meltwater floods that flowed across the entire region as the mountain ridges were being uplifted (with headward erosion of what is now the west-oriented Shamokin Creek downstream valley beheading and reversing south-oriented flood flow in the now north-oriented Shamokin Creek valley to create today's north- and west-oriented Shamokin Creek drainage route).

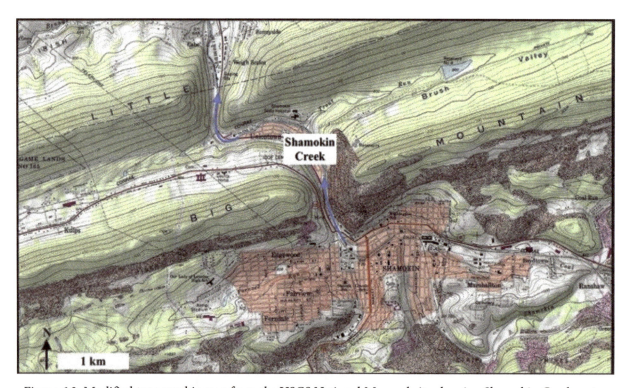

Figure 6.2: Modified topographic map from the USGS National Map website showing Shamokin Creek water gaps in the Susquehanna River drainage basin (figure 6.2 is located to the north and east of figure 6.1). The contour interval is 20 feet (6 meters). Top left corner: 40° 49' 00.291" N, 76° 36' 54.263" W.

Streams and rivers flowing across mountain ridges are found throughout the Appalachian Mountains. One interesting drainage system puzzle can be seen in figure 6.3, where Flaugherty Creek flows in a northwest direction across a high northeast-trending ridge and to the west of the figure joins the Casselman River, which then flows in a northwest direction through another water gap before turning in a southwest direction to join the north-oriented Youghiogheny River (as a barbed tributary). The Youghiogheny River then flows through some more water gaps with its water eventually reaching the Ohio and Mississippi Rivers and the Gulf of Mexico.

Adjacent to the Flaugherty Creek drainage basin is northwest-, northeast-, and southeast-oriented Wills Creek, which to the southeast of the figure has cut water gaps across still other high ridges before reaching the Potomac River that eventually reaches the Atlantic Ocean. Not only is there the problem of how Flaugherty Creek eroded its valley across a high ridge, but there is the problem of how the northwest-, northeast-, and southeast-oriented Wills Creek drainage route developed. In addition, there is the problem of how did the Ohio River-Potomac River drainage divide form.

The Flaugherty and Wills Creek puzzle evidence exists, so there must be a solution, but that solution probably requires the drainage routes to have been developed during immense and prolonged south-oriented floods which occurred as the ridges were emerging (by uplift, removal of surrounding materials, or both). Continental icesheet meltwater floods could explain the evidence; however, according to the accepted paradigm, the ridges and the drainage systems developed long before continental icesheets formed, and continental icesheet meltwater did not reach this southwestern Pennsylvania location. To explain the figure 6.3 evidence, geologists need a different Cenozoic geology and glacial history paradigm than the paradigm they have today.

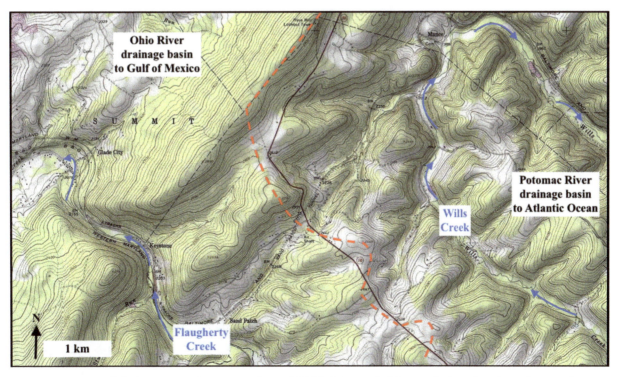

Figure 6.3: Modified topographic map from USGS National Map website showing the southwest Pennsylvania Flaugherty Creek water gap and Ohio River-Atlantic Ocean drainage divide (red dashed line). The contour interval is 20 feet (6 meters). Top left corner: 39° 50' 07.076" N, 79° 00' 28.531" W.

59

The Rocky Mountain region contains spectacular canyons where rivers flow across high mountain ranges. Atwood (p. 316) noted that "there are at least twenty-five notable canyons or water gaps in the middle and southern portions of the Rocky Mountains in the United States that are the result of the superposition of streams." Figure 6.4 shows where the north-oriented Wind River has carved a kilometer-deep canyon across Wyoming's east-west-oriented Owl Creek Mountains. Atwood's superposition hypothesis requires the Wind River to have originated on a sedimentary cover, which buried the high Owl Creek Mountains and which must have filled the Wind River Basin (to the south of the figure). That hypothesized sedimentary rock cover has since been almost completely removed, so today there is little or no evidence of the cover's existence (e. g. see Pelletier, 2009).

An alternate antecedence hypothesis requires the Owl Creek Mountains to have been uplifted around a preexisting Wind River, but that hypothesis has problems because, before reaching Wind River Canyon, the Wind River flows in a southeast direction and then, for no apparent reason, abruptly turns in a north direction to flow across the Owl Creek Mountains (see figure 8.1). The southeast-oriented Wind River headwaters are like a barbed tributary flowing to the north-oriented Wind River and suggest the Owl Creek Mountains were uplifted while a powerful and prolonged south-oriented stream of water flowed across the rising mountain range. However, the accepted Cenozoic geology and glacial history paradigm does not permit such an interpretation, and as a result (while stratigraphic units exposed along the Wind River Canyon walls have been extensively studied), Wind River Canyon as an erosional feature has not been satisfactorily explained.

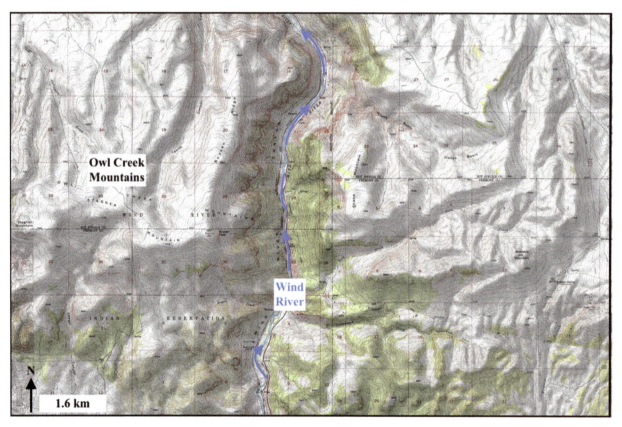

Figure 6.4: Modified topographic map from the USGS National Map website showing Wind River Canyon where the Wind River cuts across the Wyoming Owl Creek Mountains. The contour interval is 20 feet (6 meters). Top left corner: 43° 30' 23.884" N, 108° 15" 26.152" W.

Downstream from Wind River Canyon the Wind River name changes to become the Bighorn River which flows in a north direction across Wyoming's Bighorn Basin before eroding another deep canyon across the Bighorn Mountains northern end and eventually reaching the northeast-oriented Yellowstone River (as seen in figure 2.2). Between its two major canyons the Bighorn River has eroded water gaps across several other geologic structures the most prominent of which is the Sheep Mountain anticline seen in figure 6.5. Geologists know the Bighorn River's Sheep Mountain water gap exists because illustrations of it often appear in introductory geology textbooks.

The most frequently cited Sheep Mountain water gap origin explanation is the Bighorn River eroded down through a sedimentary rock cover. Unlike in the Appalachian Mountain region the Bighorn Basin does contain evidence that a sedimentary cover may have once existed. However, that sedimentary cover explanation does not explain why Bear Creek, Dry Bear Creek, and other streams flow in south directions to join the north-oriented Bighorn River as barbed tributaries.

The barbed tributaries (and there are many others in the Bighorn Basin) suggest Bighorn Basin drainage was once in a south direction. Uplift of the region and adjacent mountain ranges must have been occurring as massive floods of south-oriented meltwater carved deep canyons across the rising Bighorn and Owl Creek Mountains and the Sheep Mountain anticline and probably also removed significant amounts of easily eroded sedimentary rock from the Bighorn Basin floor.

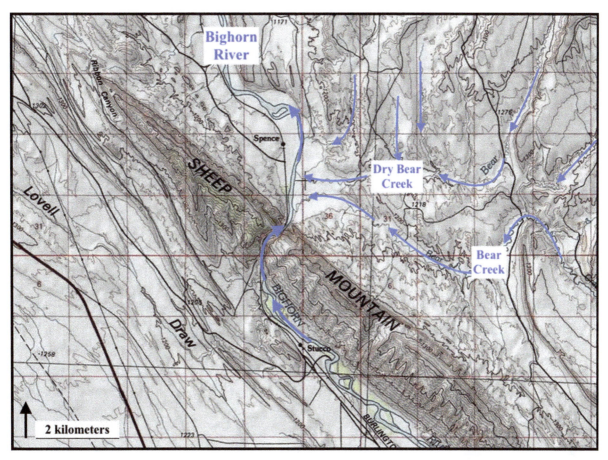

Figure 6.5: Modified topographic map from the USGS National Map website showing the water gap where the north-oriented Bighorn River crosses the Sheep Mountain anticline. The contour interval is 20 meters. Top left corner: 44° 39' 49.799" N., 108° 13' 29.640" W.

61

Not as well-known as Wind River Canyon and probably not on Atwood's list of the twenty-five or more notable Rocky Mountain canyons are the valleys seen in figure 6.6, where Deer and Box Elder Creeks flow across the northwest-to-southeast oriented northern Laramie Mountains (which are to the north of figure 4.9). Deer and Box Elder Creeks both begin in the northern Laramie Mountains as south-oriented drainage routes and flow to the southern margin of the mountainous area before making U-turns to flow in north directions in canyons completely across the Laramie Mountains to reach the east- and southeast-oriented North Platte River valley (to the west and north of the figure the North Platte River as seen in figure 8.2 cuts across the Laramie Mountains northwest end as it turns from flowing in a north direction to flow in an east and southeast direction).

Also, as seen in figure 6.6, the north-oriented Deer and Box Elder Creek valleys are joined by south-oriented (barbed) tributaries. The multiple valleys which are cut completely across the northern Laramie Mountains, the drainage route U-turns, and the barbed tributaries are evidence suggesting that as the Laramie Mountains were being uplifted large and prolonged south-oriented floods flowed across the region and the floods were beheaded and reversed (in sequence from east to west) by the headward erosion of what is now the east- and southeast-oriented North Platte River valley. However, as mentioned, the accepted paradigm considers the Laramie Mountains to have been uplifted before any continental icesheets existed, and without a water source, most geologists consider the above interpretation to be impossible.

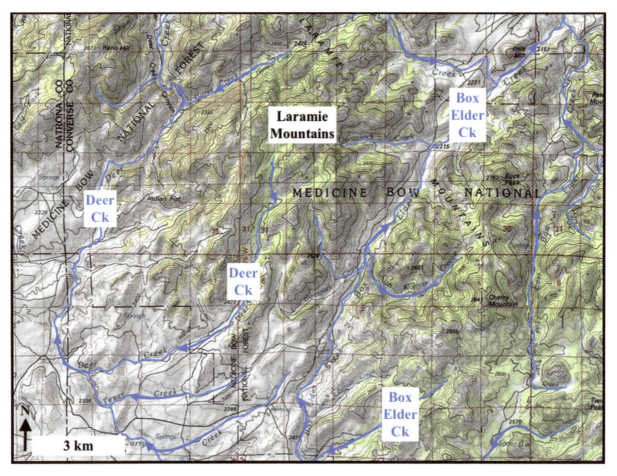

Figure 6.6: Modified topographic map from the USGS National Map website showing where Deer and Box Elder Creeks cross the northwest-southeast oriented northern Laramie Mountains. The contour interval is 20 meters. Top left corner: 42° 35' 16.809" N, 106° 05" 47.008" W.

Small local streams like Barnhart Creek in figure 6.7 have eroded valleys across numerous uplifted mountain areas. Barnhart Creek is a relatively short east- and north-oriented drainage route located in the Arkansas Ouachita Mountains and flows to the east-oriented Fourche LaFave River, which flows to the Arkansas River which then joins the Mississippi River. Figure 6.7 shows much, but not all, of the Barnhart Creek drainage basin, which hardly seems large enough to generate enough water to erode the 100- to 200-meter-deep water gaps through which it flows. Similar water gaps are common in all folded mountain regions yet the geologic literature almost never explains them.

If pressed, some geologists might argue for an antecedent origin while other geologists might argue for a superposition origin, although in both cases, the geologists would want to avoid providing any details. The Barnhart Creek water gaps, like thousands of similar water gaps, exist, but the accepted Cenozoic geology and glacial history paradigm does not provide the tools (such as a source for immense and prolonged floods that must have been flowing across the region as mountain uplift was occurring) needed to explain the water gap origins.

In the case of figure 6.7, the Barnhart Creek water gaps can be explained by the reversal of large and prolonged south-oriented meltwater floods. The flow reversal was caused by regional uplift and headward erosion of the deep Fourche LaFave River valley to the north. Headward erosion of the Fourche LaFave River valley was from the east to the west and would have beheaded and reversed flow on south-oriented channels in sequence, with the reversed flow on newly beheaded channels capturing south-oriented flood flow still moving further to the west (west of the actively eroding Fourche LaFave River valley head) so as to erode the north-oriented valley.

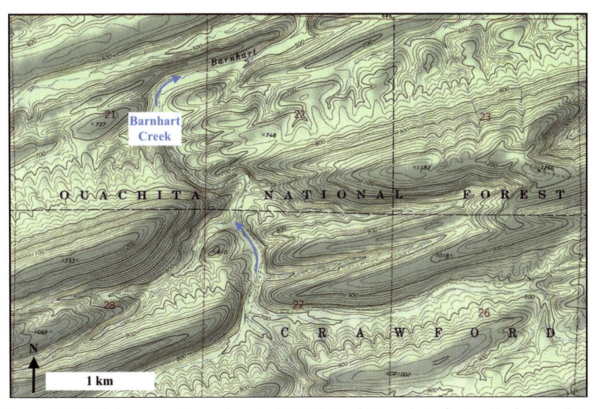

Figure 6.7: Modified topographic map from the USGS National Map website showing Barnhart Creek in Arkansas cutting across 200-meter-high Ouachita Mountain ridges. The contour interval is 20 feet (6 meters). Top left corner: 34° 54' 13.592" N, 93° 27' 51.798" W.

63

In another example, the Washita River in Oklahoma, after flowing in east and southeast directions, turns in a south direction to flow across the deeply eroded Arbuckle Mountains, as seen in figure 6.8. Today Arbuckle Mountains ridges are only a few hundred meters high, although the regional stratigraphy suggests at least 4,500 meters of bedrock has been removed. Whether that thickness of bedrock material was removed as the Arbuckle Mountains were being uplifted or after the mountains had risen to a considerable elevation is not known, nor do geologists know how the Washita River established its course across what is today a deeply eroded mountain range.

North of figure 6.8, north-oriented tributaries flow from the Arbuckle Mountains to join a southeast-oriented Washita River segment as barbed tributaries. The barbed tributaries can be explained if immense south-oriented floods flowed across the region (including across what may have been a rising but possibly previously eroded area) with headward erosion of the south-oriented Washita River valley beheading the diverging channels. Under such a situation, north-oriented reversals of flow on the beheaded south-oriented flood flow channels would form north-oriented tributaries.

From the accepted paradigm perspective, such an interpretation is impossible because there is no accepted paradigm link between Arbuckle Mountains uplift and continental icesheets and because preglacial drainage routes (now Mississippi River tributaries) to the north of Oklahoma would have prevented any continental icesheet meltwater floods from reaching Oklahoma, although interestingly, at least some geologists (e. g., Suneson, 2020) consider Oklahoma rivers to have developed during the Quaternary when continental icesheets were present.

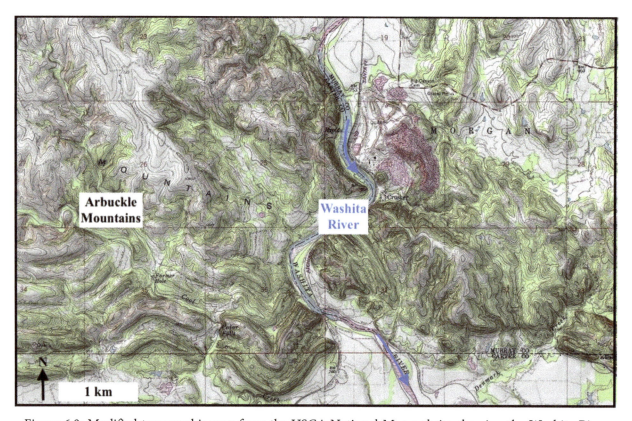

Figure 6.8: Modified topographic map from the USGA National Map website showing the Washita River cutting across Oklahoma's Arbuckle Mountains. The contour interval is 10 feet (3 meters). Top left corner: 34° 22' 14.062" N. 97° 04' 52.965" W.

Chapter 7:
Valleys Eroded across Drainage Divides

Through valleys (valleys now crossed by drainage divides) are easy to recognize on detailed topographic maps. Most through valleys are former drainage routes which no longer exist. Through valleys are common in and near recognized glaciated regions and the geology literature correctly describes some of those through valleys as having been eroded by former meltwater rivers and streams. But the geology literature rarely discusses through valleys found far beyond any recognized glaciated locations, yet such through valleys are also common.

For example, north of the south-oriented Big Hole River segment seen in figure 3.7, Deer Lodge Pass (seen in figure 7.1) is a through valley now crossing the east-west continental divide. Drainage to the north flows to the north- and northwest-oriented Clark Fork River, while drainage to the south flows to the Big Hole River. Most geologists would agree that water once flowed across what is now the continental divide, although the accepted paradigm might cause them to suggest the water flowed in a north direction. However, barbed tributaries flowing to the now north-oriented Clark Fork River (see figure 3.10) and the north-oriented Beaverhead River (see figure 3.7) suggest south-oriented flow.

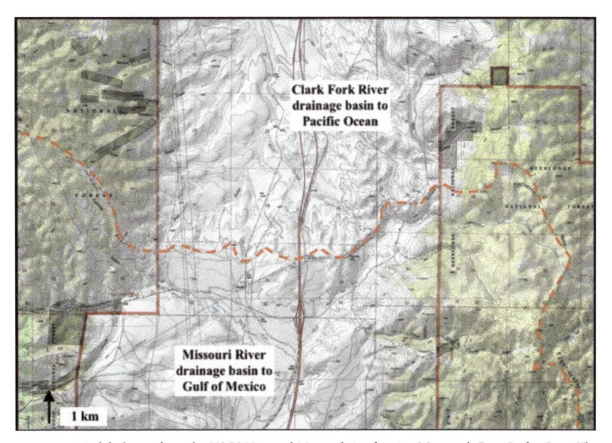

Figure 7.1: Modified map from the USGS National Map website showing Montana's Deer Lodge Pass. The contour interval is 40 feet (12 meters). The red dashed line shows the east-west continental divide location. Top left corner: 45⁰ 55' 45.585" N, 112° 45' 14.936" W.

Drainage divides can cross valleys in the most unlikely places, as in figure 7.2, which shows an area near the South Dakota Black Hills' highest elevations. The Black Hills are a domal uplift straddling the South Dakota-Wyoming border and rise more than 1000 meters above the surrounding plains. Spearfish and Whitewood Creeks in figure 7.2 drain to the southeast-oriented Belle Fourche River, which in turn drains to the northeast-oriented Cheyenne River. Rapid and Elk Creeks drain directly to the northeast-oriented Cheyenne River (see figure 4.8), which is often described as a preglacial river, although some geologists suggest a more recent origin (e.g., Stamm et al. 2013).

Red numbers in figure 7.2 identify points, where water flowed across what are now drainage divides with numbers 1 and 2 identifying valleys crossing the Spearfish Creek-Rapid Creek drainage divide. Number 6 identifies a drainage divide now separating diverging and converging channels within the Spearfish Creek drainage basin. Those and other abandoned diverging and converging channels suggest a large and probably long-lived flood crossed what are now some of the Black Hills' highest regions. There are no higher areas of any size, so the southeast-oriented floodwaters must have come from the northwest and flowed across the region before the uplift, which raised the Black Hills more than 1000 meters above the surrounding plains. While Black Hills geology has been extensively studied, these abandoned diverging and converging valleys are rarely mentioned because, from the accepted paradigm perspective, there is no way large floods from the northwest could have flowed across this now high-elevation Black Hills region.

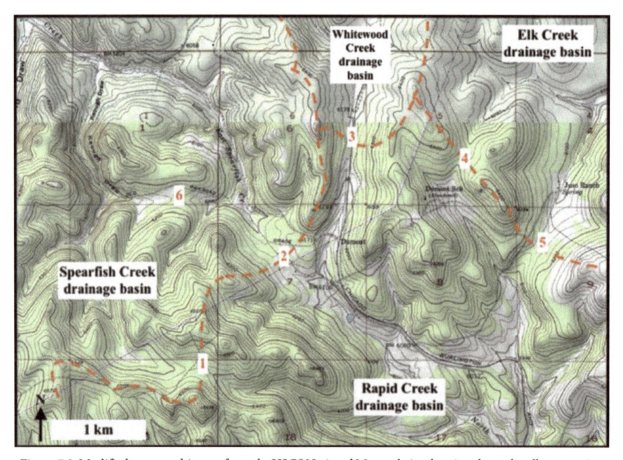

Figure 7.2: Modified topographic map from the USGS National Map website showing through valleys crossing some of the Black Hills' highest drainage divides (red dashed lines). The contour interval is 20 feet (6 meters). Top left corner: 44° 15' 35.165" N, 103° 50' 31.064" W

Figure 7.3 shows a modified and reduced-sized detailed topographic map of the region to the east of the Black Hills and located between the abandoned valleys now crossing some of the Black Hills' highest drainage divides (seen in figure 7.2) and the Scenic and Sage Creek escarpment-surrounded basins (seen in figures 4.7 and 4.8). As seen in figure 4.8, Rapid Creek joins the northeast-oriented Cheyenne River to the northwest of the Scenic Basin escarpment-surrounded basin, and (while not seen in figure 4.8) Boxelder Creek joins the northeast-oriented Cheyenne River directly to the northwest of the Sage Creek escarpment-surrounded basin. Note how, in figure 7.3, Elk, Boxelder, and Rapid Creeks are separated by asymmetric drainage divides, which suggests headward erosion of the Boxelder Creek valley captured southeast-oriented drainage which had been flowing to the Rapid Creek valley and that headward erosion of the Elk Creek valley next captured southeast-oriented drainage which had been flowing to the Boxelder Creek valley.

The development of these asymmetric drainage divides is difficult to explain unless the valleys were eroded headward in a progressive sequence across massive and prolonged southeast-oriented floods as Black Hills uplift gradually forced southeast-oriented floodwaters to flow around the rising domal area. Floodwaters flowing across this region eroded the Scenic and Sage Creek escarpment-surrounded basins before being captured by Cheyenne River headward erosion. Geologists have conducted extensive studies in the Black Hills region and surrounding regions, and the landforms illustrated in figures 4.7, 4.8, 7.2, and 7.3 are well known. However, from the accepted paradigm perspective, no large floods flowed across or around the Black Hills as the domal area was being uplifted so the topographic map evidence is either ignored or explained in other ways.

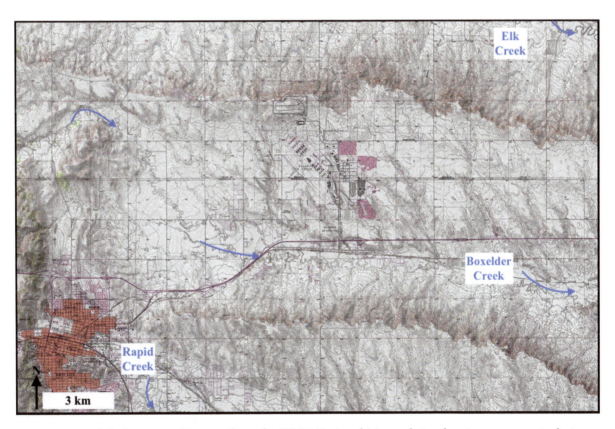

Figure 7.3: Modified topographic map from the USGS National Map website showing asymmetric drainage divides to the east of Rapid City and of the Black Hills. The contour interval is 10 feet (3 meters). Top left corner: 44° 11' 54.642" N, 103° 14' 47.906" W.

Sweetwater Gap, seen in figure 7.4, is a deep through valley eroded across the crest of what are now Wyoming's Wind River Mountains and links north-oriented Middle Popo Agie River headwaters, which flow to the Wind River and then through Wind River Canyon (as seen in figures 6.4 and 8.1) with the south-oriented Sweetwater River headwaters. Sweetwater River headwaters now flow parallel to the east-west continental divide (shown with a red dashed line in figure 7.4) and turn to flow in a southeast direction (seen in figure 5.7) and an east direction before joining the north-, northeast-, east, and southeast-oriented North Platte River. Middle Popo Agie River and Sweetwater River water eventually ends up in the Missouri River, although the routes traveled are quite different. Clasts of volcanic rocks transported from regions to the north of the Wind River Range are now found in conglomerates on the Wind River Mountains' southern flank (Steidtmann et al, 1989) and are evidence that large volumes of south-oriented water probably eroded the deep Sweetwater Gap valley into what must have been a rising Wind River Mountain Range.

Eventually, uplift must have outpaced the rate of erosion which resulted in the formation of the Middle Popo Agie River-Sweetwater River drainage divide and a reversal of flow to the north of Sweetwater Gap. From the accepted paradigm perspective, Sweetwater Gap and the volcanic clast evidence exist but are difficult to explain because Wind River Mountain uplift occurred before North American continental icesheets developed. This means continental icesheet meltwater floods could not have eroded Sweetwater Gap as the Wind River Mountains were being uplifted, which means the Wind River Mountains uplift was not related to a continental icesheet's presence. Based on these considerations, the accepted paradigm does not provide a water source large enough to erode Sweetwater Gap.

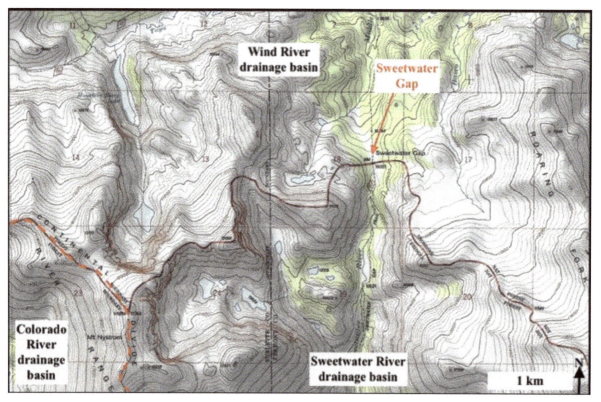

Figure 7.4: Modified topographic map from USGS National Map website showing Sweetwater Gap in Wyoming's Wind River Mountains. The red dashed line shows the continental divide. The contour interval is 40 feet (12 meters). Top left corner: 42° 40' 25.614" N, 109° 06' 40.916" W.

After starting near the Colorado River and flowing in a north direction, the Yampa River makes an abrupt turn at Steamboat Springs, Colorado, to flow in a west direction to reach the deep south-oriented canyon, which the south-oriented Green River has cut across the Uinta Mountains (the Green River then continues in a south direction to join the Colorado River). A through valley (marked by the red number 1 in figure 7.5) to the north of Steamboat Springs links the north-oriented Yampa River headwaters valley with the south-oriented Elk River valley. Figure 5.8 shows a mountain pass crossing the east-west continental divide, which links the north-oriented Encampment River and North Platte River valley with the west- and south-oriented North Fork Elk River.

Today, the Elk River turns in a southwest direction to bypass the through valley (at the red number 1) and joins the west-oriented Yampa River as seen in figure 7.5. However, the through valley at the red number 1 may have once been a channel used by south-oriented floodwaters, which flowed along the present-day north-oriented Encampment River alignment, the modern-day south-oriented Elk River alignment, and then along what is now the north-oriented Yampa River alignment to Egeria Park (seen in figure 7.6) before reaching what is now the Colorado River valley. If so, uplift of the Colorado region eventually enabled the west-oriented Yampa River valley to capture the south-oriented flood flow, which reversed the flow in the now north-oriented Yampa River valley. While a logical interpretation based on topographic map evidence, the accepted paradigm does not recognize any large and prolonged south-oriented floods that flowed across Wyoming and Colorado, and most geologists simply ignore through valleys such as the through valley linking the south-oriented Elk River and north-oriented Yampa River.

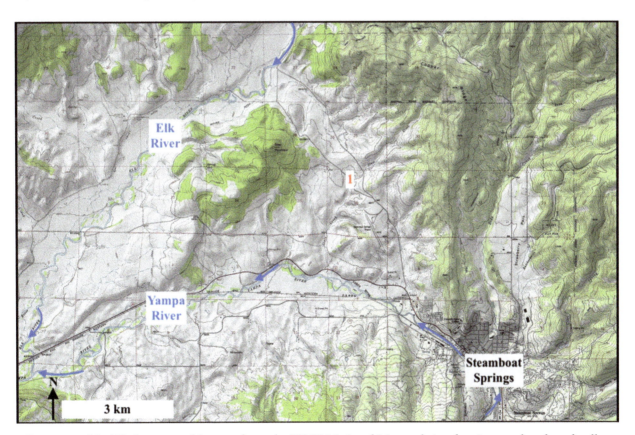

Figure 7.5: Modified topographic map from the USGS National Map website showing an abandoned valley linking the south-oriented Elk River and north-oriented Yampa River valleys. The contour interval is 40 feet (12 meters). Top left corner: 40° 33' 38.631" N, 106° 58' 18.247" W.

The Yampa-Colorado River drainage divide crosses northcentral Colorado's Egeria Park (seen in figure 7.6), which, like Deer Lodge Pass (seen in figure 7.1), is a structural feature as well as an erosional landform. The drainage divide marks the boundary between drainage to northwest-oriented Chimney Creek which flows to the north-oriented Yampa River headwaters from drainage to southeast-oriented Egeria Creek, which eventually reaches the Colorado River. After flowing in a north direction, the Yampa River turns in a west direction, as seen in figure 7.5. And after flowing in a southeast direction, Egeria Creek joins south-oriented Rock Creek, which then joins the Colorado River as a barbed tributary at a point where the Colorado River turns from flowing in a northwest direction to flow in a west and then southwest direction. This topographic map evidence suggests headward erosion of the southwest- and west-oriented Colorado River valley beheaded and reversed south-oriented flood flow, which had been moving across what is now Colorado.

While geologists have wondered why the Yampa River would first flow in a north direction away from the Colorado River valley and then turn in a west direction to join a south-oriented Colorado River tributary, the accepted paradigm has not permitted a good explanation. Kucera (1962), in an unpublished PhD thesis, suggested water in the Chimney Creek drainage basin once flowed in a south direction to reach the Colorado River but did not see a reversal of flow further to the north along what is now the north-oriented Yampa River alignment. Again, the problem is a reversal of large and prolonged south-oriented floods is needed to explain the Egeria Park topographic map drainage system evidence, and from the accepted paradigm perspective, such large and prolonged south-oriented floods did not flow across Colorado.

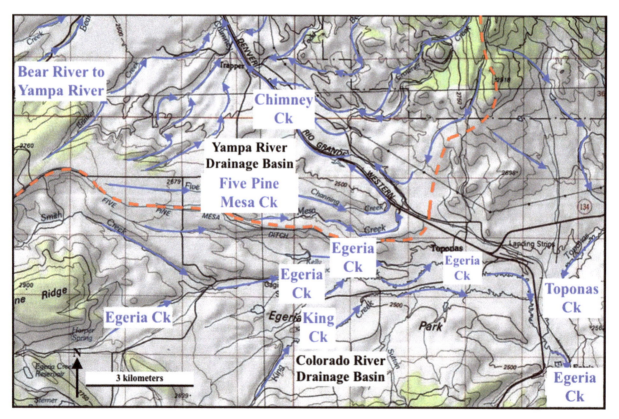

Figure 7.6: Modified topographic map from USGS National Map website showing Egeria Park linking north-oriented Yampa River headwaters with south-oriented Colorado River drainage. The contour interval is 50 meters. Top left corner: 40° 06' 55.899" N, 106° 57' 39.160" W.

The term through valley was first coined more than a century ago to describe deep narrow valleys in Upstate New York, which extend in a north-to-south direction across the St. Lawrence River-Susquehanna River drainage divide. Bloom (2018, p. 133) describes one commonly accepted paradigm interpretation by stating, "The general theory is that preglacial fluvial erosion had established opposing river drainage networks between which were uplands. Then glacial erosion exploited the north-south trending valleys and broke through the uplands." During a subsequent glacial event, ice advanced southward to where the St. Lawrence River-Susquehanna River drainage divide is today and deposited in the through valleys what are usually referred to as valley head moraines. Lakes subsequently formed in the valleys as the ice front receded northward from the valley head moraines, with lake water overflowing southward through the valleys.

This accepted paradigm interpretation explains some of the evidence seen in figure 7.7 where the dashed red line shows the St. Lawrence River-Susquehanna River drainage divide. However, the interpretation assumes a continental icesheet, which preceded the valley head moraine icesheet, extended southward into Pennsylvania, and did not otherwise destroy the so-called preglacial valley system which, as seen in figure 7.7, contained barbed tributaries. While those barbed tributaries suggest a major drainage reversal took place, the interpretation does not explain why regions to the north of the figure were lowered in elevation so as to enable north-oriented valleys to erode headward into what had been a south-oriented drainage region.

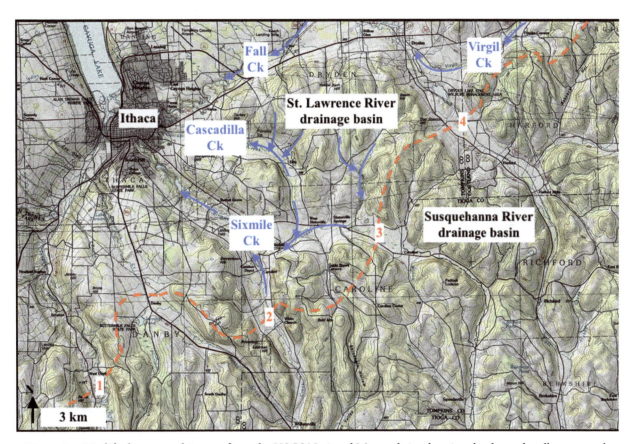

Figure 7.7: Modified topographic map from the USGS National Map website showing the through valley network located to the east of Ithaca, NY. The red dashed line shows the approximate St. Lawrence River-Susquehanna River drainage divide location. The contour interval is 20 meters. Top left corner: 42° 29' 06.946" N, 76° 34' 22.626" W.

Figure 7.8 illustrates selected drainage routes in the through valley complex as seen to the north of the figure 7.7 map area. Cayuga Lake is the largest of the New York State Finger Lakes and fills a deep trough, which, from the accepted paradigm perspective, was carved and deepened (like the other Finger Lakes troughs) by south-oriented continental icesheet movement into a northward sloping upland surface. From the accepted paradigm perspective, south-oriented drainage routes flowing into the Cayuga Lake basin, such as Salmon and Fall Creeks, developed during a preglacial reversal of drainage caused by the headward erosion of a north-oriented stream valley on what is now the Cayuga Lake trough alignment.

That interpretation has several important implications, the first of which is the preglacial drainage system looked somewhat like the drainage system seen today. A second implication is the icesheet responsible for carving the Cayuga Lake trough did not significantly alter the adjacent upland region drainage routes or landscapes. These implications require a continental icesheet able to deeply erode in some places and then to daintily tiptoe over other places, which, if one thinks about it, defies common sense logic. When White (1972) suggested that continental icesheets should have eroded the underlying bedrock much deeper than what glacial geologists were describing, he was sharply criticized by glacial geologists, including Sugden (1976), who laid out the case against deep continental icesheet erosion. However, common sense logic suggests a continental icesheet able to carve the deep Cayuga Lake trough and then continue southward into Pennsylvania should also have been able to destroy the complex upland drainage system illustrated in figure 7.8.

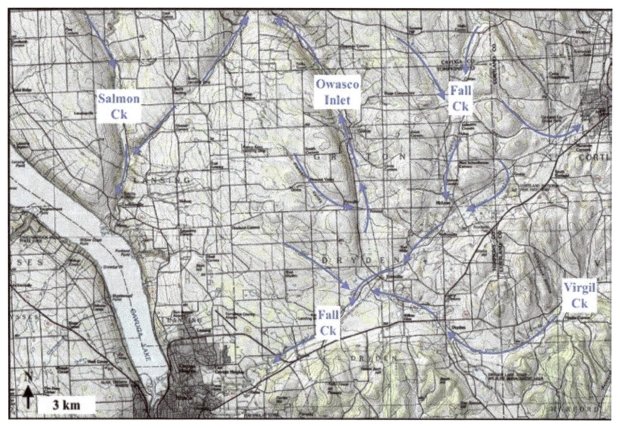

Figure 7.8: Modified topographic map from the USGS National Map website showing selected drainage routes in the region to the north of the figure 7.7 area. The contour interval is 20 meters. Top left corner: 42° 38' 58.389" N, 76° 36' 52.641" W.

Another group of intriguing valleys eroded across drainage divides that the accepted Cenozoic geology and glacial paradigm cannot satisfactorily explain are valleys crossing the Ohio River-Atlantic Ocean drainage divide. Figure 7.9 is located to the southeast of figure 6.3 and illustrates an erosional valley linking the north- and northwest-oriented Flaugherty Creek valley, which in figure 6.3 flows through a water gap and the north-northeast oriented Laurel Run valley which to the north of figure 7.9 joins southeast-oriented Wills Creek (also seen in figure 6.3). Figure 7.9 clearly shows an erosional valley crossing the Ohio River-Atlantic Ocean drainage divide, which means water once flowed across what today is a major drainage divide. Figure 7.9 evidence is not unique as numerous other erosional valleys also cross the Ohio River-Atlantic Ocean drainage divide, although the published geologic literature rarely mentions much less explains such evidence.

The geologic research community does not like to discuss erosional valleys crossing the Ohio River-Atlantic Ocean drainage divide any more than it likes to discuss mountain passes eroded across the east-west continental divide. Figure 7.9 topographic map evidence can be explained if massive and long-lived floods flowed across the region as the mountain ridges emerged through uplift and/or erosion. However, from the accepted paradigm perspective, such an interpretation is impossible because the mountain ridges emerged long before any of North America's continental icesheets existed, and preglacial drainage system valleys would have prevented any continental icesheet meltwater floods from reaching the figure 7.9 southern Pennsylvania location. Instead, most geology researchers simply ignore the evidence and opt to study something else.

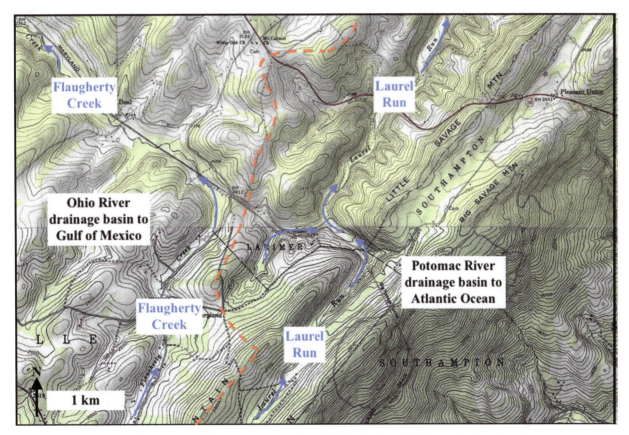

Figure 7.9: Modified topographic map from the USGS National Map website showing a southern Pennsylvania section of the Ohio River-Atlantic Ocean drainage divide (red dashed line). The contour interval is 20 feet (6 meters). Top left corner: 39° 46' 19.785" N, 78° 56' 45.595" W.

This discussion of through valleys crossing drainage divides concludes with a brief look at a section of southeastern Pennsylvania's Chester Valley seen in figure 7.10. The Chester Valley is a 100-kilometer-long structurally-defined northeast-to-southwest oriented through valley now crossed by about seven south-oriented streams or rivers. The Chester Valley section seen in figure 7.10 is located between the southeast-oriented Schuylkill River to the east and the south-oriented East Branch Brandywine Creek to the west. Note how Valley Creek East and Valley Creek West begin almost right next to each other and then flow adjacent to each other in north directions down the Chester Valley's south wall before turning to flow in completely opposite directions.

To the northeast of the figure Valley Creek East turns in a north direction to erode a water gap across the Chester Valley's north wall and to join the Schuylkill River as a barbed tributary. To the southwest of the figure Valley Creek West turns in a south direction to erode a water gap across the Chester Valley's south wall and to join East Branch Brandywine Creek. The letter "A" locates a shallow through valley between Valley Creek East and Valley Creek West. To the northeast of the figure there are through valleys between Valley Creek East and the Schuylkill River. To the southwest there is a through valley between Valley Creek West and the East Branch Brandywine Creek. This drainage history puzzle can be solved if during immense and prolonged southwest-oriented floods East Branch Brandywine Creek valley headward erosion captured the floodwaters with Schuylkill River valley headward erosion subsequently beheading and reversing the flow to create Valley Creek East.

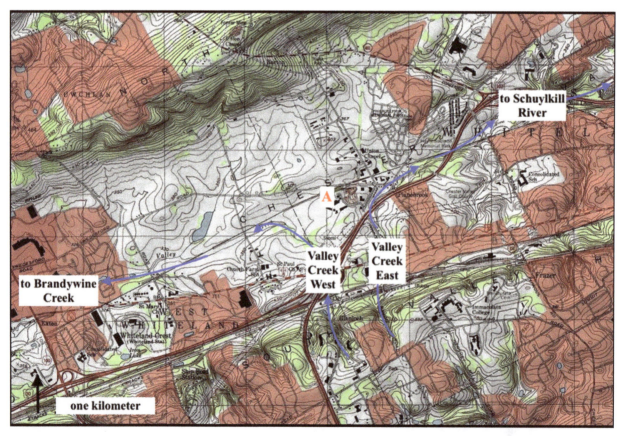

Figure 7.10: Modified topographic map from the USGS National Map website showing the through valley between Valley Creek East and Valley Creek West in Pennsylvania's Chester Valley. The contour interval is 10 feet (3 meters). Top left corner: 40° 03' 37.804" N, 75° 37' 54.268" W.

Chapter 8:
Rivers that Change Direction for No Apparent Reason

Rivers and streams sometimes change their flow direction for no apparent reason. Historical qualitative geomorphologists noted many such direction changes some of which the late 19th-century geologists thought they could explain. As noted in chapter 2 continental icesheets were interpreted to have blocked north-oriented rivers and streams which now join the south-oriented Ohio and Missouri Rivers. That interpretation became an important pillar in how future geologists explained North America's middle and late Cenozoic history, including North America's glacial history. That interpretation also became a major problem when topographic maps subsequently became available and historical qualitative geomorphologists tried to explain other river and stream direction changes—especially in regions far to the south of the Ohio and Missouri Rivers.

Previous chapters illustrated some unusual river direction changes. In addition to the Ohio and Missouri headwaters and tributary direction changes illustrated in figures 2.1 and 2.2 early geologists also considered the northeast-oriented Knife, Heart, Cannonball Rivers (seen in figure 2.7) to be preglacial north-oriented drainage routes which a continental icesheet had blocked. That interpretation explained why those rivers now join the south-oriented Missouri River as barbed tributaries, but did not explain why those rivers flow in southeast directions before turning in northeast directions. The accepted paradigm did not a provide satisfactory reason for why the Knife, Heart, and Cannonball Rivers change from southeast- to northeast-oriented drainage routes.

While accepted paradigm interpretations can explain at least some river and stream direction changes seen along and near former continental icesheet southern margins those interpretations do not explain most river direction changes seen to the south of recognized glaciated regions. For example, the North Platte River seen in figure 2.2 flows in a north direction before turning in a southeast direction. There is no geologic reason why the North Platte River could not have continued in a north direction. As a result, geologists typically avoid discussing the North Platte River direction change just as they avoid discussing many other similar river direction changes

What the geology research community needs is a paradigm able to explain river and stream direction changes throughout the United States and not just along and near former continental icesheet margins. Such a paradigm will require rethinking the late 19th-century interpretation that continental icesheets blocked preglacial north-oriented drainage systems. Obviously, a continental icesheet did block north-oriented drainage routes, but the origin of those blocked drainage routes needs to be rethought. An alternative to blocked preglacial north-oriented drainage routes is the blocked north-oriented routes were formed when a previous continental icesheet melted. Such an alternative requires the previous continental icesheet to have been located in an icesheet created deep "hole" and to have opened-up deep "hole" space as it melted. This chapter explores how such an alternative interpretation explains topographic map evidence for several obvious, but yet to be satisfactorily explained river and stream direction changes.

One of the most intriguing river direction changes is Wyoming's Wind River which after flowing in a southeast direction (as seen in figure 8.1) turns in a northeast and north direction to flow through Wind River Canyon (see figure 6.4), which is cut across the Owl Creek Mountains. From the accepted paradigm perspective, the Wind River's direction change is a mystery because there is no reason why the Wind River could not have continued to flow in a southeast or east direction to join the North Platte River. But rather than continuing in a southeast or east direction, the Wind River turns in a north direction to cut a deep canyon through a kilometer-high mountain range.

A common interpretation in the geologic literature is sediments once buried the Owl Creek Mountains by filling the Wind River Basin (and the Big Horn Basin to the north of Owl Creek Mountains) and a north-oriented stream which had developed on that sediment cover captured the southeast-oriented Wind River and then eroded down into the underlying Owl Creek Mountains (and also removed the sediments which had buried the Owl Creek Mountains). A simpler but ignored explanation is Wind River Canyon was eroded during large south-oriented continental icesheet meltwater floods that flowed across Wyoming as the Owl Creek Mountains and the entire Wyoming region were being uplifted which eventually forced a major drainage system reversal. However, the accepted paradigm requires Wyoming uplift to have occurred before any continental icesheets.

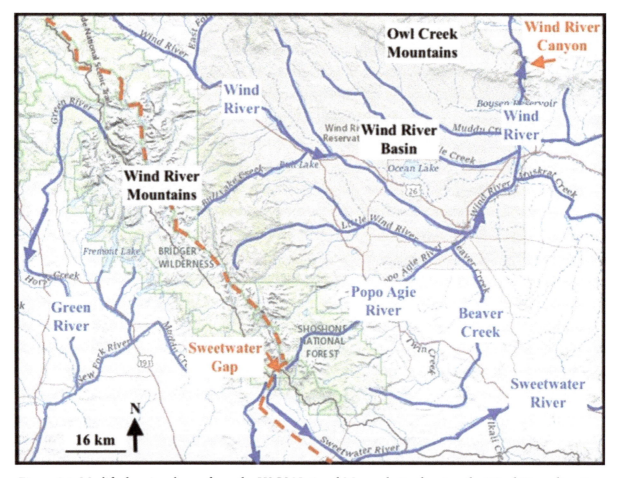

Figure 8.1: Modified regional map from the USGS National Map website showing the Wind River direction change in relation to Wind River Canyon and Sweetwater Gap locations. Top left corner: 43° 34' 57.349" N, 110° 10' 47.230" W. Red dashed line shows the east-west continental divide.

Located to the east of the Wind River's turn from a southeast direction to a north direction is the previously mentioned North Platte River's turn from a north direction to a southeast direction which is seen in figure 8.2 (note the east-oriented Sweetwater River in both figures 8.1 and 8.2). North of figure 8.2 is the Powder River Basin and the north-oriented Powder River, but the North Platte River turns to cut a water gap across the Laramie Mountains northwest end and to flow in an east and southeast direction. Other remarkable direction changes seen in figure 8.2 include Deer and Box Elder Creeks (seen in more detail in figure 6.6) and the North Laramie River which flows in a south direction to enter the Laramie Basin northeast corner before turning in an east direction to cut a canyon across the Laramie Mountains. None of these direction changes make sense from the accepted paradigm perspective, which means the geologic literature rarely discusses such evidence.

Most geomorphologists ignore such evidence and assume these abrupt river and stream direction changes are unimportant. There are ways to explain the direction changes, but those ways require the reversal of immense south-oriented floods which flowed across the region as the Laramie Mountains (and the entire region) were being uplifted. From the accepted paradigm perspective, there is no water source large enough to produce long-lived floods of the size required, although the accepted glacial history paradigm probably causes geologists to seriously underestimate the amount of meltwater that a large continental icesheet could produce. Further, the accepted paradigm does not see a relationship between continental icesheets and the uplift of the Laramie Mountains and of the larger Wyoming region. In other words, from the accepted paradigm perspective, figure 8.2 river and stream direction changes are not satisfactorily explained.

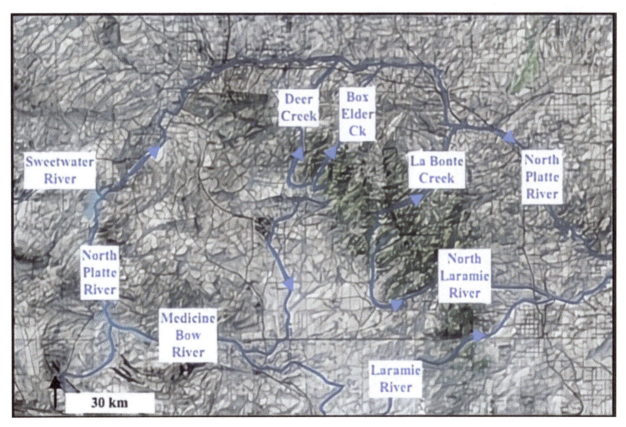

Figure 8.2: Modified map from the USGS National Map website showing the North Platte River changing from a north direction to a southeast direction and direction changes on several North Platte River tributaries. Top left corner: 43° 01' 58.725" N, 107° 17' 24.138" W.

77

The Tennessee River makes an interesting direction change (seen in figure 8.3) by flowing in a southwest direction toward the Gulf of Mexico and then, after entering Alabama, turning to flow in a northwest direction before turning in a north direction to join the west-oriented Ohio River (which then joins the south-oriented Mississippi River). The Tennessee River-Gulf of Mexico drainage divide is crossed by several sets of northeast-to-southwest oriented valleys (one set of which is seen in figure 8.4), so excellent evidence suggests that large volumes of water once flowed across that drainage divide. The geologic literature does include papers suggesting the Tennessee River once flowed directly to the Gulf of Mexico and speculating on reasons why the Tennessee River no longer does so (e.g., Hayes and Campbell, 1894). Such an interpretation has not been shared by all researchers, as there are papers providing different interpretations (e.g., Johnson, 1905).

Neither group of researchers mentions any connection between the Tennessee River direction changes and North American continental glaciation, and both groups of researchers probably have not considered the possibility that large continental icesheet meltwater floods might have once flowed across the Tennessee River drainage basin or the possibility that the weight of a thick continental icesheet might have raised what is now the Tennessee River-Gulf of Mexico drainage divide area as large meltwater floods flowed across it. These possibilities are not consistent with the accepted paradigm glacial history interpretation but offer a way to explain the Tennessee River route and the well-known evidence that large volumes of water must have once flowed across the Tennessee River-Gulf of Mexico drainage divide.

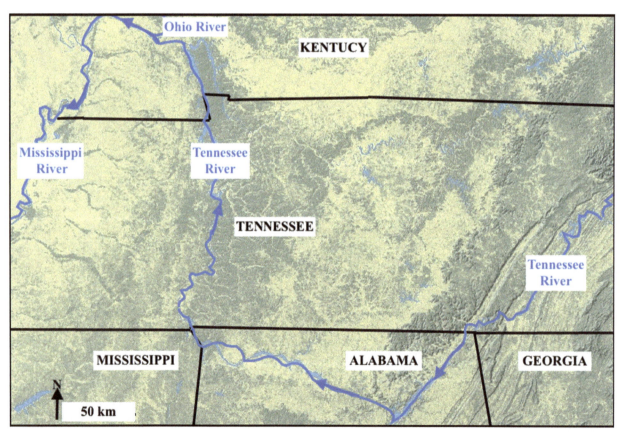

Figure 8.3: Modified map from the USGS National Map website showing how the Tennessee River changes from being a southwest-oriented river to being a north-oriented river. Top left corner: 37° 12' 57.877" N, 89° 47' 46.935" W. See figures 3.4 and 8.4 for detailed Tennessee River area maps.

Figure 8.4 illustrates one set of erosional valleys crossing what is now the Tennessee River-Gulf of Mexico drainage divide. There are lower elevation sets of valleys crossing the drainage divide both to the east and to the west of the figure, some of which have been suggested as possible abandoned Tennessee River routes. In addition, less well-defined low points along the drainage divide suggest large amounts of water probably once flowed across almost all, if not all, of the drainage divide.

From the accepted paradigm perspective, geomorphology researchers have looked for where a small number of former south-oriented drainage routes (or rivers) once crossed the drainage divide and have not considered the possibility of immense and long-lived south-oriented floods which occurred when uplift of the drainage divide area was also occurring. This failure to consider massive and prolonged south-oriented floods was due to the accepted paradigm's interpretation that all continental icesheet meltwater flowed down the icesheet marginal Ohio River valley. This failure to consider the alternative interpretation that the now north-oriented Ohio River tributaries developed when a large icesheet melted led to confusion as to where (and even if) the Tennessee River and its southeast-oriented tributaries once flowed directly to the Gulf of Mexico.

The four parallel north-northeast to south-southwest oriented valleys seen in figure 8.4 are difficult to explain due to an accepted paradigm assumption that rivers and streams in the past looked like rivers and streams of today (and flowed in one valley and not in four or more parallel valleys). The four parallel valleys suggest erosion by large volumes of south-southwest oriented water flowing in diverging and converging channels, and the presence of other sets of similarly oriented valleys crossing the same drainage divide suggests immense south-southwest oriented floods once crossed what is now the Tennessee River-Gulf of Mexico drainage divide.

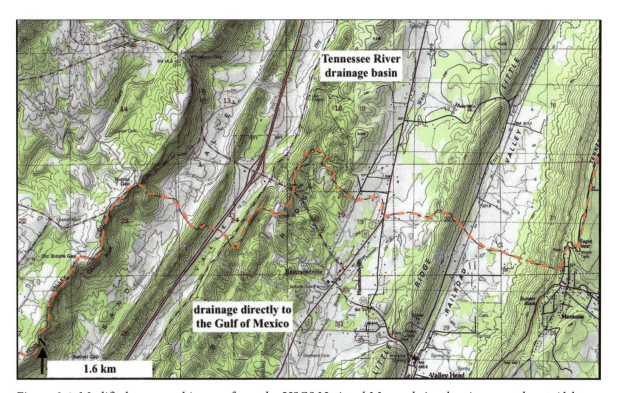

Figure 8.4: Modified topographic map from the USGS National Map website showing a northeast Alabama segment of the Tennessee River-Gulf of Mexico drainage divide (red dashed line). The contour interval is 20 feet (6 meters). Top left corner: 34° 36' 51.018" N, 85° 40' 45.589" W.

Another river that makes interesting direction changes is the New York State Delaware River which begins in the Catskill Mountains as two southwest-oriented branches seen in figure 8.5. Near the Pennsylvania border, the West Branch turns abruptly to flow in a south-southeast direction to join the southwest-oriented East Branch so as to form the Delaware River which flows in a southeast direction along the New York-Pennsylvania border. The Delaware River West and East Branch abrupt turns both suggest headward erosion of the southeast-oriented Delaware River valley first captured the southwest-oriented East Branch and subsequently captured the West Branch. Also of interest, to the north of the figure, Susquehanna River headwaters flow in a southwest direction before turning in a south direction to enter the figure's northwest corner.

Supporting the Delaware River valley headward erosion and capture hypothesis is an abandoned valley now leading from the West Branch's abrupt turn to the south-oriented Susquehanna River valley (and now drained by streams flowing in opposite directions) and a northeast-oriented (barbed) Delaware River tributary leading to the East Branch's abrupt turn. While such an interpretation explains some map evidence, the southeast-oriented Delaware River and south-oriented Susquehanna River have other barbed tributaries, a few of which are marked in the figure. The West Branch-East Branch drainage divide is also asymmetric with long south-oriented East Branch tributaries, which suggests the southwest-oriented East and West Branch valleys eroded headward across multiple south-oriented channels (or across massive south-oriented flood flow).

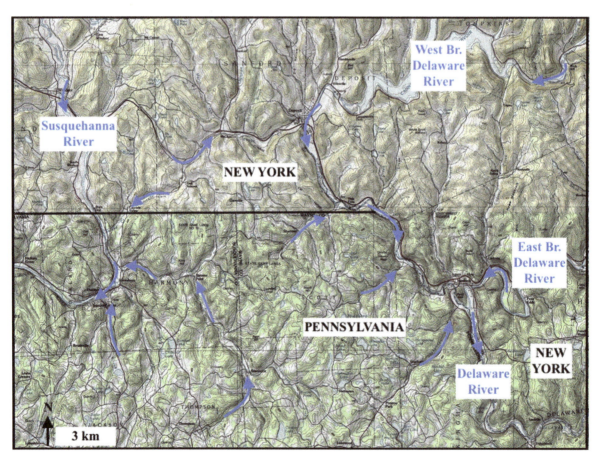

Figure 8.5: Modified topographic map from the USGS National Map website showing Delaware River and Susquehanna River direction changes and barbed tributaries. The contour interval is 20 meters, Top left corner: 42° 07' 22.421 N, 75° 40' 50.979" W.

80

The Delaware River flows from the figure 8.5 map area in a southeast direction until reaching the New Jersey border, where the river turns to flow in a southwest direction to reach the figure 8.6 map area where the river abruptly turns in a southeast direction to carve the Delaware River Water Gap across Kittatinny Mountain (named Blue Mountain further to the southwest where it is crossed by the Susquehanna River in figure 6.1). Published geological literature describing Delaware River Water Gap geologic history often only discusses the bedrock geology and says little about how, why, and when the water gap itself was eroded. One commonly stated interpretation suggests headward erosion of the downstream southeast-oriented Delaware River valley captured a southwest-oriented stream of water in the upstream valley. However, there is no reason why a southeast-oriented stream in the downstream valley would have eroded headward across the Kittatinny Mountain erosion-resistant bedrock so as to capture a larger southwest-oriented stream flowing in the upstream valley, especially since the now northeast-oriented Cherry Creek valley is formed on much easier to erode bedrock.

Another interpretation suggests the Delaware River developed on a surface of Cretaceous age marine sediments which buried Kittatinny Mountain and which have been completely eroded away. The big stumbling block for geologists when trying to explain how the Delaware River Water Gap (and other regional water and wind gaps) originated is the accepted paradigm interpretation that Kittatinny Mountain and the Delaware River predate North American continental glaciation. The water gap can be explained by headward erosion of the Delaware River valley across immense and long-lived southwest-oriented floods, which occurred as Kittatinny Mountain, and other regional ridges were emerging (either by uplift or by erosion of surrounding bedrock or both), but from the accepted paradigm perspective such large southwest-oriented floods did not occur.

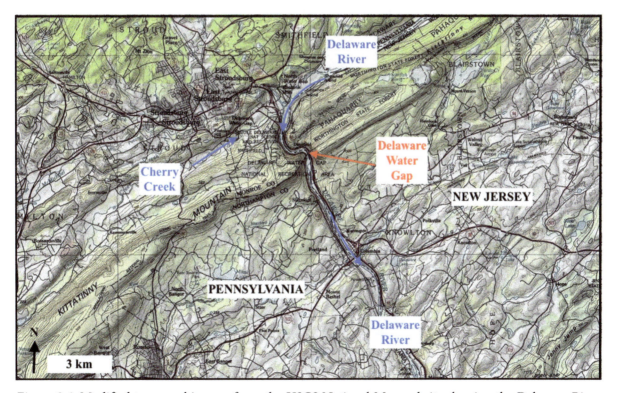

Figure 8.6: Modified topographic map from the USGS National Map website showing the Delaware River direction change at the Delaware River Water Gap. The contour interval is 20 meters. Top left corner: 41°01' 51.082" N, 75° 17' 57.207" W.

Downstream from figure 8.6, the Delaware River changes direction several times and has cut additional water gaps across igneous intrusions and ridges of folded sedimentary rock (but not as high as Kittatinny Mountain) to reach the sharp turn (near Trenton, New Jersey) seen in figure 8.7. Braun et al. (2003) explain the Trenton area direction change by saying, "The upper Cenozoic stratigraphy and sedimentology of the lower Delaware valley and Coastal Plain indicates that the Hudson [River] drained through that region and the Delaware [River] was a very minor tributary of that system until the Plio-Pleistocene time." This interpretation suggests the Hudson River, turned to flow in a southwest direction across New Jersey and then along the southwest-oriented Delaware River alignment seen in figure 8.7 and that upstream (from Trenton) the Delaware River valley eroded headward across multiple ridges and igneous intrusions to reach the Delaware River Water Gap.

What is missing from the interpretation is an explanation of how the Delaware River valley eroded headward from the Trenton area to the Delaware River Water Gap area and then across Kittatinny Mountain. Headward erosion of the Delaware River valley would have been possible if, while Kittatinny Mountain and other ridges were being uplifted, immense and prolonged southwest-oriented floods flowed across New Jersey and into eastern Pennsylvania. If so, the valleys of southeast-oriented drainage routes seen in figure 8.7 would have eroded headward across the southwest-oriented floods in sequence: Schuylkill River, Wissahickon Creek, Tacony Creek, Pennypack Creek, Neshaminy Creek, and the Delaware River. Topographic map evidence supports that sequence, but the accepted paradigm does not see southwest-oriented floods of the required magnitude.

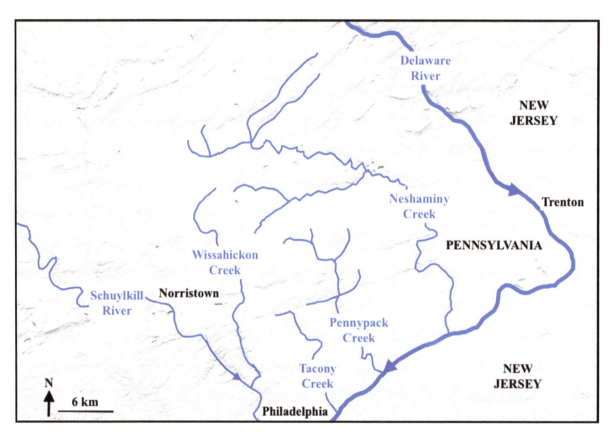

Figure 8.7: Modified map from the USGS National Map website showing the Delaware River direction change a short distance downstream from Trenton, New Jersey. Not all drainage routes are shown. Top left corner: 40° 25' 24.691" N, 75° 33' 47.662" W.

In a puzzling Great Plains area river direction change the Kansas Smoky Hill River turns from a southeast direction to a north and then east direction (see figure 8.8). That turn has been interpreted from the accepted paradigm perspective to have resulted from the capture of the ancestral southeast- and south-oriented Smoky Hill River by the east-oriented Kansas River (into which the Smoky Hill River now flows). Prior to being captured, the Smoky Hill River is usually thought to have flowed southward in what is now a buried bedrock channel (marked in figure 8.8) to reach the Arkansas River (located south of the figure). Evidence for the south-oriented bedrock channel is good, and hypotheses have been proposed to explain how and when the bedrock channel formed. Cooper (2001) added new evidence, identified other channels the ancestral Smoky Hill River and its tributaries may have eroded, and concluded by saying the Smoky Hill River was probably captured by a river near Salina, but like in previous reports, left most of the details unexplained.

Since the late 1800s, geologists have tried to explain the Smoky Hill River direction change, with some geologists suggesting a continental icesheet blocked a preglacial Kansas River, and the resulting lake overflowed in a south direction, although other geologists rejected that idea and explained the buried bedrock channel in other ways. While flowing toward a recognized former continental icesheet margin, the east- and southeast-oriented Smoky Hill River headwaters drainage basin is located in higher elevation regions to the west of continental icesheet-occupied regions, and from the accepted paradigm perspective, continental icesheet meltwater should not have played a role in developing the ancestral Smoky Hill River. However, a study of detailed topographic maps (1:24,000 scale maps, as seen in figure 8.9) suggests the entire Smoky Hill River headwaters valley—upstream from the buried bedrock channel—eroded headward across massive south-oriented floods.

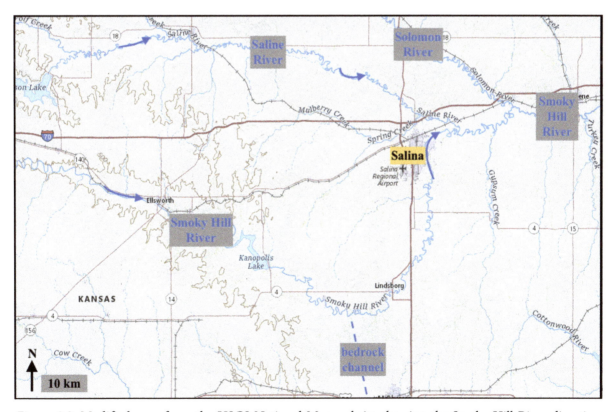

Figure 8.8: Modified map from the USGS National Map website showing the Smoky Hill River direction change near Salina, Kansas. Top left corner: 39° 04' 14.200" N, 98° 34' 51.493" W.

Figure 8.9 zooms in on a detailed topographic map of one of the abandoned valleys now crossing the Saline River-Smoky Hill River drainage divide area seen in figure 8.8. The red dashed line shows the Saline River-Smoky Hill River drainage divide location, and the red numbers identify two significant north-to-south oriented abandoned valleys. The deepest valley, which has a depth of approximately 50 meters, is at the red number 1 and links the south- and north-oriented East Elkhorn Creek valley with the south-oriented Clear Creek valley. East Elkhorn Creek begins to the north of the figure and flows in a south direction before making a U-turn to flow in a north direction and to be joined by West Elkhorn Creek (to the north of the figure). North of the figure, East and West Elkhorn Creeks combine to flow northward to join the east-oriented Saline River. Clear Creek flows in a south direction from the red number 1 to join the Smoky Hill River.

The red number 2 identifies a valley with a depth of about 25 meters linking a north-oriented tributary valley leading to the West Elkhorn Creek valley direction change from a southeast to a northeast orientation with the south-oriented East Spring Creek valley which drains to the Smoky Hill River. Detailed topographic maps show similar divide crossings present along the entire length of the Saline River-Smoky Hill River drainage divide, with those divide crossings linking now north-oriented Saline River tributary valleys with now south-oriented Smoky Hill River tributary valleys. These divide crossings and the secondary stream U-turns are best explained if the Smoky Hill River valley eroded headward across massive south-oriented floods, which were subsequently beheaded and reversed by the headward erosion of the east-oriented Saline River valley.

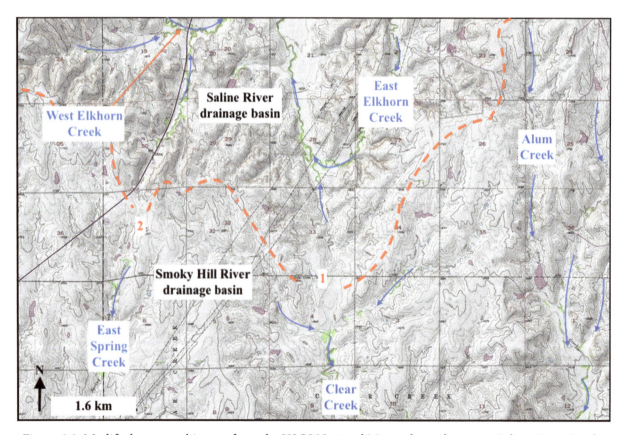

Figure 8.9: Modified topographic map from the USGS National Map website showing a Saline River-Smoky Hill River drainage divide segment to the west of Salina, Kansas. The contour interval is 20 feet (6 meters). Top left corner: 38° 49' 36.007" N, 98° 10' 08.184" W.

Chapter 9:
Poorly Explained Erosional Escarpments

An escarpment is a long, more or less continuous cliff or relatively steep slope facing in one general direction which breaks the general continuity of the land by separating two level or gently sloping surfaces and which was usually created by either erosion or faulting. Erosional escarpments can range from a few meters to hundreds of meters in height and from a few kilometers to many hundreds of kilometers in length. Sometimes erosional escarpment slopes have a cliff-like appearance but erosional escarpments can also have gradually sloping faces. Erosional escarpments like drainage divides are large-scale landforms which the geology research community typically ignores.

The geology research community does know erosional escarpments exist and, in a few cases has even developed controversial hypotheses to explain how specific erosional escarpments were created. In other cases, including for erosional escarpments that extend for hundreds of kilometers in length the geology research community appears to be satisfied with generalized descriptions and to have little or no interest in determining when and how those escarpments were formed.

This lack of geology research community interest is puzzling because erosional escarpments are often significant landform features. For example, the Pine Ridge Escarpment seen in figure 9.1 is one of South Dakota's and Nebraska's largest and most prominent landform features. How can the geology research community claim to understand South Dakota and Nebraska Cenozoic history and not understand the Pine Ridge Escarpment's erosion history? One or more significant, but yet unrecognized geologic events must have carved the Pine Ridge Escarpment.

In another example the Missouri Escarpment seen in figures 9.3 and 9.4 is crossed by what the geology research community claims are north-oriented preglacial valleys as the escarpment extends from south central South Dakota northward into central North Dakota and then in a northwest direction into and across southern Saskatchewan to reach eastern Alberta. How can the geology research community build its accepted paradigm on the assumption that those north-oriented valleys predate the continental icesheets without understanding the Missouri Escarpment's erosion history?

This chapter explores how topographic maps provide information which can be used to determine erosion histories for several well-known erosional escarpments. Map information includes drainage systems which now cross and/or flow adjacent to the escarpment faces. Those drainage systems have histories which the maps record in the form of direction changes, barbed tributaries, and other characteristics. And those drainage system histories tell a completely different Cenozoic geology and glacial history than what the geology research community's accepted paradigm has told to date.

Tree-covered northwest Nebraska Pine Ridge Escarpment upper slopes seen in figure 9.1 are approximately 300 meters higher than the lower plains regions to the north, with the escarpment continuing in a northeast and then east direction into and across southern South Dakota almost to the Missouri River valley. In Wyoming, the escarpment is known as the Hat Creek Breaks and marks the Cheyenne River drainage basin's southern boundary. The escarpment is sometimes assumed to have retreated in a southward direction and Fenneman (1931, p. 18–9) stated, "how far this escarpment has retreated southward is not known, but it must be at least 200 miles [320 km] because remnants of the same formation are found near the boundary between North and South Dakota. Locally the strata in this escarpment dip south and form a monoclinal ridge or cuesta."

Since that statement was made geomorphologists have not advanced their knowledge of the Pine Ridge Escarpment history much beyond what was known in 1931. Figure 9.1 suggests a giant flood carved a 300-meter-deep valley between the Black Hills to the north and the high plains to the south. If massive and prolonged southeast-oriented floods flowed across and then around a rising Black Hills upland, Cheyenne River valley headward erosion would have captured southeast-oriented floodwaters that had been flowing in the figure 9.1 area to the previously eroded White River valley. Such a situation explains how after the Scenic and Sage Creek Basin knickpoints seen in figures 4.7 and 4.8 had been "frozen" floodwaters could still reach the White River valley and spill in a northwest direction into what was still an actively eroding Cheyenne River valley.

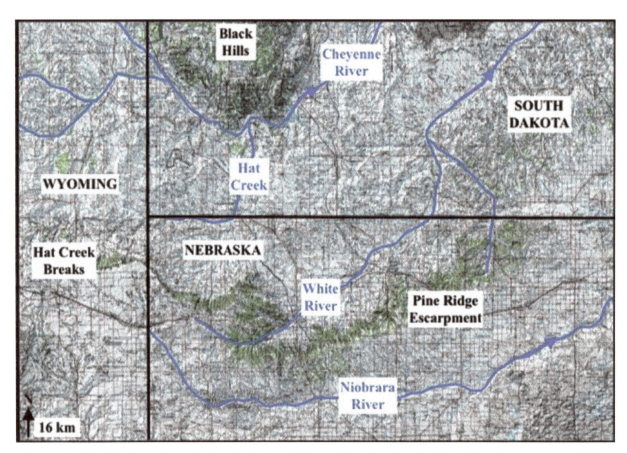

Figure 9.1: Modified map from the USGS National Map website showing the Pine Ridge Escarpment and Hat Creek Breaks relationship to the Black Hills and major drainage routes. Top left corner: 43° 35' 56.431" N, 104° 37' 09.591" W. See figure 4.8 for further discussion.

Proceeding north and east from the Pine Ridge Escarpment into glaciated northeast South Dakota figure 9.2 shows the escarpment-surrounded Prairie Coteau northern end. The east-facing Missouri Escarpment (seen in figures 9.3) is located about 100 kilometers to the west of the Prairie Coteau upland.

Escarpment-surrounded uplands are found to the north and east of the Missouri Escarpment and include the Turtle Mountains (partially seen in figure 9.4), the Prairie Coteau (seen in figure 9.2), the Riding and Duck Mountain uplands in Manitoba, and the Moose and Last Mountain uplands in Saskatchewan. Bluemle (1991, p. 45) says, "Before they were glaciated, the Turtle Mountains and Prairie Coteau were erosional outliers–probably low mesas—of Cretaceous and Tertiary sandstone formations that stood above the surrounding plain. The location of the Missouri Escarpment was marked by a more diffuse rise in elevation to the west than today."

It is puzzling why glacial geologists, like Bluemle, would assume the Prairie Coteau escarpments and the other regional escarpments predate the continental icesheets that covered the region. Bluemle and others interpret the Missouri Coteau to be covered by hummocky collapsed ice-stagnation moraines. Similar ice-stagnation moraines cover the Prairie Coteau, Turtle Mountains, and other upland surfaces, while thinner glacial deposits typical of mobile wet-based icesheets cover the escarpment slopes and most lowland areas. In South Dakota, the south-oriented James River now drains the 100-kilometer-wide lowland (sometimes referred to as the James River lowland) located between the east-facing Missouri Escarpment and the west-facing Prairie Coteau escarpment.

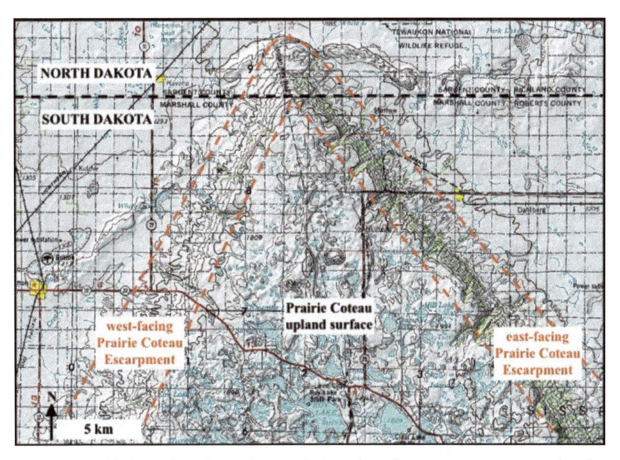

Figure 9.2: Modified map from the USGS National Map website showing escarpments surrounding the Prairie Coteau northern tip and upland surface ice-stagnation moraines. The contour interval is 50 meters. Top left corner: 45° 59' 33.495" N, 97° 46' 30.690" W.

The Missouri Escarpment in South Dakota (seen in figure 9.3) and southcentral North Dakota has a north-to-south orientation, but in central North Dakota, the 1000-kilometer-long Missouri Escarpment turns and has a northwest-southeast orientation as it continues into northcentral and northwest North Dakota (see figure 9.4) and then across southern Saskatchewan and into eastern Alberta. The Missouri Coteau in North and South Dakota is located between the southeast- and south-oriented Missouri River and the Missouri Escarpment. Glacially deposited debris now partially filling abandoned valleys, which can be traced across the North and South Dakota Missouri Coteau and Escarpment, is used as evidence that those valleys and the Missouri Escarpment, which the valleys cross, must predate continental glaciation.

If the escarpments (in some form) existed in preglacial time, as many glacial geologists claim, the problem of how the escarpments formed is simply pushed back in time and is left unexplained. Easily eroded bedrock underlies the northern prairie regions in southwest Manitoba, southern Saskatchewan, and North and South Dakota where the Missouri Escarpment and other isolated escarpment-surrounded uplands are located, which means the accepted paradigm requires geologists to assume continental icesheets expanded across the region without deeply eroding the easily-eroded underlying bedrock. According to White (1972), this assumption defies common sense logic and requires continental icesheets to have daintily tiptoed across the region. However, glacial geologists such as Sugden (1976) list what they view as convincing evidence which they interpret to say continental icesheets did not deeply erode the underlying bedrock.

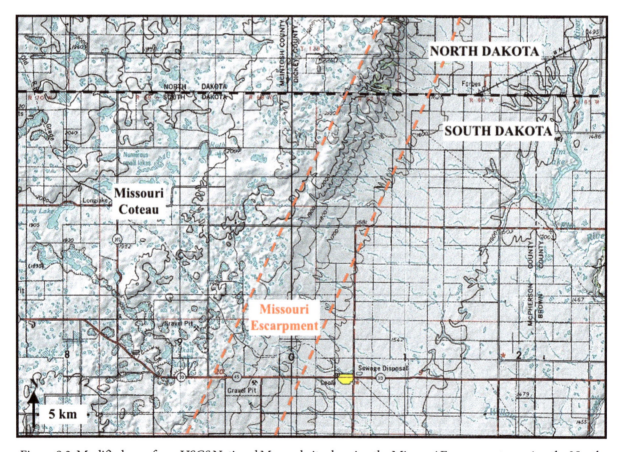

Figure 9.3: Modified map from USGS National Map website showing the Missouri Escarpment crossing the North Dakota-South Dakota border 100 km west of the Prairie Coteau northern tip. The contour interval is 100 meters. Top left corner: 45° 59' 45.516" N, 99° 18' 50.271" W.

In addition to defying common sense logic with regard to how deeply continental icesheets eroded the northern prairie regions, the accepted paradigm interpretation raises questions about the difference between the usually thick ice-stagnation moraines found on the Prairie Coteau, Missouri Coteau, and Turtle Mountain upland surfaces (and on the escarpment-surrounded southwest Manitoba and southern Saskatchewan upland surfaces) and the usually thinner glacial moraines (characteristic of mobile icesheets) found on the escarpment slopes and covering the intervening lowland areas. Why are ice-stagnation moraines found on the Prairie Coteau, Missouri Coteau, Turtle Mountains, and other escarpment-surrounded upland regions, while moraines found on the escarpment slopes and lowland areas suggest deposition by a more mobile icesheet?

Glacial geologists abiding by accepted paradigm assumptions do not consider the possibility that northern prairie region escarpments might be what remains of the walls of giant ice-walled and bedrock-floored canyons that supraglacial rivers sliced into the surface of what was a decaying continental icesheet. If that decaying icesheet had previously created (by deep erosion and uplift of surrounding regions) and occupied a deep "hole," as that icesheet melted icesheet-marginal water would have flowed in north directions into opened-up deep "hole" space. Once in that opened-up space the water would have first flowed in south directions and later in north directions. If that reversal of flow changed the climate so as to cause north-oriented drainage to freeze around decaying first icesheet remnants, a second thin icesheet might have formed with mobile wet-based ice located between decaying first icesheet remnants. Such an interpretation might explain the difference between ice stagnation and the more mobile icesheet glacial moraines.

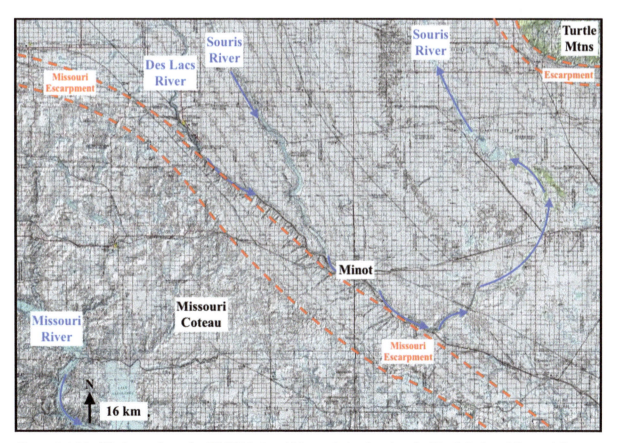

Figure 9.4: Modified map from the USGS National Map website showing the North Dakota Missouri Coteau, Missouri Escarpment, and Turtle Mountains just south of the Canadian border. The contour interval is 100 meters. Top left corner: 48° 58' 38.941" n, 102° 50' 47.083" W.

The rim of the north-facing central Wyoming escarpment known as the Beaver Divide for a significant distance, serves as the Wind River Basin southern boundary and also as the Wind River-Sweetwater River drainage divide in the region to the east of the Wind River Mountains (see figure 8.1). The regional bedrock geology has been described in some detail, but the accepted paradigm has yet to provide a good explanation for the 300-meter-high north-facing Beaver Divide escarpment other than to say the Beaver Divide marks the Wind River Basin's southern and southeastern boundary. Figures 9.5 and 9.6 illustrate the Beaver Divide escarpment origin problem. Note how in figure 9.5, West Fork Long Creek headwaters begin almost along the Beaver Divide escarpment rim and then flow in an east direction to reach the figure 9.6 map area where the West Fork Long Creek flows almost to the Beaver Divide escarpment rim (which has curved around in a northward direction to enlarge the Sweetwater River drainage basin area).

A short and abandoned valley leads from the West Fork Long Creek valley to a deep notch in the Beaver Divide escarpment rim, but instead of flowing through that abandoned valley and into the notch, the West Fork Long Creek turns in a south direction and eventually reaches the Sweetwater River. Further to the east (and not seen), the East Fork Long Creek begins as a west-oriented stream in an abandoned valley leading to an east-oriented notch carved into the Beaver Divide escarpment rim before turning in a southwest direction to reach the Sweetwater River. The West Fork Long Creek and East Fork Long Creek evidence (and other similar evidence) suggests large volumes of south-oriented water once crossed what is now the north-facing Beaver Divide escarpment. Love (1970) described evidence for a powerful south-oriented river that had once flowed across the region but did not explain how the Beaver Divide escarpment had been eroded.

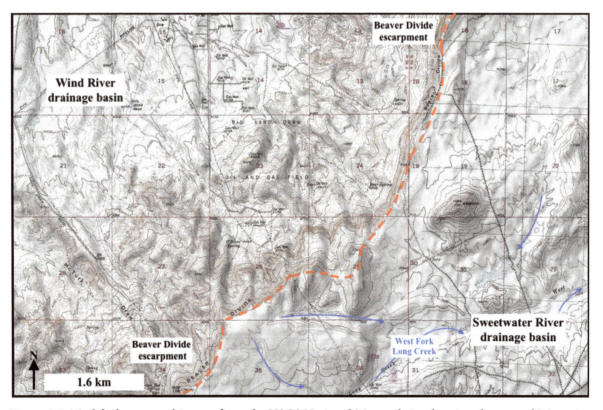

Figure 9.5: Modified topographic map from the USGS National Map website showing the central Wyoming Beaver Divide escarpment with the Sweetwater-Wind River drainage divide at its rim. The contour is 20 feet (6 m). Top left corner: 42° 45' 17.375" N, 108° 12' 24.002" W.

Large volumes of north-oriented water were needed to erode the north-, northwest- and northeast-facing Beaver Divide escarpment, but to the south is the Sweetwater River drainage basin and Wyoming's Great Divide Basin (which is located along the east-west continental divide). Also, as seen in figures 9.5 and 9.6, south-oriented water eroded the area to the south of the Beaver Divide north-facing escarpment. Where did the north-oriented water needed to erode the north-facing Beaver Divide escarpment and the south-oriented water to erode the area to the south of the Beaver Divide escarpment come from? The Wind River's abrupt direction change from flowing in a southeast direction to a north direction, which is seen in figure 8.1, provides some clues. As previously mentioned, that direction change suggests a major drainage reversal occurred and that the southeast-oriented Wind River headwaters once joined the south-oriented water that had once flowed through what is now the north-oriented Wind River Canyon.

If large enough volumes of south-oriented water were flowing across the region at the same time that regional and mountain range uplift was occurring, the uplift may have been responsible for reversing the south-oriented floodwaters, with the reversed water (and captured southeast-oriented water still flowing into the region from further to the west) being responsible for eroding the Wind River Basin so as to create the north-facing Beaver Divide escarpment. Such an interpretation is impossible from the accepted paradigm perspective because the regional and mountain range uplift occurred before any continental icesheets existed, and Wyoming's elevation after that uplift would have prevented continental icesheet meltwater floods from reaching what is now a high-elevation Rocky Mountain intermontane basin. As a result, the Beaver Divide escarpment remains a poorly explained large-scale landform that geomorphologists rarely discuss.

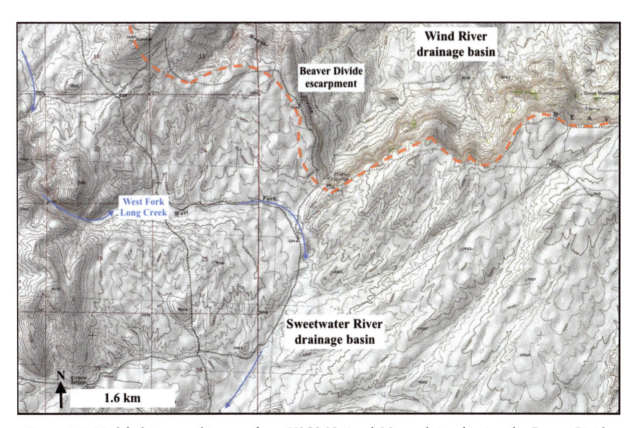

Figure 9.6: Modified topographic map from USGS National Map website showing the Beaver Divide escarpment and West Fork Long Creek to the east of figure 9.5. The contour interval is 20 feet (6 meters). Top left corner: 42° 44' 58.543" N, 108° 03' 878" W.

In the eastern United States Banks (2001, p. 1) describes the Blue Ridge Escarpment as being "a striking land feature in the southern Appalachian Mountains of Virginia and North Carolina. For over 450 km, this escarpment separates the Piedmont and Blue Ridge physiographic provinces, reaches a height of over 550 meters, and forms the drainage divide between the Gulf of Mexico and Atlantic Ocean. The landform is atypical of the subdued topography found throughout most of the Appalachians, in that it consists of very rugged, steep slopes, [and] it also lies in a mountain belt in which orogenesis ceased over 270 million years ago. . . Despite a wide variety of hypotheses that attempt to explain its origin, however, none have become dominant, and the escarpment's development is still poorly understood."

The topographic map in figure 9.7 illustrates a Blue Ridge Escarpment segment east of Boone, North Carolina, with the escarpment slope located in the east half of the figure. Red lines on the map outline the Blue Ridge Parkway corridor which is located along and near the Escarpment rim. The east-oriented Elk Creek drainage basin has eroded a large escarpment-surrounded basin similar in size and shape to the escarpment-surrounded basins discussed in chapter 4. The Elk Creek escarpment-surrounded basin probably required large volumes of east- or southeast-oriented water to erode, although no upland water source is apparent as the South Fork New River flows in a north direction just to the west and northwest of the Escarpment rim. Note how northwest-oriented South Fork New River tributaries originate at gaps (low points along the rim) near the Escarpment rim. These northwest-oriented tributary valleys and the gaps could be interpreted as evidence that multiple streams of southeast-oriented water once flowed across the escarpment but were beheaded and reversed by headward erosion of the South Fork New River valley. But such a hypothesis is alien to the accepted paradigm and is not considered.

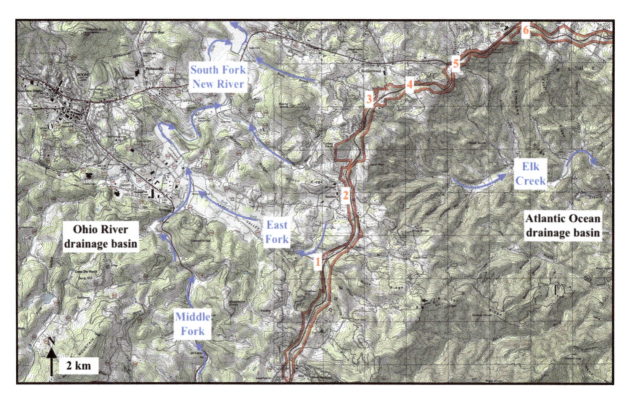

Figure 9.7: Modified topographic map from the USGS National Map website showing a Blue Ridge Escarpment segment to the east of Boone, NC. Red numbers identify gaps. The contour interval is 40 feet (12 meters). Top left corner: 36° 13' 58.694" N, 81° 41' 37.461" W.

In southern Virginia, a Blue Ridge Escarpment segment has an east-to-west orientation, as seen in figure 9.8. Numerous gaps (numbers identify some deeper gaps) are cut into this Blue Ridge Escarpment rim segment and link north-oriented New River tributary valleys with stream valleys draining in a south direction down the escarpment slope. The south-oriented streams have much steeper gradients than the north-oriented streams and, for that reason, are frequently interpreted to be causing the escarpment to retreat in a north or northwest direction. While some escarpment retreat may be occurring today, the south-oriented streams did not erode the numbered (and other) gaps seen in figures 9.7 and 9.8 (and along the entire Blue Ridge Escarpment rim). Those gaps were eroded by south- and southeast-oriented streams of water flowing from what is now the north-oriented New River drainage basin across the Blue Ridge Escarpment rim. However, the geologic literature rarely, if ever, mentions the gaps which suggest large numbers of closely-spaced streams of south- and southeast-oriented water once flowed across the Blue Ridge Escarpment rim.

Even though numerous barbed tributaries in the New River drainage basin to the north and west of the Blue Ridge Escarpment suggest a major drainage reversal took place, the accepted paradigm considers the New River to be a geologically old river, which prevents geologists from seeing the gaps as evidence that immense south- and southeast-oriented floods flowed across the Blue Ridge Escarpment rim. Such floods may have contributed significantly to the Escarpment's erosion as well as to the development of drainage systems now found in lowlands to the south and east along the Escarpment base and also in higher regions, which are located to the north and west of the Escarpment's rim. The Blue Ridge Escarpment and gaps along its rim represent poorly explained and unexplained (yet easily observed on topographic maps) landform features, which add to the geology research community's topographic map mystery.

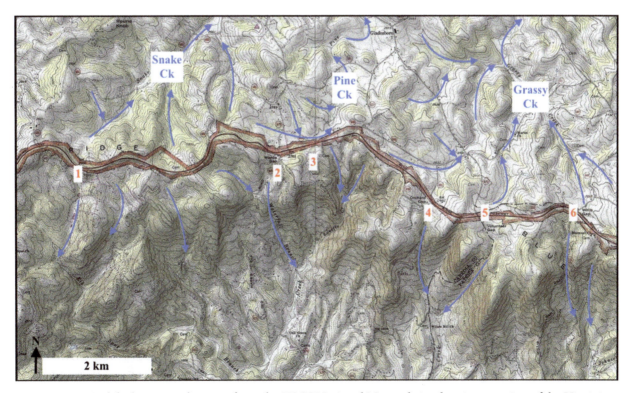

Figure 9.8: Modified topographic map from the USGS National Map website showing a section of the Virginia Blue Ridge Escarpment. Red numbers identify gaps along the escarpment rim. The contour interval is 20 feet (6 meters). Top left corner: 36° 41' 20.522" N, 80° 45' 45.348" W.

Intense erosion of the Colorado Plateau physiographic province caused Thornbury (1965, p. 436) to state, "Probably the one outstanding fact about the Colorado Plateau province is that here, erosion has been carried out on a scale unmatched in any other part of the United States. . .Hunt (1956) estimated that 80 percent of the province has been eroded to formations below the Upper Cretaceous; that 60 percent has been eroded below the base of the Cretaceous; that 35 percent has been eroded below the base of the Jurassic; and that 25 percent has been eroded below the base of the Triassic." Whether Colorado Plateau erosion was greater than in other regions can be debated; however, there is no reason to question the magnitude of Colorado Plateau erosion. One small example of Colorado Plateau erosion is seen in figure 9.9, which illustrates a topographic map of a region upstream from the Arizona Grand Canyon, showing how more than 600 meters of sedimentary rock has been stripped from the area surrounding Vermillion Cliffs.

In the Colorado Plateau physiographic province, erosional remnants such as the Vermillion Cliffs escarpment-surrounded upland preserve a record of nearly horizontal sedimentary strata that geologists can safely assume once extended across a much larger region. There are other North American regions where the surface bedrock consists of much older rocks but which lack similar erosional remnants. Without such erosional remnants, geologists have no easy way of determining what, if anything, has been eroded. As a result, geologists frequently assume younger bedrock units were never deposited or if younger bedrock units had been deposited that the younger bedrock units had been thin. Such an assumption is frequently made for North America's Canadian Shield (which is mostly in Canada), where North America's continental icesheets were centered. Such an assumption leads to the commonly stated accepted paradigm interpretation that the continental icesheets did not deeply erode the Canadian Shield area.

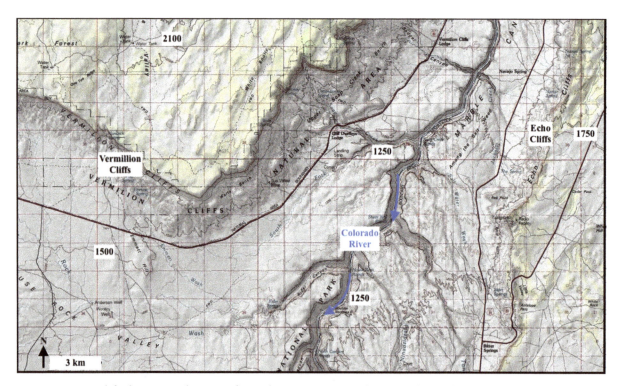

Figure 9.9: Modified topographic map from the USGS National Map website showing the Vermillion and Echo Cliffs area. The contour interval is 50 meters, with numbers showing selected contour line elevations in meters. Top left corner: 36° 47' 58.289" N, 111° 57' 39.709" W.

Among the poorly explained features seen in figure 9.9 are side canyons draining in north directions to the south-oriented 400-meter-deep and narrow Colorado River canyon. These barbed tributaries suggest a drainage reversal has taken place, although what drainage was reversed is difficult to determine. The magnitude of erosion that has taken place in the Colorado Plateau region and which was required to carve the Grand Canyon (seen in figure 9.10) has always impressed geomorphologists and has resulted in a variety of differing hypotheses, with most hypotheses being generalized descriptions of erosion over long periods of time by streams and rivers acting like streams and rivers act today as tectonic activity raised the region.

Why would the Colorado River flow in a south direction and then turn in a northwest direction to cross a north-to-south oriented arch (and to carve the Grand Canyon) when as seen in figure 9.10, it could have continued in a south direction in the valley now drained by the north-oriented Little Colorado River? The barbed tributaries seen in figure 9.9 and elsewhere in figure 9.10, and the Colorado River direction changes from south to northwest to southwest to south and then to northwest again (as seen in figure 9.10), suggest drainage reversals have taken place, not just in one locality, but across the entire region. Immense south-oriented floods, possibly of continental icesheet meltwater, which flowed across the Colorado Plateau as uplift was raising the entire region might explain the barbed tributaries and Colorado River direction changes, but the barbed tributaries and river direction changes are usually ignored because the accepted paradigm does not see any continental icesheet meltwater floods ever flowing across the Colorado Plateau.

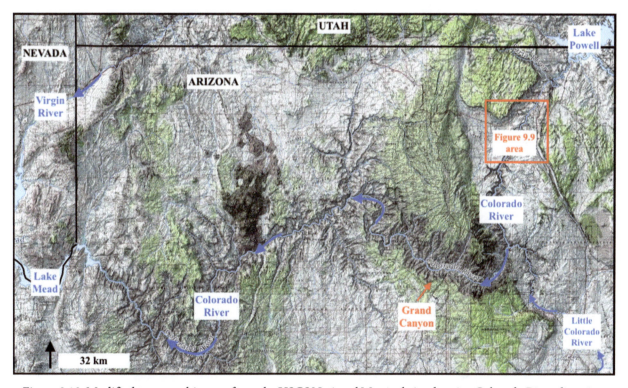

Figure 9.10: Modified topographic map from the USGS National Map website showing Colorado River direction changes in the northern Arizona Grand Canyon area. The red rectangle shows the figure 9.9 area. Top left corner: 37° 07' 59.479" N, 114° 22' 34.701" W.

To conclude this chapter figure 9.11 provides an interesting drainage history puzzle. The area is in southeast Montana and the town shown in yellow is Ekalaka. Little Beaver Creek and Boxelder Creek are both northeast-oriented tributaries flowing to the north-oriented Little Missouri River. The north-oriented Powder River flows to the northeast-oriented Yellowstone River (see figure 2.2 for a big picture map). To the north of Beaver Flats, which is in the Little Beaver Creek drainage basin, the north-oriented streams flow directly to the Yellowstone River. Note how each of the four major drainage basins has developed its own distinctive surface level and topography.

Erosion of this region began on a surface as high or higher than the highest points in the Ekalaka Hills and Chalk Buttes uplands which today are held up by small patches of horizontal erosion-resistant bedrock. Massive southeast-oriented floods next eroded the area as headward erosion of the northeast-oriented Boxelder Creek and the northeast-oriented Little Beaver Creek drainage basins diverted the southeast-oriented flood flow in a northeast direction to the north-oriented Little Missouri River valley. Southeast-oriented flood flow moving to the Boxelder Creek drainage basin between Chalk Buttes and the Ekalaka Hills ended with headward erosion of the Little Beaver Creek drainage basin while the Boxelder Creek drainage basin continued to erode headward (in a southwest direction) and to have its floor lowered. Headward erosion of the much deeper northeast-oriented Yellowstone River valley and its north-oriented tributary Powder River valley next beheaded and reversed all flood flow to the northeast-oriented Little Missouri River tributaries and produced the drainage systems and topography seen today. A more detailed discussion of this Ekalaka region erosion history interpretation is provided in Clausen 2018d.

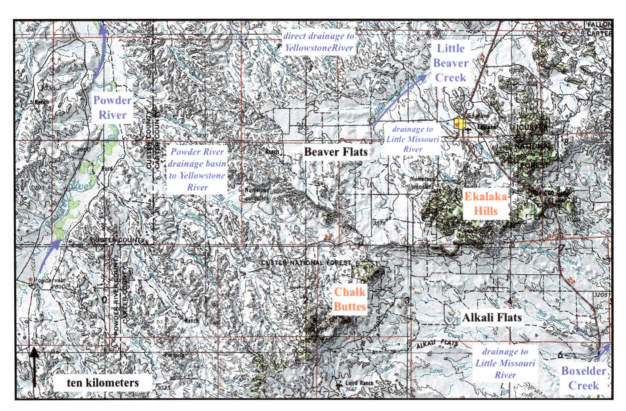

Figure 9.11. Modified map from the USGS National Map website showing the escarpment between the Beaver Flats and Alkali Flats erosion surfaces in the Ekalaka, Montana area. The contour interval is 100 feet (30 meters). Top left corner: 45° 58' 39.675" N, 105° 06', 43.866" W.

Chapter 10
Searching for a Topographic Map
Mystery Solution: Part I

Previous chapters described how I now use topographic map evidence to interpret origins for different types of large-scale drainage system and erosional landform features which the geology research community's accepted paradigm does not satisfactorily explain. But there was a time when I was just as lost about how to interpret map evidence as most geology research community members are now. After completing graduate studies at the University of Wyoming I moved to North Dakota and began teaching geology in a then new geology program at the institution now known as Minot State University. Minot is located near the center of the North American continent which provided a unique perspective that few geomorphologists have, but first I had to learn something about North Dakota geomorphology.

Arriving in North Dakota after studying at Columbia University and the University of Wyoming was like landing in an alien world. At the time I was convinced commonly used geomorphology textbooks and published geology literature contained all of the information needed to explain North Dakota geomorphology. But almost immediately I ran into a major obstacle. That obstacle was the Missouri Escarpment seen in figure 9.4 (the figure also shows Minot's location). Teaching geology at Minot State meant I needed to know what the Missouri Escarpment was and I did not have a clue.

At that time USGS Professional Paper 325 (Lemke, 1960) was the most detailed publication describing Minot area landforms. In that professional paper Lemke suggested the Missouri Escarpment might be a fault line of some sort. Yet, Lemke's evidence was not convincing and North Dakota Geological Survey (NDGS) publications and maps gave no indication the Missouri Escarpment could be associated with any known fault line. Unable to explain the Missouri Escarpment origin I spent ten years working on unrelated projects and trying to learn something about North Dakota geology and geomorphology. It was not until 1979 that I attempted to tackle the Missouri Escarpment origin problem.

I was prompted into action when Alan Kehew, who had then recently been employed by the University of North Dakota (after working in Idaho) described evidence for a catastrophic flood which had flowed across the Minot area (see Kehew, 1979). Some of his prime evidence was an anastomosing channel complex (seen in figure 10.1) which floodwaters had carved into the prairie about five kilometers to the east of where for the past ten years I had been teaching and living. I knew the channel complex was there but had ignored it. I had read interpretations of the channel complex given in USGS Professional Paper 325 which suggested water flowing around decaying blocks of ice had eroded the channels. I had not liked Lemke's interpretation, but had never bothered to develop a better interpretation.

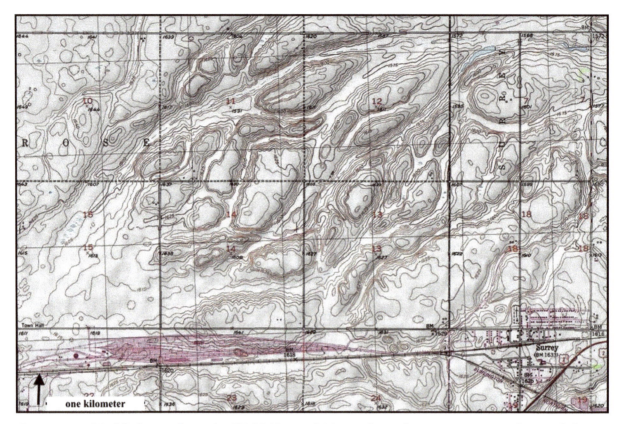

Figure 10.1: Modified map from the USGS National Map website showing a section of a much larger anastomosing channel complex located on the prairie just to the east of Minot, North Dakota. The contour interval is 5 feet (1.5 meters). Top left corner: 48° 16' 13.623" N, 101° 12' 34.010" W.

In addition to a lack of curiosity about what I should have recognized as important geomorphological evidence (located practically on my doorstep) my failure to recognize the importance of the evidence can be attributed to two other factors. The first was no professor or textbook during my geology training at Columbia University and at the University of Wyoming had mentioned catastrophic floods, much less provided me with the knowledge needed to recognize catastrophic flood evidence. Kehew attributed the Minot area catastrophic flood to the rapid draining of a large glacially dammed lake, with floodwaters flowing in a southeast direction along the Missouri Escarpment base from Canada into North Dakota. I then knew my geomorphology education had been incomplete and that I needed to learn how to recognize catastrophic flood evidence. As I learned about catastrophic flood evidence, I also began to learn why my geology education had been incomplete.

The second factor for my failure to recognize the Minot area anastomosing channel complex catastrophic flood origin was I had seen anastomosing channels far from any glacially dammed lakes. The evidence that bothered me the most were anastomosing canyons now crossing the Wyoming Laramie Mountains (seen in figure 4.2). Figure 4.2 does not show most of the diverging and converging canyons located to the west of the Goshen Hole basin (seen in figure 4.1), but I knew Kehew's explanation for the Minot area anastomosing channels should also explain how those Laramie Mountains anastomosing canyons and the Goshen Hole basin had originated and I had no clue as to how that could have happened.

Kehew's unexpected explanation for what I now recognize as obvious Minot area catastrophic flood evidence convinced me that 1.) I needed to learn about catastrophic floods and why my education had omitted any mention of catastrophic floods, and 2.) I needed to get started on determining how the Missouri Escarpment had formed. With respect to the Missouri Escarpment, I began by noting glacial geologists had suggested lobes of glacial ice had streamlined "preglacial" northern prairie region escarpments such as the escarpments surrounding the Prairie Coteau northern end (see figure 9.2). By that time, I also knew the regional bedrock for the most part is easily eroded material.

With those observations as starting points I prepared a manuscript for publication in which I proposed glacial lobes had developed in valleys of icesheet marginal rivers (which had formed at the front of an advancing icesheet) and had subsequently widened and streamlined those valleys when the icesheet advanced. I sent the manuscript to two North Dakota glacial geologists for review and both reviewers sent back comments strongly criticizing my hypothesis. The major problem identified by both reviewers was my hypothesis did not adequately address evidence for the abandoned valleys of "preglacial" rivers that can be traced across the Missouri Escarpment and the lowlands to the north and east.

Thankfully, because it was a flawed paper, that manuscript never got published, but the reviewer comments forced me to look at the so-called north-oriented "preglacial" valleys that cross the Missouri Escarpment. Abandoned valleys partially filled with glacially deposited debris do cross the Missouri Escarpment and I kept asking myself how could "preglacial" valleys which were cut in easily eroded bedrock survive being buried by one or more large continental icesheets? After a search of the geologic literature, I discovered that White (1972) was asking the same question, although several glacial geologists had severely criticized his deep erosion by continental icesheets hypothesis.

White's hypothesis did not explain the Missouri Escarpment origin but his deep erosion by continental icesheets concept did explain North Dakota's northeast-oriented slope. North Dakota is an east-to-west oriented rectangle. The state's highest point is near its southwest corner where buttes and localized and generally thin alluvial deposits sometimes containing Eocene, Oligocene, and Miocene fossils are above hundreds of meters of Paleocene rocks which are on top of hundreds of meters of Cretaceous rocks. Proceeding down the northeast-oriented slope the Paleocene and most Cretaceous rocks disappear leaving only the oldest Cretaceous sediments present as the state's northeast corner is approached.

Then available NDGS published cross sections showed the erosional origin of North Dakota's northeast-oriented slope but did not say when or how the erosion had occurred. Except in the state's southwest area (which was not glaciated) glacially deposited sediments now cover the northeast-oriented slope's erosional surface. For this reason, combined with the presence of abandoned valleys containing glacially deposited debris, continental glaciation is usually assumed to have occurred after the state's northeast-oriented slope had been eroded. I found White's hypothesis intriguing because it suggested deep continental icesheet erosion might have created North Dakota's northeast-oriented slope.

At that time (1980) the North Dakota Geological Survey (NDGS) had just published a new geologic map of North Dakota. The map showed mapped southwest North Dakota Oligocene sediments and other late Cenozoic deposits of questionable age contained igneous alluvium which had been derived from either the Black Hills or the Rocky Mountains. I searched the geology literature to determine why the source area was controversial and found vertebrate paleontologists since the early 20th-century had assumed the Black Hills were the source. No alluvium trail leading to the Black Hills had ever been reported although the Black Hills are the closest igneous rock outcrop location and the Little Missouri River flows in a north direction from the western Black Hills into southwest North Dakota.

The controversy developed when Denson and Gill (1965) in a USGS report said the distinctive southwest North Dakota alluvium igneous rocks did not match Black Hills igneous rocks and suggested the correct source was in the Montana Beartooth Mountains. They confused their report by including a map showing the route along which the alluvium might have been transported as being from the Absaroka Mountains (which are south of the Beartooth Mountains). Further confusing the issue was a PhD dissertation subsequently published as an NDGS report in which it was reported that the Absaroka Mountain source was not correct and the suggestion made that the southwest North Dakota igneous rock alluvium had come from Black Hills outcrops which had been completely eroded away. That report went on to suggest the North Dakota alluvium could be used to reconstruct Black Hills area igneous history.

The distinctive alluvium igneous rock source confusion fascinated me and I trusted the USGS report which said the Black Hills were not the source and I also trusted the PhD thesis which said the alluvium did not come from where the USGS geologists had suggested. I studied geologic maps and concluded the Montana Bear Paw Mountains were a possible alternate source. Based on literature descriptions the Bear Paw Mountains contained rock types similar to those found in the southwest North Dakota alluvium and southeast-oriented continental icesheet meltwater flowing along a recognized icesheet margin would have logically flowed from the Bear Paw Mountain location to southwest North Dakota.

Convinced the Bear Paw Mountains must be the correct source area I then collected a representative sample of distinctive southwest North Dakota alluvium igneous rock types and drove directly to the Bear Paw Mountains. Once in the Bear Paw Mountains I unsuccessfully searched for matching igneous rock outcrops. Finally, I was forced to conclude the Bear Paw Mountains were not the correct source. Convinced the southwest North Dakota distinctive alluvium igneous rocks had come from somewhere I then began to zig zag across eastern Montana and to check alluvium at every stream bed I encountered. My goal was to determine where the distinctive alluvium igneous rock types would first appear.

Alluvium containing the distinctive igneous rock types was first encountered in the Redwater River drainage basin. In fact, the Redwater River drainage basin was full of the stuff. The Redwater River is a local northeast-oriented Missouri River tributary located just to the west of the northeast-oriented Yellowstone River in eastern Montana and drains an area which has no known igneous rock outcrops. Continuing east I found thick and extensive alluvium deposits containing distinctive igneous rock types capping the Redwater River-Yellowstone River drainage divide along which eastern Montana's highest elevations are now found. The distinctive igneous rock types were abundant and I could not understand why previous geologists had not reported seeing what I was seeing.

On subsequent trips I proceeded upstream along the Yellowstone River checking all tributary valleys to determine where the distinctive igneous rock alluvium originated. That strategy enabled me to trace the most distinctive alluvium to dikes and sills in the Beartooth Mountains right where the 1965 USGS report had suggested. After additional trips and learning about Beartooth Mountain geology I concluded immense volumes of northeast-oriented water had transported the alluvium in a northeast direction from the Beartooth Mountains on a surface as high or higher than the highest Redwater River-

Yellowstone River drainage divide elevations today to near a recognized continental icesheet margin where at least some alluvium had been diverted in an east and southeast direction into southwest North Dakota.

The distinctive alluvium trail said a continental icesheet had been present when southwest North Dakota sediments containing the alluvium had been deposited. The trail also suggested a continental icesheet was present before the now deep north-oriented Yellowstone and Little Missouri River valleys had been eroded. But more surprising was the trail said a continental icesheet had been present when the mapped southwest North Dakota Oligocene rocks had been deposited. I knew those rocks were fossiliferous. I had seen the fossils and did not question their existence. I also knew those fossils had been correlated with fossils in other Oligocene sediments throughout the Great Plains and Rocky Mountains.

At that time (from 1980 to 1998) I gave progress reports most years to the North Dakota Academy of Sciences and at various other professional meetings. Almost immediately those reports encountered stiff resistance from the vertebrate paleontology community. Repeatedly I was reminded the Oligocene sediments had been deposited approximately 30 million years before any continental icesheet had reached into North Dakota. However, while critical of my reports no vertebrate paleontologist has since demonstrated the existence of a different alluvium source or of a different alluvium trail.

My first hypothesis to explain the alluvium trail suggested valley glacier rapid melting in the Beartooth Mountain canyons (in which the source dikes and sills are exposed) provided the water needed to transport alluvium 600 kilometers to southwest North Dakota deposition areas. However, after thinking about the amount of alluvium, the size of some of the cobbles and small boulders, and the distances involved (and also after observing melting alpine glaciers in the Canadian Rockies on hot summer days) I rejected that hypothesis because I thought much larger water volumes were needed.

Initially I thought the southwest North Dakota Oligocene sediments were in some way different from other Great Plains and Rocky Mountain Oligocene sediments. The alluvium in the North Dakota Oligocene sediments is different, but vertebrate paleontologists objected to my suggestion that North Dakota Oligocene sediments might be different and insisted North Dakota Oligocene fossils could be correlated with fossils at other Great Plains and Rocky Mountain Oligocene sediment locations. Their insistence that the southwest North Dakota Oligocene sediments could be correlated with other Great Plains and Rocky Mountain area Oligocene sediments suggested to me that perhaps the vertebrate paleontologists were misinterpreting those other Oligocene sediments as well. With that thought in mind I started to explore a hypothesis in which a continental icesheet was present when all of the other Great Plains and Rocky Mountain Oligocene sediments had been deposited.

My second attempt to explain the alluvium trail used a volcanic eruption under an icecap on the Yellowstone Plateau to generate immense floods which flowed in multiple directions including across what are now mountain passes leading from the Yellowstone Plateau to the Beartooth Mountain canyons. I was not aware such an event had ever been reported and before proposing that hypothesis I spent a summer hiking across the mountain passes involved, taking a special course on Yellowstone volcanic history, and trying to learn as much as possible about Yellowstone glacial history.

That second hypothesis provided what I thought was a large enough water source to transport the volumes of cobble-sized alluvium present in southwest North Dakota over the 600-kilometer-long route before deposition. The hypothesis also provided a water source able to produce large floods flowing in other directions which could have reached Oligocene sediment sites in other Great Plains and Rocky Mountain states. The published literature describing many of those other Oligocene sediment sites mentioned the presence of what I thought might be flood transported coarse-grained alluvium.

Literature related to the Reva Gap Oligocene sediments in northwest South Dakota also caught my attention. An unpublished 1925 PhD thesis (Toepelman, 1925) described landslide blocks along walls of a northwest-to-southeast oriented valley. In 1959 Malhotra and Teglund used heavy minerals to reject the Black Hills as a sediment source. Gill in 1962 mapped landslide blocks at Reva Gap and other northwest South Dakota and southeast Montana Oligocene sediment sites, including the Jumpoff seen in figure 4.3. Yet, Lillegraven (1970) who described Reva Gap vertebrate fossils, claimed there was no evidence a river had flowed through the area, and reported subsidence faulting tilted the sediments.

Intrigued, I visited Reva Gap and the other Oligocene sediment sites where Gill had mapped landslide blocks. The distinctive Beartooth Mountain alluvium was absent at those sites, although other alluvium including rounded cobbles and small boulders was present. At some sites I had to look hard to find alluvium, although at Reva Gap I had no trouble finding rounded cobbles and small boulders at the base of the large landslide block Gill had mapped. Because alluvium found at the northwest South Dakota Oligocene sediments sites was not distinctive like at the North Dakota sites I was unable to identify a source area. Based on the Toepelman, Malhotra and Teglund, and Gill papers (which a reviewer told me should not be trusted because Lillegraven's paper was more recent) and on present-day drainage routes seen on detailed topographic maps I thought floodwaters from the Yellowstone Plateau flowing along a route to the south of the Beartooth Mountain alluvium route could have been responsible for the northwest South Dakota northwest-to-southeast oriented valleys and alluvium.

Floodwaters produced during a major volcanic eruption underneath a large Yellowstone Plateau icecap could have easily flowed in multiple different directions. Using that knowledge, I could see how such floodwaters could have reached many other Great Plains and Rocky Mountain Oligocene sediment sites. Of particular interest were Oligocene sediment sites located along or near the recognized continental icesheet southwest margin which include the Cypress Hills in southwest Saskatchewan and southeast Alberta, the southwest North Dakota and northwest South Dakota sites, and the South Dakota Badlands. I found Oligocene sediments at each of those sites contained interesting but different types of alluvium.

The Cypress Hills Oligocene sediments were intriguing because they include coarse-grained alluvial deposits capping isolated uplands located just to south of the recognized continental icesheet margin. Geomorphologists have been puzzled as to why and how large concentrations of alluvium were deposited in what appears to be the middle of nowhere. Similar large and isolated concentrations of alluvium are found to the east at progressively lower elevations also near the recognized continental icesheet margin in southern Saskatchewan (the Wood Mountain gravels) and in northeast Montana (the Flaxville gravels). Based on fossil evidence the Wood Mountain gravels are usually considered to be Miocene in age and the Flaxville gravels to be Pliocene in age, although a close reading of the literature suggests fossils of different ages have been found in all three of those isolated alluvial deposits.

The Cypress Hills, Wood Mountain, and Flaxville gravels immediately impressed me as being possible places where large floods radiating out from the rapid melting of a Yellowstone Plateau icecap might have encountered an icesheet margin. Those isolated alluvium deposits later became important clues that led to the development of my current Missouri Escarpment origin hypothesis, but it took considerable further research before that hypothesis emerged. In the meantime, I kept looking to see how floodwaters from the rapid melting of a Yellowstone Plateau icecap could have transported coarse-grained alluvium to still other Great Plains and Rocky Mountain Oligocene sites. While not impossible the solutions I found were not as clean cut as I would have liked. While the second hypothesis explained large amounts of evidence, the hypothesis did not satisfactorily explain all of the evidence it should have been able to explain. As a result, the second hypothesis was rejected.

The decision to reject the second hypothesis was not made easily. I had liked the second hypothesis, although it did not explain the Missouri Escarpment origin. However, even though rivers now radiate from the Yellowstone Plateau in several different directions I was unable to find satisfactory routes to what I thought was flood deposited alluvium at a number of Oligocene and Miocene sediment sites. Further, what according to the second hypothesis was flood deposited alluvium is found on top of isolated uplands which stand one hundred meters or more above surrounding regions. To reach many of what I interpreted to be flood deposited alluvium sites the floodwaters would have had to also flow across what are now deep valleys. While a major volcanic eruption underneath a Yellowstone Plateau icecap would produce tremendous amounts of water, I realized much larger amounts of water were needed to explain the amount of erosion that has occurred since the alluvium had been deposited.

My second hypothesis had been promising and it had been extremely productive in terms leading me to large amounts of poorly explained evidence. Thomas Kuhn refers to such evidence as anomalous evidence which is evidence an accepted scientific paradigm cannot satisfactorily explain. It seemed as though everywhere I looked there was anomalous evidence which the accepted geology and glacial history paradigm could not explain and which geologists were ignoring and perhaps unconsciously or consciously covering up. There were controversies related to some of the anomalous evidence I encountered. But, if I was going to satisfactorily explain that anomalous evidence, a completely different approach using completely different and previously unstudied evidence was needed.

Chapter 11
Searching for a Topographic Map
Mystery Solution: Part II

While searching for a new approach and a large and yet-to-be-studied set of evidence which could answer my still unresolved research questions I spent two weeks exploring the Colorado River of Texas drainage basin. My goal was to compare northern Great Plains and Rocky Mountain drainage systems and alluvium with a drainage system and alluvium located far to the south of where at that time I thought large glacially related floods could have reached. My comparison did not note any significant differences and concluded either I was wrong about northern Great Plains and Rocky Mountain evidence (which I did not think was the case) or that somehow large catastrophic floods had flowed through the Colorado River of Texas drainage basin (in which case I did not know where the water came from). As a result, there was no annual progress report that year.

Trails of distinctive alluvium that could be traced from the eastern Montana Redwater River-Yellowstone River drainage divide across the now deep north-oriented Yellowstone River and Little Missouri River valleys into southwest North Dakota and then in a southeast direction along the southwest margin of mapped glacial erratic materials into the South Dakota Moreau River drainage basin still intrigued me. That evidence had convinced me that large amounts of southeast-oriented water had flowed along the southwest margin of the icesheet which had deposited the glacial erratic materials now located to the south and west of the North Dakota and South Dakota Missouri River. Those alluvium trails became the starting point for my new research approach.

First, I needed to understand why in North and South Dakota fine-grained glacial till is not found to the south and west of the Missouri River although fine-grained glacial till is abundant to the north and east of the river. Flint (1955) compared glacial erratic boulder weathering on both sides of the Missouri River and concluded the same icesheet deposited the boulders. He proposed the Missouri River valley (which he assumed had already been eroded) acted as a baffle preventing the icesheet's lowest layers (which contained finer-grained till material) from advancing beyond the river valley while the icesheet's upper layers (which only contained coarse-grained debris) advanced further to south and west.

Flint's explanation for the difference in glacially deposited material on opposite sides of the Missouri River impressed me as being unreasonably complicated and as being unlikely to have happened, but his suggestion that the same icesheet deposited the erratic boulders now found on both sides of the Missouri River intrigued me. Flint compared boulders in South Dakota and I decided to compare boulders in North Dakota. My boulder comparison results were the same as Flint's but I concluded that finer-grained glacial tills had been deposited to the south and west of the Missouri River and had subsequently been completely eroded away (probably by icesheet-marginal meltwater floods).

Combining my then new knowledge that meltwater had probably removed almost all finer-grained glacial till sediments in the region to the south and west of the Missouri River with my previously obtained knowledge of distinctive Beartooth Mountains igneous alluvium trails across southwest North Dakota enabled me to construct a geomorphic history for southwest North Dakota. That history began with an erosion surface now preserved (if it is preserved at all) by the tops of the highest southwest North Dakota buttes. A continental icesheet deposited glacial tills on that erosion surface while probably at the same time high energy rivers flowing along the icesheet's southwest margin cut deep valleys into that surface and filled at least some sections of those valleys with sediments which included distinctive Beartooth Mountain alluvium. Continued erosion lowered the entire southwest North Dakota landscape with the exception of erosional remnants which today stand as isolated buttes. Finally, north-oriented Little Missouri River valley headward erosion ended the regional erosion.

My southwest North Dakota geomorphic history was based on what I considered to be solid evidence, although I doubt my progress report that year convinced other geologists. Next, I expanded and reinforced the geomorphic history by building a case for the diversion of water from the now northeast- and north-oriented Yellowstone River across southwest North Dakota and northwest South Dakota. The case for these Yellowstone River diversions was built by noting the distinctive alluvium trails, the alignment of secondary drainage routes seen on topographic maps, the alignment of some buttes, the presence of rounded cobbles and small boulders at the mapped Oligocene sediment sites, cross beds in some of the mapped Oligocene deposits, and an analogy with the commonly accepted interpretation that the Missouri River had been formed as water was forced to flow along an icesheet's margin.

Even though my new approach was to only use what I considered to be noncontroversial evidence my vertebrate paleontology critics continued to remind me of a 30-million-year time gap between when the Oligocene rocks had been deposited and when a continental icesheet first advanced into North Dakota. Age dates for the southwest North Dakota Oligocene sediments were based on fossil correlations and not radiometric dating, although there were a few published radiometric age dates for some Yellowstone River (and tributary river) terraces. While I thought the Yellowstone River valley had been eroded headward much more rapidly than incision rates calculated from the terrace age dates suggested I used published terrace age dates to calculate Yellowstone River incision rates which indicated southwest North Dakota Oligocene sediments were deposited somewhere between 1.0 and 14.3 million years ago (not more than 30 million years ago as my vertebrate paleontology critics kept insisting).

At the same time, I became fascinated with topographic map evidence showing aligned southeast- and northwest-oriented drainage routes (like those seen in figures 2.5 and 2.6) that I had observed when constructing the southwest North Dakota geomorphic history. Divide crossings like those seen in figure 2.6 could be used to reconstruct drainage routes that existed prior to erosion of the present-day north-oriented trunk stream valleys. The drainage reconstructions required viewing detailed evidence on several hundred hard-copy 1:24,000-scale topographic maps. I constructed large mosaics of photographically reduced 1:24,000-scale topographic maps so as to be able to see evidence over large areas of eastern Montana and adjacent areas (and which extended beyond the mosaic areas in all directions). The reconstructions convinced me north-oriented trunk stream valleys eroded headward across a gigantic complex of diverging and converging southeast-oriented flood channels which must have been located along a continental icesheet's southwest margin. However, at that time I did not know why north-oriented valleys would have eroded headward from an icesheet location.

Once I knew how to recognize former diverging and converging channels on detailed topographic maps, I used the maps to trace the flood route headward to where previous geologists had described large glacially dammed lakes. I also read everything I could find about how to recognize catastrophic flood evidence and the controversy which had developed in the 1920s when J Harlan Bretz proposed a now well-recognized catastrophic flood had flowed across the Washington State Channeled Scablands area. What impressed me most about that earlier controversy was W. C. Alden and R. F. Flint had both strongly opposed the Bretz flood hypothesis. I had used references by both when trying to learn about North Dakota area geomorphology. Alden (1932) wrote a major reference describing eastern Montana geomorphology and Flint (1955) wrote an important reference describing eastern South Dakota glacial geology. I began to wonder, if Alden and Flint could not recognize catastrophic flood evidence in the Channeled Scabland area would they have recognized the evidence in the regions they studied?

Following the flood route headward led toward the Rocky Mountain front area along the Alberta-Montana border and not to the Yellowstone Plateau. Catastrophic failure of one of the glacial lakes that previous geologists had described in that region was initially considered as a possible water source. Almost immediately that hypothesis failed because topographic maps suggested floodwaters had flowed across present-day drainage divides with elevations higher than the previously reported probable glacial lake outlet elevations. One of my students looked to see if Glacial Great Falls might have been much higher than previously reported. She found evidence the glacial dam might have been as much as 100 meters higher than previously reported. However, I rejected an even higher than reported Glacial Lake Great Falls flood source because topographic map evidence suggested floodwaters had crossed even higher divides and then flowed around the Black Hills southern end (see figure 9.1).

Divide crossings or low points along drainage divides seen on detailed topographic maps could also be used to determine the downstream flow route which suggested floodwaters had flowed to the west of the Ozark Mountains to reach the Gulf of Mexico. That flood flow route helped to explain some of the puzzling Texas field evidence I had seen. But that flood flow route also introduced questions which at the time I could not answer. Specifically, that flood flow route crossed what are today northeast- and east-oriented Missouri River tributary valleys and then further to the south, east-oriented Mississippi River tributary valleys, And, at that time I still expected to find higher elevation regions which floodwaters had not crossed. I could not explain why and how valleys could erode headward from an icesheet location across large floods and then into higher unflooded regions.

Asymmetric drainage divides, geology's principle of cross cutting relationships, and 1:250,000-scale topographic maps showed that Missouri River tributary drainage basins now crossing my then identified south-oriented flood flow route had been formed in a sequence starting in the southeast and progressing to the northwest. At that time, I used topographic maps to also determine that eastern United States rivers draining to the Atlantic Ocean had also developed in a progressive sequence from the south to the north. My efforts to interest other geologists in what I thought were easily identified drainage basin formation sequences were unsuccessful even though those observed drainage basin formation sequences impressed me as being important evidence needing to be explained.

Determining that Missouri River tributary valleys had eroded headward in sequence made the northwest-oriented streams now draining the South Dakota Scenic and Sage Creek Basin floors (see figures 4.7 and 4.8) stand out as anomalous evidence. The escarpment-surrounded Scenic and Sage Creek Basins appeared to be "frozen" knickpoints which had been eroded headward from a deep east-oriented White River valley in a northwest direction by two large and parallel rivers or streams of southeast-oriented flood flow. The knickpoints had been "frozen" when Cheyenne River valley headward erosion across the southeast-oriented flood flow had captured those two large streams of southeast-oriented water. What the large southeast-oriented floods initially did not appear to explain were the northwest-oriented valleys now draining the Scenic and Sage Creek Basin floors.

Eventually a solution to the Scenic and Sage Creek Basin drainage history puzzle emerged. The solution required southeast-oriented floods flowing across and around an emerging Black Hills upland (emerging by uplift and/or by deep erosion of the surrounding region). First the White River valley must have eroded headward in a west and then southwest direction as it captured southeast-oriented flood flow while the Sage Creek and Scenic Basin knickpoints must have eroded headward in a northwest direction from where the actively eroding White River valley turned to erode headward in a southwest direction. Cheyenne River valley headward erosion next beheaded the southeast-oriented flood flow moving to the Sage Creek and Scenic Basin knickpoints, but did not erode headward fast enough to capture the flood flow which was moving around the Black Hills southern end to reach the still actively eroding White River valley head. A flood flow surge filled the White River valley and the water briefly spilled across the then "frozen" Sage Creek and Scenic Basin knickpoints into the newly eroded Cheyenne River valley and eroded the northwest-oriented valleys which now drain the basin floors.

Solving the Scenic and Sage Creek escarpment-surrounded basin drainage history puzzle helped confirm my previous interpretation that immense southeast-oriented floods had flowed around the Black Hills southern end and had carved the Pine Ridge Escarpment seen in figure 9.1. Recognizing the Scenic and Sage Creek Basins as "frozen" knickpoints I next scanned topographic maps to locate similar escarpment-surrounded basins some of which are discussed in chapter 4. A plot of the basins and their orientations was made similar to figure 4.11 to determine probable flood flow routes. Basins on the previously determined flood flow route helped to confirm my flood flow route interpretations, but some basins required previously unrecognized flood flow routes through what are now high elevation Rocky Mountain intermontane basins. Bates Hole and the Beaver Divide were puzzling because they open in north directions and required north-oriented flood flow to be explained.

Efforts to interest other geologists in the Great Plains and Rocky Mountain flood routes which had been identified from topographic map drainage system and drainage divide evidence and then confirmed by the presence of large flood eroded "frozen" knickpoints continued to be unsuccessful. That lack of interest was discouraging because it meant I would have trouble when trying to publish my findings. I was also aware that my training had not introduced me to any catastrophic flood evidence and the geology literature showed no hint that other geologists had seen what my study of topographic map evidence was forcing me to recognize. With the help of the escarpment-surrounded basins, asymmetric drainage divides, and other topographic map evidence the identified flood flow routes were expanded into the Rocky Mountain region and to the Colorado River drainage basin. Flood flow routes could also be traced across high drainage divides to reach the Colorado Plateau areas seen in figures 9.9 and 9.10.

Map evidence could also be used to show how valley headward erosion had systematically diverted the south-oriented floodwaters so as to create present-day drainage systems.

By the early 1990s I was using divide crossings (low points along drainage divides), asymmetric drainage divides, barbed tributaries, through valleys (valleys now crossing drainage divides) and similar evidence seen on topographic maps of the lower 48 states to trace flood flow routes and how those flood flow routes had been diverted to flow in new directions. The map evidence could be used to determine how present-day western United States drainage systems had progressively evolved as valleys eroded headward from the Gulf of Mexico and from the Pacific Ocean to capture massive south-oriented flood flow and how eastern United States drainage systems had progressively evolved as valleys eroded headward from the Gulf of Mexico and the Atlantic Ocean. Again, my efforts to interest other geologists were unsuccessful. They were not interested in looking at the topographic map evidence.

Throughout my topographic map investigations, I frequently checked the geologic literature to see how previous geologists interpreted large-scale landforms seen on the topographic maps I was studying. In many cases there was no literature in which the landforms were mentioned much less explained. And, in the rare cases where an explanation was provided the explanation was usually not consistent with the topographic map evidence. What impressed me most during those geologic literature searches was the almost complete absence of studies in which topographic map evidence was even mentioned. Those literature searches convinced me I was interpreting evidence previous geologists had never studied (or if they had, previous geologists for some reason had chosen not to report what they found).

One major problem with the newly discovered flood flow routes was I still did not know how meltwater floods from a continental icesheet could flow across high mountain areas when much lower areas exist between the icesheet location and the high mountain ridges which maps showed the floodwaters had crossed. I spent several years exploring different hypotheses before concluding the only way to explain the drainage system and drainage divide evidence was if the icesheet had been located in a deep "hole" which had been created by deep icesheet erosion of the underlying bedrock and by surrounding region uplift. That solution explained the map evidence. That solution also required the northeast-oriented northern Missouri River drainage basin slope to have been eroded when icesheet melting opened up deep "hole" space into which icesheet-marginal meltwater floods flowed. The solution also explained why north- and northeast-oriented valleys would erode headward from the icesheet location.

The previously determined southeast to northwest sequence of northern Missouri River tributary valley headward erosion suggested deep "hole" space had been opened-up in the south first and then opened-up progressively in a northwest direction. Meltwater floods at first appeared to have been diverted to flow into deep "hole" space and once in the deep "hole" to flow toward southern exits with deep "hole" rim uplift progressively closing off the southern exits until only the south-oriented Mississippi River valley remained. Later as icesheet melting continued meltwater floods were diverted across the decaying icesheet floor toward northern oceans which ended almost all of the south-oriented flow. I interpreted the reversal of meltwater floods from flowing in a south direction to flowing in a north direction to have caused a major climate cooling event which froze north-oriented meltwater and other drainage around decaying first icesheet remnants so as to create a second and much thinner icesheet and an "ice age."

The deep "hole" interpretation provided answers to many previously asked research questions including the Missouri Escarpment origin question and also led to explanations of yet-to-be considered evidence. Using the deep "hole" interpretation, I determined valleys of what are now north-oriented northern Missouri River tributaries had not eroded headward from an icesheet margin, but from what must have been a giant northwest-to-southeast ice-walled canyon that a large supraglacial meltwater river must have carved into the decaying first icesheet's surface. The now isolated Cypress Hills, Wood Mountain, and Flaxville Gravel upland alluvial sediments suggested they had been deposited where north- and northeast-oriented valleys had eroded headward across the decaying icesheet surface and into surrounding bedrock that was subsequently removed. Present-day elevations of those isolated alluvial capped uplands suggest subsequent southeast-oriented icesheet-marginal meltwater floods removed as much as several hundred meters of bedrock from regions to the south and west of the icesheet.

Based on the deep "hole" interpretation the Missouri Escarpment could be interpreted to be what remains of the southwest and west wall of the giant ice-walled and bedrock-floored canyon. The Prairie Coteau west-facing escarpment and the Turtle Mountains southwest-facing escarpment (seen in figures 9.2-9.4) are remnants of that ice-walled and bedrock-floored canyon's northeast and east wall. What must have been a giant southeast and south-oriented river (which I named the Midcontinent River) flowed on the floor of that giant southeast- and south-oriented ice-walled canyon to the icesheet's margin near where the James River now joins the Missouri River in southern South Dakota (which explained why downstream from that location the Missouri valley is larger than it is upstream from that location).

Similar escarpments found throughout southwest Manitoba and southern Saskatchewan suggested a complex of similar diverging and converging ice-walled canyons sliced into at least a section of the icesheet so as to create a number of detached and semi-detached icesheet masses. Present-day river U-turns along the former Midcontinent River route (such as the Souris River U-turn seen in figure 9.4) appeared to record how the southeast-oriented Midcontinent River had been systematically captured and diverted to flow in a north direction. Those captures occurred when water in a south-oriented tributary ice-walled canyon was reversed to flow on a newly opened-up route toward northern oceans.

What previous geologists had interpreted to be valleys of a preglacial north-oriented drainage system were instead valleys eroded into the first thick icesheet's floor as the southeast- and south-oriented Midcontinent River (flowing in an ice-walled and bedrock-floored canyon) had been repeatedly captured and diverted to flow in a north direction. Those captures occurred first in southeast North Dakota, next in northcentral North Dakota (the figure 9.4 area) and then again in Saskatchewan where the North Saskatchewan River now makes an abrupt direction change as it leaves the former Midcontinent River route. Evidence for the Midcontinent River captures helped to confirm my previous interpretation that as the first thick icesheet melted what had been south-oriented meltwater floods were diverted fairly rapidly to flow toward north-oriented oceans. I interpreted that fairly rapid flood flow reversal to have triggered a major climatic change which created the second thin icesheet.

Midcontinent River diversions to the north when combined with the interpretation that north-oriented drainage had frozen around decaying first icesheet remnants to form a second icesheet explained the presence of ice-stagnation glacial moraines on escarpment-surrounded uplands (such as the Prairie Coteau seen in figure 9.2) and thinner moraines associated with wet-based icesheets which are found between the escarpment-bounded ice-stagnation moraine upland areas. The escarpment-bounded ice-stagnation upland area glacial moraines are generally located where detached and semi-detached first icesheet remnants included in the second icesheet had slowly melted. Glacial moraines associated with a wet-based icesheet are generally where north-oriented drainage had been frozen on floors of the ice-walled canyon network that separated the detached and semi-detached first icesheet remnants.

Up until the early 1990s I had been trying to find ways to tweak the accepted geology and glacial history paradigm to explain what had become the growing mass of topographic map and other evidence I was attempting to explain. Anyone following my progress reports which were presented to the North Dakota Academy of Science and at national and international professional meetings might have reasonably been confused because my hypotheses to explain where the massive floods had originated evolved as new evidence was studied. This process of describing different floodwater sources ended in the early 1990s when I determined the floodwaters must have come from a thick icesheet that had created and then occupied a deep "hole" in the North American continent.

By the early 1990s I had read Thomas Kuhn's book *The Structure of Scientific Revolutions.* The book helped me understand what had happened when qualitative historical geomorphologists could not explain most of the well-mapped topographic map drainage system and erosional landform evidence. The unexplained evidence was anomalous evidence which Kuhn describes as being evidence an accepted paradigm cannot satisfactorily explain. With the help of Kuhn's ideas, I also recognized that by trying to explain anomalous evidence I was in fact developing a new and fundamentally different geology and glacial history paradigm which could explain what the accepted paradigm could not explain. The new paradigm that my search led to described a Cenozoic geology and glacial history in which there were two linked icesheets with the first icesheet being thick and being located in an icesheet created deep "hole" and the second much thinner icesheet being formed when north-oriented drainage froze on the deep "hole" floor around first icesheet remnants.

Up until 1998 I gave annual progress reports to the North Dakota Academy of Science and at a variety of other professional meetings, although trying to describe how a new paradigm explains previously unexplained or poorly explained evidence in a 15-to-20-minute presentation and in a one-page abstract or communication was challenging. Adding to the challenge was the fact that much of my evidence was on detailed topographic maps and required the use of dozens and even hundreds of hard copy maps to properly see. At the time I was hoping to interest other geologists, but while other geologists attended sessions where I gave presentations and probably read the abstracts and communications no serious interest was expressed. One prominent catastrophic flood expert following one of my presentations said I was not being reasonable and then walked away.

Problems with my professional meeting presentations, abstracts, and communications came to a head in 1999 when the North Dakota Academy of Science rejected the two one-page communications I had submitted. A vertebrate paleontologist was the Academy of Science President that year and vertebrate paleontologists had always been among my strongest critics. I had been the Academy President some years earlier and knew the rejection of my submissions was an unusual step. The rejection notice included two letters written by anonymous reviewers which pointed out how the two communications violated accepted paradigm interpretations (which the reviewers regarded as unquestionable facts) and they claimed I had not used real data in my research.

Kuhn in his book describes how advocates of two fundamentally different and competing paradigms have extreme difficulty when trying to communicate. I understood what was happening in that my research had led to a new paradigm that accepted paradigm advocates did not understand. However, the rejection stung because the reviewers claimed my research was not based on real data which was definitely not the case. After licking my wounds, I decided that if the reviewers wanted to see real data, I would document every drainage divide (between streams large enough to be shown on USGS 1:100,000 scale topographic maps) in the Missouri River drainage basin in a test of the new paradigm implication that the Missouri River drainage system had evolved as valleys eroded headward across massive continental icesheet meltwater floods.

My resulting Missouri River drainage basin study used hard copy topographic maps and took 17 months of almost full-time work to complete. I had retired from teaching by that time but had a part time job administering unrelated National Geographic Education Foundation and other grants. To the best of my knowledge my Missouri River drainage basin study was the first time anyone had systematically gone through detailed topographic maps covering the entire Missouri River drainage basin and several adjacent river drainage basins to determine how each valley in those drainage basins had been eroded. The resulting database documented 42,360 different drainage divides and stream valleys. Each stream valley encountered could reasonably be interpreted to have been eroded headward by floodwaters that had flowed across what are now adjacent drainage divides. The study also confirmed the new paradigm perspective did explain almost all of the Missouri River drainage basin topographic map drainage system and erosional landform evidence.

Chapter 12
A Paradigm Able to Explain the Topographic Map Drainage System and Erosional Landform Evidence

North Dakota of Academy of Science reviewers rejected a communication submitted midway during my Missouri River drainage basin study and a communication submitted after the study's completion. Cover letters sent with both of my submitted communications offered to provide upon request a computer disc with the database on which my conclusions were based. No request was made to see the disc, but rejection notices for each communication included multiple reviews some of which were mocking comments written over my submitted text. Reviewer comments appeared to be more than a rejection of the submitted communications, but an effort to kill the new paradigm which the Missouri River drainage basin study strongly supported and which explained most if not all of the topographic map drainage system and erosional landform evidence I had observed.

The two submitted communications probably deserved to be rejected, but not for the reasons the reviewers gave. Like with my 1999 submitted communications which the North Dakota Academy of Science had previously rejected, I had tried to pack too much information into those one-page submissions. Having a submission rejected is not pleasant no matter what the reason, but the reviewer comments included statements such as "doesn't appear to be a report of research", "it appears that USGS map is being used as both a source of data and reference support, assertions which lack scientific foundation", and "current theories on the effect of tectonic activity on these drainage basins is alluded to, but not addressed and clearly refuted by the data presented." Those statements suggested the reviewers were rejecting USGS topographic maps as a valid evidence source.

During my research (most of which communications to the North Dakota Academy of Science described) I discovered that reading detailed topographic map drainage system and erosional landform evidence is like reading an unknown language. Until the language is learned, it has no meaning, but if the language is known, it has great meaning. Historical qualitative geomorphologists, most of whom were excellent map interpreters, could not use the geology research community's accepted paradigm to determine what much of the topographic map drainage system and erosional landform evidence was saying. As previous chapters have hinted, there is a different paradigm perspective from which topographic map drainage system and erosional landform evidence can be understood, but that different perspective leads to a completely different Cenozoic geologic and glacial history than what the accepted paradigm perspective has permitted the geology research community to describe. North Dakota Academy of Science reviewers rejected that different geologic and glacial history. I was being told the topographic map drainage system and erosional landform evidence was not real evidence and was not worth considering.

The new Cenozoic geology and glacial history paradigm which is able to explain the topographic map drainage system and erosional landform evidence (which North Dakota Academy of Science reviewers rejected as not being valid scientific evidence) emerged when I interpreted all Missouri River drainage basin drainage system and erosional landforms (large enough to show on the 1:100,000 scale USGS topographic maps). Prior to that successful interpretation, I spent many years using mosaics of hard-copy paper topographic maps testing preliminary sets of rules and assumptions that might explain the observed topographic map evidence. More than ten years after the North Dakota Academy of Science's rejection, National Geographic TOPO digital maps and software—which by that time had become available—were used to redo the Missouri River drainage basin study by determining how every Missouri River drainage basin drainage divide (between streams large enough to be shown on 1:24,000 scale topographic maps) had been formed. More than 550 non-peer-reviewed research notes in blog format for that successful Missouri River drainage basin test are available in 2024 at geomorphologyresearch.com.

The new paradigm explains Missouri River drainage basin detailed topographic map drainage system and erosional landform evidence by interpreting low points along drainage divides (unless there is reason to think otherwise) to be where water once flowed across the drainage divides and large numbers of closely-spaced low points along a drainage divide to be evidence that large floods flowing in anastomosing channel complexes once crossed the drainage divide. Recognition of drainage divide low points and of anastomosing channel complex evidence leads to an interpretation that the headward erosion of deep valleys repeatedly beheaded and reversed massive and prolonged floods (in progressive sequences identifiable by the valley headward erosion direction) so as to create the drainage divides. The interpretation that most, if not all, drainage divides—large enough to be seen on 1:24,000 scale topographic maps—originated as the headward erosion of deep valleys captured immense and prolonged floods means a large flood source is needed. The Missouri River drainage basin is located to the southwest of where large North American continental icesheets once existed, and drainage divide evidence can be used to trace floodwaters in headward directions to continental icesheet locations. With these interpretations, the Missouri River drainage basin topographic map drainage system and erosional landform evidence can be explained.

The resulting new paradigm emergence was helped by also interpreting the large numbers of south-oriented or barbed tributaries flowing to what are now north-oriented Missouri River tributaries (examples are in figures 2.5 and 2.6) to indicate that the headward erosion of deep north-oriented valleys had captured large and prolonged south- and southeast-oriented floods and had diverted the floodwaters in a north direction toward what must have been a continental icesheet location. In all cases, elevations at the southern ends of the north-oriented drainage basins are much higher than at the northern ends, meaning the continental icesheet must have been located in a deep "hole" and probably that uplift had been occurring as immense meltwater floods flowed across rising regions to the south and west of the continental icesheet margin. These interpretations became new paradigm requirements and represented significant breaks from the accepted paradigm rules and assumptions, but they are needed if the topographic map drainage system and erosional landform evidence is to be understood, and the topographic map mystery is to be solved.

The new paradigm requires most drainage systems in the lower forty-eight states to have been developed as deep valleys eroded headward across immense and prolonged meltwater floods and that the floods had initially flowed across tectonically rising regions and mountain ranges, which implies a relationship between the floods and the uplift of the regions and mountain ranges over which the floodwaters flowed. A long-lived and thick North American continental icesheet—perhaps as thick as today's Antarctic Icesheet and located where North American continental icesheets are usually reported to have been—explains the map evidence, especially if the thick continental icesheet deeply eroded the underlying bedrock and was heavy enough to cause the uplift of surrounding regions and mountains so as to form and occupy a deep "hole."

The accepted paradigm does not recognize any comparable continental icesheet created deep "hole," nor does the accepted paradigm see immense and long-lived continental icesheet meltwater floods flowing across tectonically rising regions and mountain ranges. Yet, topographic map drainage system and erosional landform evidence found to the south of the thick continental icesheet's southern margin (shown in figure 12.1 with a dashed blue line) documents how uplift of a deep "hole" rim (shown with a red line) diverted what must have been immense floods that had been flowing across the rising deep "hole" rim to flow toward the Mississippi River valley and later in north directions into deep "hole" space the melting thick continental icesheet had once occupied.

Figure 12.1: Modified map from the USGS National Map website showing the approximate deep "hole" rim location (red line), approximate thick icesheet southern margin (blue dashed line), the Arkansas River drainage basin location, and the Mississippi River location.

The accepted paradigm has been used to describe four or more late Cenozoic continental icesheets where the new paradigm's thick icesheet was located; however, the accepted paradigm does not consider any of those multiple icesheets to have been located in a deep "hole" or see evidence that gigantic meltwater floods flowed across most deep "hole" rim locations or were later diverted into space one or more of those multiple continental icesheets once occupied. The new paradigm's deep "hole" rim in the western United States followed what is now the east-west continental divide from the Canada-Montana border in a south and southeast direction into southern Colorado and then the Sangre de Cristo Mountains crest line into northeast New Mexico before turning in an east direction to follow what is now the Arkansas River drainage basin (probably along the Arkansas River drainage basin southern margin). In the eastern United States, the deep "hole" rim followed what are today the Ohio River-Atlantic Ocean and Ohio River-Gulf of Mexico drainage divides.

Deep "hole" rim uplift probably was gradual and occurred as massive and long-lived south-oriented meltwater floods flowed across it. As time progressed in the western United States, deep "hole" rim uplift forced meltwater floods to flow in southeast and east directions and in the eastern United States deep "hole" rim uplift forced meltwater floods to flow in southwest and west directions both toward the Mississippi River valley, which eventually became the deep "hole's" only southern exit. Valleys eroded headward from that deep "hole" southern outlet to capture the massive meltwater floods and progressively developed what is today the Mississippi River drainage system.

Topographic map drainage system and erosional landform evidence records how the above-described thick continental icesheet decayed, which probably began as deep "hole" rim uplift was still occurring. Icesheet decay in what is now North Dakota, South Dakota, southwest Manitoba, southern Saskatchewan, and probably also in other regions, occurred as massive south-oriented supraglacial meltwater rivers sliced giant ice-walled and ice-floored (and later bedrock-floored) canyons into the decaying icesheet surface. What is now the poorly explained 1000-kilometer-long Missouri Escarpment, which extends in a southeast direction from eastern Alberta across southern Saskatchewan and northwest North Dakota and which, in central North Dakota, turns in a south direction and continues to southcentral South Dakota, is probably what is left of the southwest and west wall of an ice-walled and ice-floored (and later bedrock-floored) canyon, which eventually detached the icesheet's southwest margin (the detached icesheet mass was located where the Missouri Coteau ice-stagnation moraine area is now).

Other northern prairie region escarpments (such as seen in figures 9.2, 9.3, and 9.4) are remnants of other ice-walled and ice-floored (and later bedrock-floored) canyon walls, which formed as the thick icesheet decayed with those ice-walled canyons eventually detaching other decaying icesheet ice masses where North Dakota, South Dakota, southwest Manitoba, and southern Saskatchewan ice-stagnation moraine areas now cover the Prairie Coteau, the Turtle Mountains, Riding Mountain, Duck Mountain, the Moose Mountains, Last Mountain, and other upland areas.

Being located in a deep "hole" means that in what is now the North American northern prairie region the thick continental icesheet floor was lower in elevation than the elevations of the large icesheet-marginal meltwater floods, which flowed along the icesheet's southwest margin. Eventually, the floor of the ice-walled canyon located near the icesheet's southwest margin—the one associated with the Missouri Escarpment—became low enough that icesheet-marginal floods could breach the icesheet's semi-detached southwest margin and spill into the southeast-oriented ice-walled canyon (the more than 1000-kilometer-long Missouri Escarpment is what remains of that ice-walled canyon's southwest and west wall). At first, all flow in the ice-walled canyon network moved in a south direction, with one of the outlets being in southeast South Dakota where the Missouri River valley now greatly widens (with the water eventually reaching the Gulf of Mexico).

The immense south-oriented meltwater floods in addition to raising sea level must have caused an ever-increasing climatic warming which further increased the thick ice sheet's decay. As the thick icesheet decay progressed north-oriented ice-walled and bedrock-floored canyons which offered much shorter routes to sea level intersected with the expanding south-oriented ice-walled and bedrock-floored canyons and systematically diverted the immense icesheet-marginal meltwater floods and other drainage toward northern oceans. What are now north-oriented Ohio and Missouri River tributary drainage systems and their associated north-oriented regional slopes developed as north-oriented valleys eroded headward from the ice-walled canyon complex. As icesheet decay progressed water flowing in the ice-walled canyon complex was diverted in a series of steps from routes leading to the Gulf of Mexico to newly opened-up and shorter routes leading to the North Atlantic and Arctic Oceans.

The opening-up of ice-walled canyon routes leading to the North Atlantic and Arctic Oceans caused the large south-oriented meltwater floods and other drainage, which had been flowing to the Gulf of Mexico to flow along newly opened-up routes across the deep "hole" floor so as to reach northern oceans. Diversion of massive meltwater floods and other drainage from the Gulf of Mexico to northern oceans ended what had been progressively warming northern hemisphere climatic conditions and introduced cold climatic conditions, which eventually caused north-oriented drainage which entered the deep "hole" to freeze around detached and semi-detached thick icesheet remnant masses. This freezing created what became a second and much thinner continental icesheet. This second thinner icesheet blocked the newly formed north-oriented drainage systems which had formed when the headward erosion of valleys from the deep "hole" into regions to the south of the decaying icesheet captured icesheet marginal meltwater floods. Water from these north-oriented drainage systems was then forced to flow along the second icesheet's southern margin so as to form the icesheet-marginal Ohio and Missouri Rivers. Unlike the first thick continental icesheet, the second thin continental icesheet did not deeply erode or further develop the already formed deep "hole," but the cold climatic conditions led to what the geology research community refers to as an "Ice Age" and caused alpine glaciers to form in higher mountain regions (which had been uplifted as the first thick icesheet had raised its deep "hole" rim).

The above-described new paradigm like every scientific paradigm is incomplete and needs to be fleshed out. Fleshing out scientific paradigms is what most scientists do. Scientific paradigms are fleshed out when scientists use the paradigm to explain previously unexplained evidence. Those explanations, if successful, can become paradigm pillars which are then used to help explain additional sets of new evidence. According to Kuhn this process of fleshing out paradigms (which Kuhn refers to as normal science) is essential if a scientific community is to advance.

The geology research community which now consists of many thousands of research geologists has been fleshing out the accepted geology and glacial history paradigm for the past 150 years. In contrast the new paradigm except for my research has yet to be fleshed out. Why I am so brash as to suggest the geology research community has an unrecognized paradigm problem? The North Dakota Academy of Science reviewers provided the answer. The geology research community does not consider USGS topographic map drainage system and erosional landform evidence to be real evidence worthy of reporting and addressing in scientific reports. Yet, drainage systems and erosional landforms blanket almost all continental areas. There is no way the geology research community can properly understand Cenozoic geology and glacial history without understanding how those well-mapped drainage systems and erosional landforms originated.

117

Chapter 13
Demonstrating How a New Paradigm Explains Topographic Map Evidence

Not seeing any scientific merit in the North Dakota Academy of Science reviewer comments that claimed my 17-month-long study of topographic map evidence "was not real research", that "a study based on topographic map evidence lacks a scientific foundation", and that data in my database (which reviewers never asked to see) "refuted" what my study had found I responded. My response consisted of an 80-page book titled "Evolution of a Scientific Paradigm" which was prepared and mailed at my expense to all North Dakota Academy of Science members. Included in that book were an informal essay describing the research path which led to the new paradigm (similar but in more detail to chapters 10 and 11 in this book), my rejected communications, all reviewer comments as I had received them, and my review of the reviewer comments.

About a year later the North Dakota Academy of Science President made contact with me and said I could again submit communications for presentation at North Dakota Academy of Science meetings. I thanked him, but the North Dakota Academy of Science was no longer the audience I wanted to reach. I wanted to reach the much larger geology research community. Using Kuhn's book, *The Structure of Scientific Revolutions* I had studied how other scientific paradigms had been changed and realized that continuing to present my work at scientific meetings and in scientific journal articles (assuming I could convince geology journals to accept my submissions) was unlikely to have any significant impact. A completely different approach was needed.

One immediate problem was a growing realization the geology research community did not value the topographic map drainage system and erosional landform evidence upon which the new paradigm was based. While perhaps not as blunt as the North Dakota Academy of Science reviewers, other geologists, funding agencies, geology journal editors and reviewers, and the geologic literature were all conveying the same message. Consciously or unconsciously the geology research community was not just ignoring the topographic map drainage system and erosional landform evidence (which did not agree with accepted paradigm interpretations), but it was actually dismissing that evidence as being unimportant and not worth considering.

Another problem was the database constructed during my 17-month Missouri River drainage basin study had been constructed using evidence seen on hundreds of the hard copy detailed topographic maps. The data entries identified the maps by name and state and provided brief descriptions of specific features to document that water had once flowed across what are now drainage divides. While constructing the database was valuable to me in determining how the drainage divides had formed anyone else trying to use the database would have had to obtain the hard copy maps in question and then find the specified features on those maps. That cumbersome process limited the database's usefulness when trying to convince other geologists to seriously review my work.

In addition, the database used software that was becoming obsolete, the Internet was becoming a tool for the communication of scientific information, and topographic maps were being digitalized and each year fewer geologists were having access to large hard copy topographic map collections. The database could always document the Missouri River drainage basin study had been done, but otherwise was becoming of questionable value. I decided not to upgrade the database software and looked for another more user-friendly way to document that the Missouri River drainage basin study had been done. My goal was to find a way to post user-friendly Missouri River drainage basin study results on a public website, but it took almost ten years before I did so.

I had retired from teaching in 1997 and from 1995 until 2006 administered on a part time basis National Geographic Education Foundation and other grants for the North Dakota Geographic Alliance (an organization of North Dakota K-12 geography teachers). Administering those grants introduced me to geography educators from around the country and made me aware that physical geographers as well as geologists should be interested in what the topographic map drainage system and erosional landform evidence has to say. From 2001 until 2006 the North Dakota Geographic Alliance published a quarterly magazine which I edited and provided some content for.

Thinking the National Geographic Society could be a powerful ally in my paradigm change effort I tried to interest the National Geographic Society and North Dakota Geographic Alliance in the topographic map drainage system and erosional landform evidence. The Alliance however wanted to go in a different direction which in my opinion violated the Alliance's endowment contract terms (which I had helped write and finance). I then proposed an alternate direction based on the National Geography Standards (which the National Geographic Society helped write and which fit the endowment contract terms like a glove). My alternate proposal was rejected and I chose to resign when the Alliance governance insisted on violating the endowment contract terms.

In 2006 I thought that if the National Geographic Education Foundation could be convinced to honor the Alliance's endowment contract terms the National Geographic Society might assist in a project to convince the geology research community that topographic map drainage system and erosional landform evidence was important evidence and could not be ignored and dismissed as geologists were doing. When my protests about the endowment contract breaches had no effect, I proceeded to take legal action, but my case was dismissed because my name was not on the endowment contract. I appealed the case, but the appeal was also unsuccessful. To the best of my knowledge the contract terms were still being breached in 2023 and I have not given up hope the National Geographic Society will someday participate as a badly needed and powerful ally.

When the National Geographic Society failed to become a paradigm change ally, I looked for a different paradigm change strategy and decided to develop a public website where all Missouri River drainage basin study results could be posted. Instead of using data from the previous study I used digitalized topographic maps and completely redid the study so as to create a set of research notes specifically written for the new public website. I purchased National Geographic Topo software and a complete set of digitalized USGS topographic maps for the entire United States. Using a website on the then new Google Knol platform I began the process of again systematically studying how every Missouri River drainage basin drainage divide had been formed.

My second Missouri River drainage basin study began in 2009 and continued into mid 2013. In late 2011 Google ended its Knol platform and all of my research notes posted up until that time had to be transferred to a newly established WordPress website at geomorphologyresearch.com. That public website now contains more than 550 blogs in which the Missouri River drainage basin study evidence is presented (plus several summary and other blogs). A typical blog begins with an abstract providing summary information. A preface follows which describes the larger research project. Following the preface is an introduction to the specific blog study region which includes location maps to show how local drainage routes fit into the larger regional drainage system. Next are detailed interpretations of drainage system and erosional landform evidence including each of the major drainage divides as seen on about eight detailed topographic maps (which are shown in the blog). A sidebar provides an index for locating blogs in which various Missouri River tributary drainage basins and other physiographic features are mentioned.

The second Missouri River drainage basin study which interpreted the origins for all Missouri River drainage basin drainage divides (between streams shown on 1:24,000-scale maps) was completed in 2013, although later some other related blogs were added. Most website traffic appears to be from lay persons looking for specific geographic feature information and not from geology research community members. The website's existence was helpful in getting several of my subsequent published papers past critical reviewers, but otherwise appears to have had little or no impact. I expected critical comments and questions from geologists who had worked in the Missouri River drainage basin area, but few such comments and questions have materialized.

Following the website's completion I moved from Minot, North Dakota to Jenkintown, Pennsylvania. Minot had been my home for 45 years and its middle of the North American continent location had provided an excellent research perspective. But it was time for an edge of the continent research perspective. Jenkintown is today a tree-covered hilly suburban community located in the Pennsylvania Piedmont Province about eleven miles to the northeast of Philadelphia's city center. Near my new home and in a compact area are small-scale examples of larger-scale northern Great Plains and Rocky Mountain region drainage system and erosional landform features. Within a five-mile radius, in an area where the local relief is slightly more than 100 meters there are major drainage divides, water gaps, wind gaps, valleys crossing drainage divides, barbed tributaries, deep gorges cut in erosion resistant bedrock, and abrupt stream direction changes.

After arriving in Jenkintown, I discovered my new home was about two miles from where William Morris Davis (1850-1934) spent much of his boyhood and some of his early adulthood. During much of his adult career, Davis was a Harvard University faculty member where he helped to develop the science of geomorphology. In that capacity Davis is sometimes referred to as the "father of North American geomorphology" (Chorley et al. 1973). Davis during his lifetime published hundreds of influential scientific articles and several widely used textbooks some of which attempted to explain drainage system and erosional landform origins. Among other things Davis introduced the erosion cycle concept which is today still taught in some introductory geology and geography classes. Several key pillars upon which the present-day geology research community's accepted paradigm is based can be traced back directly or indirectly to ideas Davis first introduced. As a boy and as a young adult Davis must have observed Jenkintown area drainage systems and erosional landforms, but his publications say nothing about such observations.

Davis, as a boy growing up during the late 1850s and early 1860s, did not have access to topographic maps but he must have explored the region surrounding his home. At that time, instead of today's tree-covered suburban neighborhoods the region surrounding the Davis home was largely open fields making it much easier to see landform features than it is today. Davis grew up in a wealthy Quaker family. His father (with some partners) owned a coal mine and railroad and thousands of acres of coal lands in north central Pennsylvania and in Kentucky and was also a real estate developer who played a major role in developing entire neighborhoods that now surround the homesite where Davis lived.

The Davis home no longer stands, but a historical marker identifies the site. The historical marker is not for Davis, but is instead for his grandmother, Lucretia Mott who was a noted 19th-century abolitionist and women's rights advocate. The Mott and Davis families lived on opposite sides of Old York Road (which led in one direction to Jenkintown and in the other direction to Philadelphia). Lucretia Mott probably taught Davis many advocacy skills which he later used when promoting his drainage system and erosional landform origin ideas. Figure 14.1 shows a section of the first USGS topographic map of the Davis boyhood home region, with the red number 1 identifying where Davis grew up. The map was published in 1893, long after Davis had moved from the region to teach at Harvard, although Davis probably returned to his boyhood home regularly to visit family members.

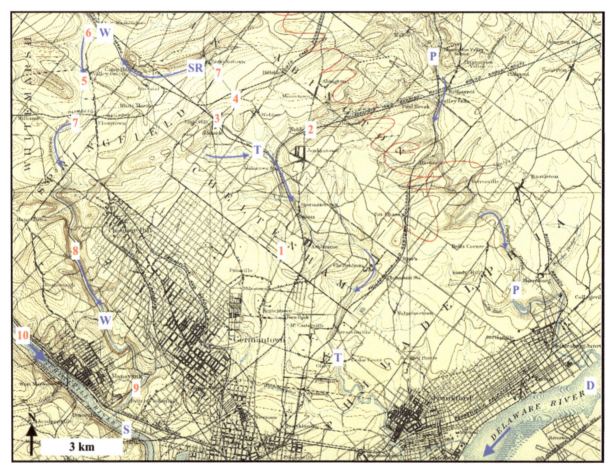

Figure 14.1: Modified section of the USGS 1893 Germantown, PA topographic map from the USGS Topoview website. The contour interval is 20 feet (6 meters). The number 1 identifies the William Morris Davis boyhood home location. Other letters and numbers identify important drainage routes and other features as described in the text. Jenkintown is south of the number 2.

Major drainage routes shown on the 1893 map (a section of which is seen in figure 14.1) which Davis must have known as a boy are identified in blue letters as follows: D-Delaware River, P-Pennypack Creek, S-Schuylkill River, SR-Sandy Run, T-Tookany Creek (downstream segments are known as Tacony and Frankfort Creeks), and W-Wissahickon Creek. When seeing the 1893 map for the first time Davis probably looked to see where he grew up (shown with the red number 1). The 1893 map was published when railroad expansion was underway and Davis probably looked to see how railroads crossed the local drainage divides. The map clearly shows a 100-meter-deep through valley (at the red number 2) linking the south-oriented Tookany and Pennypack Creek valleys which Davis must have seen as a boy and also wind gaps at the red numbers 3 and 4 all of which railroad builders used when crossing the local drainage divides.

As a boy Davis probably rode trains traveling through the wind gap at number 3 and then across the Chester Valley's eastern end to follow Sandy Run as it passes through a north-oriented water gap located to the east of the south-oriented Wissahickon Creek water gap (at red number 5). Davis should have noted that Sandy Run starts in the Chester Valley eastern end and, for a distance flows in a southwest direction, but instead of joining Wissahickon Creek in the Chester Valley (at the red number 7) Sandy Run turns in a north direction to flow through a water gap which is cut across a 100-meter-high sandstone ridge before joining south-oriented Wissahickon Creek (at red number 6) as a barbed tributary, which then flows across the same 100-meter-high ridge.

Davis must have puzzled over why Sandy Run turns in a north direction to cut a water gap across a high resistant ridge only to join a south-oriented stream as a barbed tributary and to flow across that same ridge again–especially when Sandy Run logically could have continued in a southwest direction to join Wissahickon Creek without ever having to leave the Chester Valley. Davis must have been equally puzzled by south-oriented Wissahickon Creek, which after flowing across the Chester Valley enters a narrow 100-meter-deep gorge and which just before joining the southeast-oriented Schuylkill River turns in a southwest direction (at red number 9) so as to become a barbed tributary when Wissahickon Creek could have easily flowed through the northeast-to-southwest oriented Chester Valley to reach the southeast-oriented Schuylkill River (the downstream Schuylkill River gorge is shown by the red number 10).

Chapter 2 (see figure 2.10 and related text) discussed the "A River Pirate" paper in which (Davis, 1889a) used an 1890 Doylestown topographic map advanced copy (the map directly to the north of the Germantown map) to demonstrate he knew how to interpret barbed tributary evidence, but ignored that map's most obvious barbed tributary evidence. Shortly after his River Pirate paper had been published Davis submitted a longer article titled "The Rivers and Valleys of Pennsylvania" to the then new *National Geographic Magazine*. Ideas expressed in that longer article conflicted with what the Doylestown map barbed tributary evidence should have told him. Davis commented in his "Rivers and Valleys of Pennsylvania" paper that "the history of the Susquehanna, the Juniata, or the Schuylkill is too involved with complex changes, if not enshrouded in mystery, to become intelligible to any but advanced students" And with that comment Davis pointed the geology research community and the National Geographic Society toward a flawed paradigm that could not explain most of the topographic map drainage system evidence.

Quite unintentionally by moving to Jenkintown I discovered where the topography mystery began. My move also unexpectedly opened up new paradigm change opportunities. More than ten years earlier, while still administering National Geographic Education Foundation grants, I attended a Philadelphia geography conference and joined the Pennsylvania Geographical Society. Once in Pennsylvania I attended some of the Society's annual meetings where I presented papers describing Pennsylvania topographic map evidence from a new paradigm perspective. I also published a paper in the Society's journal, *The Pennsylvania Geographer*, describing what I had learned up to that time about William Morris Davis's Pennsylvania background.

My curiosity about Davis and what he could have determined about the region where he lived as a boy and as a young man led to the decision to begin the next phase of my gradually evolving paradigm change strategy. My first step was to scour the many Philadelphia area university and other libraries searching for publications that explained how Philadelphia area drainage systems and erosional landforms had originated. My search found very little really useful information even though several Philadelphia universities have and have had nationally-recognized geology and geography programs. It was apparent that knowledge about Philadelphia area drainage system origins had not progressed much beyond what William Morris Davis had determined.

My second step was to establish a new website at phillylandforms.info on which Philadelphia area topographic map drainage system and erosional landform evidence could be illustrated and then explained in blog format. My main purpose was to use the new website's development as a way to investigate and learn about Philadelphia area topographic map drainage system and erosional landform evidence, most of which I had never studied. By that time, I realized most website traffic would come from lay people looking for specific landform or drainage feature information and a different approach would be needed to reach geology research community members.

The third step was to attempt to publish interpretations of the previously unexplained Philadelphia area topographic map drainage system and erosional landform evidence in peer reviewed geography and geology publications. The southeast Pennsylvania Piedmont Province topographic map drainage system and erosional landform evidence could be interpreted and explained from a new paradigm perspective which suggested massive southwest-oriented meltwater floods had flowed across the region. That perspective had never been used by geologists or geographers when explaining southeast Pennsylvania drainage systems and erosional landforms and required each of my manuscript submissions to include copies of the detailed map evidence that was being interpreted, which greatly limited the size of the geographic regions my reports could cover.

The strategy of including copies of the detailed topographic map evidence being interpreted in the submitted manuscripts proved to be an effective way to demonstrate how the flood interpretation explained mapped drainage system and erosional evidence. Eight such reports were published; three by *The Pennsylvania Geographer*, one by *the Middle States Geographer*, one in an Association of New Jersey Geologists fieldtrip guidebook, two by the *Journal of Geography and Geology*, and one by the *Journal of Geography and Earth Science*. At long last, I had found a strategy which at least some peer reviewers would not reject and which would enable new paradigm interpretations of topographic map evidence to be published in peer reviewed publications.

Having a way to publish new paradigm interpretations of topographic map and drainage system evidence that at least some peer reviewers would accept meant Missouri River drainage basin research results could also be published as peer reviewed reports, provided each report covered a small enough geographic region so that copies of detailed topographic maps which showed the key evidence could be included. Limiting reports to relatively small geographic regions and the size of the Missouri River drainage basin meant many dozens of such reports would be needed to publish my previously obtained Missouri River drainage basin study results and many hundreds of additional reports would be needed to demonstrate the new paradigm's ability to explain topographic map drainage system and erosional landform evidence in other regions.

Knowing there was a way to demonstrate the new paradigm's ability to explain large amounts of detailed topographic map drainage system and erosional landform evidence in the peer reviewed geology and geography literature was encouraging, but posed a challenge. I was retired and had time to prepare at least a representative sample of the hundreds of the needed small geographic region reports. The needed detailed topographic map evidence was available on the USGS National Map website and screen shots of the key map evidence could be used as images. The major challenge was in selecting geography and geology journals which would accept my submissions, make the reports accessible to the audience I wanted to reach and not expect a small fortune in return.

There was no shortage of geology and geography journals to choose from. New ones pop up every few months. Each journal is different, but authors like myself who want to publish an open access article and retain the copyright are usually expected to pay an article processing charge (APC). Some journals will publish articles without any charge, but those journals usually retain the copyright and then place the article behind a paywall. Charges to publish open access articles vary tremendously depending on the journal and on when the open access begins. The charges for each accepted article can range from a few hundred dollars to several thousand dollars. The journals encourage researchers to ask their funding agencies or their institution to pay the APC.

The option of placing my published reports behind a paywall was unacceptable. The large number of reports I needed to publish eliminated journals with high APCs (I was retired and had no research funding agency or institution willing to cover the publication costs). I also knew many journals compete based on impact ratings which are determined by the number of citations their published articles obtain. I decided high impact journals would probably not want to publish a report which interpreted a small geographic region's topographic map drainage system and erosional landform evidence. With those considerations I developed a long-term publication strategy.

With a publication strategy in place, I began to prepare and submit manuscripts in which the new paradigm perspective was used when interpreting small subsets of topographic map evidence which the blogs on my geomorphologyresearch.com website had already informally described. I soon found out that geology and geography journals expect submitted manuscripts to include a statement of the research problem, a review of previous studies related to that research problem, a description of the research method used, a description of the results obtained, a discussion section in which the author can discuss what the results might mean, and a conclusions section. Many, but not all of my submitted manuscripts tried to address those requirements.

Not knowing how many manuscripts I would ultimately write and be able to get published I cherry picked geographic regions where some of the most interesting topographic map evidence was located.

Initially my submitted manuscripts addressed previously studied Missouri River drainage basin topographic map evidence. To date (2024) more than 30 of those manuscripts have been accepted and published. More recently I have prepared and submitted manuscripts related to topographic map evidence located in geographic regions along the deep "hole" rim which I interpret to have extended eastward from the Rocky Mountains along what is now the Arkansas River drainage basin's southern drainage divide and then along the Ohio River-Atlantic Ocean drainage divide. To date eight such manuscripts have been accepted and published.

In addition to the above-described published papers, I published two summary papers aimed at helping readers better see the new paradigm big picture, a paper describing how William Morris Davis in 1889 initiated the practice of ignoring topographic map drainage and erosional landform evidence that did not fit with his erosion cycle ideas, and a paper describing how the flawed accepted paradigm contributed to a major controversy in the 1920s when J Harlan Bretz suggested an immense flood had flowed across eastern Washington State. All told since launching my publication strategy I have successfully published more than 50 papers.

Based on information from some (but not all) of the journals and from my ResearchGate and Academia.edu sites my published papers typically average several hundred views each year with about one-fourth of the views resulting in a PDF download. Once a paper is published the number of views and downloads seems to grow at about the same rate each year which means my new paradigm related published papers as a group in 2024 will receive approximately 15,000 views. For the most part I do not know who the viewers are or what they think and like with my websites I suspect many viewers are not geologists. However, unlike my websites, I suspect most viewers of scientific journal papers which are posted on my ResearchGate and Academia.edu sites are from the academic community which is the audience my publication strategy is aimed at reaching.

So far, the impact of my 50 published papers appears to have been minimal. For the most part the only researcher who is citing my papers for the purpose of fleshing out the new paradigm is myself. Even though I expected negative comments from some readers, to date very few negative comments have been received. Probably the most significant negative comment was made by a geologist who published a paper in which he blasted the interpretations I made in a paper describing Chester Valley drainage history (in southeast Pennsylvania). That geologist's paper proposed an alternate interpretation for the Chester Valley origin which does not explain any of the topographic map drainage system evidence and which shows a poor understanding of other geologic evidence.

Geology research community members should have no trouble finding my published journal articles when searching for information related to the specific geographic regions my journal articles address. However, most geology research community members have no reason to search for information related to the relatively modest-sized geographic regions my journal articles address. For that reason, this book is an effort to reach a still larger segment of the geology research community than my published journal articles are likely to reach. This revised edition also provides a more complete description of my research path than the first edition did.

Will my publication strategy succeed in convincing the geology research community to correct its unrecognized paradigm problem? Without the help of a powerful ally such as the National Geographic

Society I see little hope of short-term success. I intend to keep publishing journal articles as long as I am able, however I know most geologists have no reason to search for information related to the geographic regions my journal articles address. And, even if my journal articles are found, read, understood, and agreed with, most geologists, like myself, do not have the ability or the clout needed to correct whatever unrecognized geology paradigm problem they might see.

Construction of the accepted geology and glacial history paradigm has been on-going for at least 150 years and has been in a haphazard way with each researcher building interpretations of evidence on top of previous interpretations. Back in 1889 William Morris Davis, who had the skills, clout, and opportunity to include the then newly available topographic map drainage system and erosional evidence in his studies chose not to do so and permitted the geology research community to build its paradigm without the benefit of the well-mapped topographic map evidence. The accepted paradigm is now entrenched in the way geologists think and conduct their research and while they should, few geologists care about flawed interpretations that were made almost 140 years ago.

Think of building a geology and glacial history paradigm as a giant sudoku puzzle with an almost infinite number of squares to fill-in. Each of those almost infinite number of squares as it is filled-in influences how other puzzle squares must be filled-in. If early on a square is incorrectly filled-in, that incorrect information will cause other yet-to-be-filled-in squares to be incorrectly filled-in. With a typical sudoku puzzle a flaw may not be discovered until most squares have been filled-in at which point it becomes obvious a correct solution is not possible. In the case of the geology paradigm puzzle, the puzzle is so large the geology research community may never fill-in enough squares to recognize a solution is not possible. As a result, geologists who are otherwise doing excellent work, may in fact unknowingly be constructing an incorrect and fictious geology and glacial history.

In addition to not being taught about catastrophic floods my education did not prepare me to think in terms of different scientific paradigms, although as a graduate student I was expected to read T. C. Chamberlin's (1897) paper titled "The Method of Multiple Working Hypotheses." In that paper, which a different journal had published 7 years earlier, Chamberlin describes three scientific methods. First is a ruling theory method in which evidence is interpreted to support a favored hypothesis and no testing is done. Second is the working hypothesis method where a tentative hypothesis is proposed and tested. Third is the method of multiple working hypotheses where multiple explanations are proposed and tested to determine which hypothesis or combination of hypotheses best explains the evidence

Chamberlin points out the ruling theory method usually prevents science (or in this case geology) from advancing and the working hypothesis method has a risk of unconsciously becoming the ruling theory method. Chamberlin argues that only by using the method of multiple working hypotheses can geologists avoid the risk of letting unconscious ruling theories determine their interpretations. Throughout my research I have tried to follow this advice and even today when interpreting topographic map drainage system and erosional evidence I look for alternate explanations. However, it took many years before I became proficient in viewing evidence from different paradigm perspectives.

Being able to view evidence from the perspective of two fundamentally different paradigms means that in addition to being the new paradigm's strongest (and perhaps only) advocate that I am also one of the new paradigm's worst critics. I repeatedly ask myself if there is a way the accepted paradigm or some yet-to-be discovered paradigm might better explain the topographic map drainage system and erosional landform evidence? Even though literature searches have convinced me that to date no one has found such a way I cannot rule out the possibility. Being aware there might be other ways to explain the topographic map evidence, I try to compare in my mind how each of the two competing paradigms explains whatever drainage system and erosional landform features I might be studying.

Also, I frequently ask myself what evidence does the new paradigm not explain well? And the honest answer is there are multiple sets of evidence the new paradigm as described in this book has yet to explain satisfactorily. Such yet-to-be satisfactorily explained evidence includes the northern New Jersey and New York City and adjacent area glacial deposits which are located not too far from my new Jenkintown, Pennsylvania home. Based on geologic literature descriptions those deposits are evidence for three or more different continental icesheets which advanced across what I interpret to be the new paradigm's deep "hole" rim. According to the new paradigm as described here there were only two linked continental ice sheets, both of which should have been located inside the deep "hole."

Using just an accepted paradigm perspective the published literature claim that three or more different continental ice sheets advanced to almost the same places is a remarkable coincidence and for that reason alone should raise red flags. I strongly suspect the new paradigm's immense meltwater floods deposited at least some of the materials glacial geologists claim were deposited by one or more of those continental icesheet advances. While I seriously doubt three or more different continental icesheets deposited the northern New Jersey, New York City, and adjacent area glacial deposits I have no reason to question an interpretation that at least one icesheet did advance into the region (and the same situation may be true in the Puget Sound area in the Pacific Northwest). Yet to-be-done new paradigm tweaking is needed to explain how an icesheet could advance into regions beyond the deep "hole" rim.

The Great Lakes are another set of glacially-related evidence which the new paradigm has not yet explained to my satisfaction. Usually accepted paradigm interpretations see the Great Lakes basins being eroded during the last (Wisconsin) continental icesheet advance when icesheet erosion guided by the regional bedrock characteristics greatly deepened previously existing river and stream valleys. From the new paradigm perspective, the Great Lakes are located within the first thick icesheet created deep "hole" which means the previously existing stream and river valleys should have been eroded by thick icesheet meltwater floods and then deepened by the second icesheet's erosion. To date I have not found ways to satisfactorily explain how thick icesheet meltwater floods eroded the previously existing stream and river valleys and I also do not like an interpretation which requires a continental icesheet to deeply erode in one region and not to deeply erode easily-eroded materials in another region.

These are just two examples of evidence which the new paradigm in its present form does not explain just as the accepted paradigm does not explain all evidence. When comparing the accepted and new paradigms it is important to not only determine which paradigm explains the most evidence, but also to determine which of the two paradigms leads to the greatest amount of unexplained, or anomalous evidence. If after being fully fleshed out the new paradigm still leads to large amounts of anomalous evidence (as the much more mature accepted paradigm already does) a study of the anomalous evidence may lead to a quite different and yet-to-be recognized geology and glacial history paradigm.

Chapter 14:
What Changing the Geology and Glacial History Paradigm Might Mean

Thomas Kuhn (1970) suggests scientific evidence can always be interpreted in more than one way and that scientific paradigms sometimes change when large volumes of new evidence are added to the previous evidence mix. Topographic map drainage system and erosional landform evidence upon which the new paradigm is based represents an immense set of previously ignored but well-mapped evidence, and to date, the new paradigm provides the only paradigm perspective from which that evidence appears to have been explained. On the other hand, the geology research community can validly claim the accepted Cenozoic geology and glacial history paradigm is also based on a large set of rock, fossil, and other evidence, and at least to date, no one has adequately demonstrated how the new paradigm explains much of that evidence. Ideally, the geology research community should adopt a paradigm able to explain both types of evidence, but to date, neither paradigm has demonstrated an ability to do so.

The new and accepted paradigms are incommensurable, which means there is no common standard by which they can be compared, although some readers might want to suggest the geologic time scale as a possible common measuring stick. The geologic time scale, which the geology research community regards as one of its greatest achievements, was developed by using a variety of different relative and absolute age dating methods. Some relative age dating techniques are probably paradigm neutral and should be valid no matter which paradigm is used and involve placing events in the order in which those events occurred.

Students in introductory geology classes are taught the law of superposition which says undisturbed strata are arranged in the order in which they were laid down. Students are also taught the principle of cross-cutting relationships, which says a geologic feature that cuts another geologic feature is the younger of the two. Relative age dating of this type, if based on observations of actual rock units, geologic structures, or landforms identifiable in the field or determinable from topographic map or imagery evidence, is the geologic dating gold standard and should be valid regardless of which geology paradigm is used.

Introductory geology students are also told the principle of faunal and floral succession is an important relative age dating technique, although unlike the law of superposition and principle of cross-cutting relationship, the principle of faunal and floral succession may or may not be paradigm neutral. The principle of faunal and floral succession assumes plants and animals progressively change through time, with distinctive fossil groups being characteristic of each geologic time period. When the law of superposition is used to place stratigraphic units in order, progressive changes in the observed fossil record are seen, and in a general sense, the principle of faunal and floral succession appears to be paradigm neutral.

However, paleontologists use the accepted paradigm perspective to make assumptions when interpreting the incomplete fossil record. Those assumptions are then used to help define various geologic time divisions and to determine which fossil groups are characteristic of those time periods. As a result, geologic time, as determined by the principle of faunal and floral succession, may be paradigm-biased, and geologic time as determined from the incomplete fossil record, might or might not look the same from a different paradigm's perspective.

Relative age-dating techniques, whether paradigm neutral like the law of superposition and the principle of cross-cutting relationships or possibly paradigm-biased like the principle of faunal and floral succession, permit geologists to determine sequences of geologic events but do not provide absolute dates for which absolute age-dating techniques are used. A few absolute age-dating techniques may be paradigm neutral such as using written human records or tree rings, but they date only very recent geologic events.

Most absolute age dates are obtained by using radiometric age dating techniques, all of which are based on accepted paradigm-biased assumptions (which, from a different paradigm's perspective, may or may not be the same). The geologic literature is filled with publications describing research in which paradigm-influenced assumptions were used when collecting samples, when doing the age dating analyses, and when determining what the obtained absolute age dates mean. In brief, a different paradigm may or may not force a reconsideration of some or of most accepted paradigm obtained absolute age dates.

A study of the Geological Society of America (GSA) Geologic Time Scale, which can easily be found with a simple Internet search, suggests geologists know exactly when many geologic events occurred. The geology research community does explore alternate and new ideas; however, that exploration has limits. For example, no one in the geology research community (with rare exceptions) questions the accepted paradigm interpretation that North American continental icesheets developed late during the geologic time scale's Cenozoic Era when the Northern Hemisphere experienced multiple glacial-interglacial cycles. The very precise late Cenozoic chronology of each of those multiple glacial-interglacial cycles which has been determined from the absolute dating of oceanic sediments and fossils makes it extremely difficult for any researcher using different evidence to interpret glacial history in other ways. Yet, if the USGS topographic map drainage system and erosional landform evidence is to be explained, a completely different North American glacial history and chronology is needed.

A glacial history and chronology able to explain topographic map drainage system and erosional landform evidence requires a thick continental icesheet (located where North American continental icesheets are usually recognized to have been), which deeply eroded the underlying bedrock and which was heavy enough to raise surrounding regions including mountain ranges so as to create and occupy a deep "hole." If that continental icesheet's existence could be slotted into one of the accepted paradigm's glacial-interglacial cycles, the accepted paradigm might survive with just some tweaking. However, topographic map evidence can only be explained if immense and prolonged meltwater floods flowed across the deep "hole's" rising rim and eroded valleys now containing sediments and fossils, which from the accepted paradigm perspective, date back to as much as 50 million years before North American continental icesheets existed.

Further complicating the accepted paradigm chronology, topographic map drainage system and erosional landform evidence suggests south-oriented meltwater floods were diverted into deep "hole" space the melting icesheet once occupied and flowed around decaying thick icesheet remnants to reach northern oceans. This diversion probably caused a major climatic change which froze north-oriented drainage around the decaying thick icesheet remnants which created a second and thinner continental icesheet and an "Ice Age." That second and thinner continental icesheet probably melted when the accepted paradigm's last Wisconsin icesheet melted.

When compared, the accepted and the new paradigms describe completely different and incompatible North American glacial (and geological) histories which require quite different and incommensurable middle and late Cenozoic chronology interpretations. The new paradigm glacial history interpretation describes two linked continental icesheets which spanned what the accepted paradigm considers to be a 50 million-year or longer middle and late Cenozoic time period, while the accepted paradigm sees its numerous glacial-interglacial cycles occurring only during the most recent three million years.

Occam's Razor is a fundamental rule in science, saying the simplest explanation needed to explain all of the pertinent evidence should be preferred. If so, the ignored topographic map drainage system and erosional landform evidence may be pointing geologists toward a simpler (and possibly shorter in absolute time) middle and late Cenozoic history than what the geology research community has described to date, although the new paradigm's two linked icesheets may have existed for a much longer length of absolute time than all of the accepted paradigm's late Cenozoic glacial-interglacial cycles combined.

Absolute age dates cannot be determined from the topographic map drainage system and erosional landform evidence. However, the simplicity of the new paradigm's glacial history could mean geologists may have included more middle and late Cenozoic absolute time in their geologic time scales (such as the GSA Geologic Time Scale) than is needed. Vertebrate paleontologists, who interpreted mammalian fossil evidence, established the Cenozoic time subdivisions with the absolute age dates and magnetic polarity information subsequently added.

The GSA Geologic Time Scale gives the impression the various dating techniques agree with each other and that age dates have been precisely determined, but the possibility exists the accepted paradigm has caused absolute age dates to fit what might be flawed accepted paradigm-biased mammalian fossil evolutionary relative age approximations. Had topographic map drainage system and erosional landform evidence been interpreted before the mammalian fossil evidence, the geologic time scale might look very different than it does. While no one in the geology research community wants to consider the geologic time scale to be flawed, unrecognized problems may exist, and for that reason, the geology research community cannot afford to ignore the well-mapped detailed topographic map drainage system and erosional landform evidence.

Fossils of temperate and warm climatic region animals and plants are found in what the accepted paradigm considers to be middle Cenozoic sediments and which the new paradigm's meltwater floods probably deposited. From the accepted paradigm perspective, continental icesheets are associated with cold climatic conditions, and temperate and warm climatic region fossils suggest no continental icesheet existed. From the new paradigm perspective, temperate and even warm climatic region fossils should be found near the thick continental icesheet's southern margin because that icesheet's southern margin had flowed into temperate and possibly even warm climatic regions.

The large and long-lived new paradigm described meltwater floods suggest significant melting was occurring along the thick continental icesheet's southern margin (at least on a seasonal basis). Such melting could only have occurred if the thick continental icesheet's southern margin was located in a temperate or even a warm climatic zone. The new paradigm does not see extremely cold "Ice Age" type climatic conditions like those the accepted paradigm describes developing until after meltwater floods had been diverted to flow into and through the deep "hole" to reach northern oceans and to freeze around the first icesheet remnants so as to create a second and much thinner continental icesheet.

The new paradigm requirement to develop a large continental icesheet is not a cold climate but a climate where more snow falls than melts. A large permanent snowfield, once established, creates its own climate by reflecting sunlight and increasing precipitation (mostly snow), with snow depths and the size of the snow-covered areas progressively increasing. A large permanent snowfield can expand and develop into a large icesheet, with glacial ice flowing outward from the heaviest snowfall regions in all directions. The thickness and geographic extent of such an icesheet can continually increase until the icesheet has expanded into regions where the icesheet's marginal melting is as great as the amount of new snow being added to the icesheet's surface.

Why the new paradigm's thick icesheet formed is unknown, but that icesheet must have grown sufficiently in thickness and weight to create the new paradigm's deep "hole," which the topographic map drainage system and erosional landform evidence documents. The new paradigm's thick continental icesheet must have expanded into temperate and perhaps even into warm North American climatic zones before achieving an equilibrium where new snowfall on what would have been its high-elevation icesheet surface (probably as high or higher than some of today's highest mountain ranges) was balanced by the icesheet margin melting. Under such conditions, icesheet marginal melting every year, especially during summer months, would have generated immense amounts of meltwater which would have flowed away from the icesheet margin in whatever directions were possible.

Recognizing that enormous and long-lived (but possibly seasonal) meltwater floods flowed at one time or another across much of the continental United States (as topographic map drainage system and erosional landform evidence suggests) probably will force vertebrate paleontologists to change how they interpret middle and late Cenozoic mammalian evolution. Present-day middle and late Cenozoic mammalian evolution interpretations are based on vertebrate fossils collected from what the accepted paradigm considers to be middle and late Cenozoic sediments, which, based on the topographic map drainage system and erosional landform evidence, the new paradigm described meltwater floods probably deposited.

At least some of the accepted paradigm's middle and late Cenozoic sedimentary deposits include coarse-grained alluvium, which only powerful streams could have transported (for any distance), although much of the vertebrate paleontology literature downplays the coarse-grained alluvium's significance. As a result, the geology research community does not see large and long-lived floods playing a significant role in the transport and deposition of the middle and late Cenozoic fossiliferous sediments. The new paradigm's massive and prolonged meltwater floods, if seasonal as seems possible, could have repeatedly wiped out an entire region's fauna and flora, requiring repeated repopulation from surrounding regions. The repeated decimation and repopulation of faunas and floras over large regions may have led to much more rapid evolutionary changes than vertebrate paleontologists currently describe.

The new and accepted paradigms, in addition to having fundamentally different North American glacial history interpretations, also interpret mountain ranges differently. The geology research community sees mountain ranges developing along plate boundaries. The Rocky Mountains are not located along a plate boundary, and some researchers suggest the Rocky Mountains are high today because the North American plate has overridden another plate, although not all geologists are convinced. From the accepted paradigm perspective, the reasons for the most recent Rocky Mountain uplift and the timing of that uplift are debated and unresolved. From the new paradigm perspective, the Rocky Mountains are located along the deep "hole" rim, which was uplifted as immense south-oriented meltwater floods flowed across it (meaning a thick continental icesheet's weight probably caused deep "hole" rim uplift).

Also problematic for accepted paradigm geologists are present-day Appalachian Mountain elevations, which while not as high as Rocky Mountain elevations, are higher than most geologists think those elevations should be. Appalachian Mountain structures are usually associated with a late Paleozoic plate collision. However, most geologists think erosion over the long time period since that plate collision occurred should have reduced the Appalachian Mountains to an almost featureless plain. The reasons for today's Appalachian Mountain elevations from the accepted paradigm perspective are unresolved, although, from the new paradigm perspective, the Appalachians Mountains are also located along the deep "hole" rim.

Occam's razor suggests the geology research community eventually may have to recognize what the topographic map drainage system and erosional landform evidence appears to be saying, which is the geology research community needs to discard the accepted paradigm's complicated multiple late Cenozoic glacial-interglacial cycles, and adopt the much simpler new paradigm glacial history (just as the Copernican revolution which used a heliocentric astronomical model replaced the Earth-centered Ptolemaic astronomical model). The topographic map evidence shows how most continental United States drainage systems and erosional landform features (located to the south of the thick continental icesheet's southern margin) developed during immense and prolonged continental icesheet meltwater floods while what must have been the thick continental icesheet's tremendous weight was raising surrounding North American regions and mountain ranges.

The topographic map evidence also shows how northern prairie region erosional escarpments (such as seen in figures 9.2, 9.3, and 9.4 and discussed in Clausen 2019f) developed when during the thick icesheet's decay large supraglacial meltwater rivers sliced giant ice-walled and bedrock-floored canyons into the decaying thick continental icesheet's surface. If the new paradigm interpretation can be used to also explain rock, fossil, and other geologic evidence (in addition to the topographic map evidence), the new paradigm describes a much simpler Cenozoic geology and glacial history than the accepted paradigm has described.

Chapter 15:
Some Final Notes

During the past 250 years the geology discipline has experienced several significant paradigm changes. One major paradigm tweaking event occurred during my geology training. That training (which was at two of the then top ranked university geology departments) used textbooks in which continental drift, if it was mentioned at all, was treated as a controversial subject. I was taught about mountain building processes which most geologists today would consider ridiculous. I also remember geology professors asking questions about what the increasing amount of newly obtained oceanographic data might mean. By the time my geology teaching career began plate tectonics had been accepted and most geology textbooks were rapidly being rewritten.

For several hundred years the apparent fit of continents had attracted scientific attention. Not only did the continents fit together, but geologic and fossil evidence suggested the continents had once been together. In the early 1900s a strong case was made for continental drift, but some fifty years later in the early 1960s most North American geologists still rejected the concept. While evidence supporting continental drift was good, the problem was geologists could not explain how continents could move. During my student years many influential geologists actively opposed the continental drift hypothesis. For example, I remember as a graduate student listening in the mid 1960s to a guest lecturer from a prestigious United States university who used land bridges (like Central America) to explain the similarity of fossils in Africa and South America.

Opposition to continental drift collapsed when newly-obtained seafloor spreading and seismic evidence supported a previously-proposed convection cell hypothesis. Once plate tectonics had been accepted it rapidly led to new research opportunities some of which are still being discovered today. Acceptance of plate tectonics did not affect all geology subdisciplines evenly. What initially happened was some geology textbooks merely added a plate tectonics chapter. Other textbook chapters were not changed which suggested plate tectonics affected only selected geology subdisciplines. For many geologists the acceptance of plate tectonics as a new paradigm pillar appeared to be just an interesting geology paradigm tweaking nonevent.

The acceptance of plate tectonics did not alter the geology time scale, in fact the geologic time scale helped plate tectonics gain acceptance. Plate tectonics did not challenge the work of most paleontologists, instead some paleontological research supported the continental drift hypothesis. For most geologists plate tectonics explained what had been previously poorly-explained evidence. As such the acceptance of plate tectonics was an important paradigm tweak and not a paradigm change.

Many geologists may view the paradigm change needed to explain topographic map drainage system and erosional landform evidence (if they view such a change as being needed) as nothing more than another paradigm tweak. Most geologists have no reason to learn how today's drainage systems and erosional landforms originated. To most geologists determining those origins is an academic problem that geomorphologists should solve and any needed paradigm tweaking should not significantly affect what the other geology subdisciplines are doing. Unfortunately, several other geology subdisciplines, in addition to early geomorphologists like William Morris Davis, are responsible for developing accepted paradigm interpretations which make most of the topographic map drainage system and erosional landform evidence impossible to explain.

Failing to address topographic map drainage system and erosional landform evidence has not stopped the geology research community from doing what Kuhn refers to as normal science which is fleshing out the accepted paradigm. Normal science is what almost all research geologists have been trained to do and does not question the accepted paradigm. The goal of normal science is to use a discipline's accepted paradigm to collect and analyze new data in ways which support the discipline's accepted paradigm. That goal can cause scientists who are doing normal science to downplay the importance of any anomalous evidence their research may uncover.

But an accepted paradigm which produces large quantities of anomalous evidence may mean the scientists who are doing normal science are constructing a fictious geology history story. The Ptolemaic astronomical model represents a good example of what research geologists may now be doing. Astronomers, some of whom made excellent observations and calculations, for many centuries kept fleshing out the Ptolemaic model before finally realizing the model had become so cumbersome that a better model was needed. At some time in the future (and it may be the distant future) historians of science may liken the present generation of research geologists to the astronomers who kept fleshing out the incorrect Ptolemaic model.

Many accepted geology paradigm flaws can be traced back to the failure of late 19th-century and early 20th-century geologists to apply T. C. Chamberlin's method of multiple working hypotheses. The past and present geology literature includes many studies in which the method of multiple working hypotheses does not appear to have been used. There are even geologists who now argue modern research techniques and procedures and the geologic knowledge obtained to date eliminate any need to apply the method of multiple working hypotheses. The large quantities of anomalous evidence which I have identified suggests the geology research community has not only ignored the topographic map drainage system and erosional landform evidence, but has also repeatedly failed to use (or has incorrectly used) the method of multiple working hypotheses.

Chapters 2 and 13 discussed how William Morris Davis interpreted some barbed tributary evidence on a newly published topographic map, but omitted any mention of much more obvious barbed tributary evidence on the same map. Davis obviously did not correctly use the method of multiple working hypotheses which prevented him from developing an explanation able to explain all of that map's barbed tributary evidence. Correct use of the multiple working hypotheses method required Davis to keep on developing working hypotheses until he had found a hypothesis able to explain what the map's barbed tributary evidence showed. Correct use of the method of multiple working hypotheses would also have caused Davis to never write his "Rivers and Valleys of Pennsylvania" paper which caused future geologists to flesh out a flawed paradigm.

What Davis should have done is what I eventually did. He should have kept proposing and testing hypotheses until he found a hypothesis that could explain his easily observed evidence. In my case the successful hypothesis was far different than any of the early hypotheses I initially considered. In fact, when my study began, I probably would have rejected what ultimately became the successful hypothesis because it violated many accepted paradigm interpretations. My advice to the geology research community is, whenever large amounts of anomalous evidence are found use that anomalous evidence as a starting point and keep developing hypotheses until all or at least most of that anomalous evidence can be explained.

To the best of my knowledge the new paradigm described in this book solves the topographic map mystery, but the topographic map mystery will not really be solved until the geology research community accepts the new paradigm or another paradigm which is able to explain all or at least most of the topographic map drainage system and erosional landform evidence. A paradigm change will not be easy. Influential geologists and entire geology subdisciplines with vested interests will oppose any paradigm change. Scientific paradigm changes often occur only after a completely new generation of scientists who no longer have those vested interests has emerged.

In the meantime, the geology research community will continue to ignore topographic map drainage system and erosional landform evidence and downplay that evidence's importance. For that reason, it will be almost impossible for geologists to obtain research grants for the purpose of studying topographic map drainage system and erosional landform evidence. Most research funding goes to support normal science and not to study anomalous evidence which may lead to scientific paradigm changes. While my previously mentioned effort to interest the National Geographic Society in exploring alternate paradigms failed I may or may not have an opportunity to try again. Should the National Geographic Society become interested, funding may become available to explore and possibly flesh out the new paradigm this book describes.

Acknowledgments

This book would not have been possible without thousands of United States Geological Survey (USGS) employees and contractors who, over a period of more than a century mapped drainage system and erosional landforms and prepared and published the USGS detailed topographic maps. Up until the beginning of this century, large collections of those hard copy topographic maps could be viewed at one of a few hundred USGS map depository libraries, one of which was located at Minot State University, where I worked as a faculty member. The Minot State University map library was developed with help from library staff, other faculty members, and students, and its large flat tables where large mosaics of the hard copy topographic maps could be laid out was ideal for the study of topographic map drainage system and erosional landform evidence. Those topographic map mosaics were particularly helpful when trying to understand how drainage system and erosional landform features fit together in what eventually became understandable patterns.

During the mid-1960s, Arthur Strahler, then at Columbia University, and Brainerd Mears Jr., then at the University of Wyoming, introduced unanswered drainage system and erosional landform origin problems. At the same time, I was taught to view all geologic evidence, including topographic map evidence, from what this book refers to as the accepted Cenozoic geology and glacial history paradigm perspective. I began my professional career believing geologists wanted to solve the puzzling drainage system and erosional landform problems that Strahler, Mears, and others had introduced. As a result, I spent considerable time searching not only in the Minot State University Library but also libraries of more than a dozen large research universities looking for publications addressing drainage system and erosional landform origins. Gradually I realized the geology research community was focused on other types of geologic problems and had little or no interest in addressing the still unsolved drainage system and erosional landform origin problems.

When visiting research university libraries, I also tried to visit their map libraries, which usually housed larger map collections than Minot State. Those map libraries, while having excellent map collections, often did not have large flat tables on which topographic map mosaics could be laid out. Those observations suggested to me that researchers at those universities would have had a difficult time doing the type of topographic map research the Minot State map library permitted (today, everyone can access USGS topographic maps at the USGS National Map website). After years of searching in geology journals and books, I realized the geologic research community has an unrecognized paradigm problem and had unknowingly given up on trying to explain the well-mapped topographic map drainage system and erosional landform evidence. I knew understanding what the topographic map drainage system and erosional landform evidence had to say was essential if North America's Cenozoic geology and glacial history is to be properly understood. I also knew the geology research community is continuing to build on its Cenozoic geology and glacial history story by completely ignoring what the well-mapped USGS topographic map drainage system and erosional landform evidence is silently waiting to say.

Accepted Paradigm References Cited

References listed here were cited in the text and written by researchers who used the accepted Cenozoic geology and glacial history paradigm perspective. Pertinent publications written by Eric Clausen (the author of this book) are listed separately in the following section.

Adams, G.I. 1902. Geology and Water Resources of the Patrick and Goshen Hole Quadrangles in Eastern Wyoming and Western Nebraska. United States Geological Survey Water Supply and Irrigation Papers Number 70: 23–25.

Alden, W.C. 1932. *Physiography and glacial geology of eastern Montana and adjacent areas*. United States Geological Survey Professional Paper 174, 133. https://doi.org/10.3133/pp174

Atwood, W.W. 1940. *The Physiographic Provinces of North America*. Ginn and Company, Boston, 536.

Banks, G. C. 2001. *Testing the Origins of the Blue Ridge Escarpment*. Masters' Thesis, Virginia Polytechnic Institute and State University, 120.

Bishop, P. 1995. "Drainage rearrangement by river capture, beheading and diversion." *Progress in Physical Geography*, 19, 449–473.

Bloom, A. L. 2018. *Gorges History: Landscapes and Geology of the Finger Lakes Region*. Paleontological Research Institution, Ithaca, NY, 214.

Bluemle, J.P. 1991. *The Face of North Dakota: Revised Edition*. North Dakota Geological Survey Educational Series 21, 177.

Braun, D.D., Pazzaglia, F. J., and Potter, N. 2003. "Margin of Laurentide Ice to the Atlantic Coastal Plain: Miocene-Pleistocene landscape evolution in the Central Appalachians." In: *Quaternary Geology of the United States: INQUA 2003 Field Guide Volume* edited by D. Easterbrook. Desert Research Institute, Reno, NV, 220.

Chamberlin, T. C. 1897. "The Method of Multiple Working Hypotheses." *Journal of Geology*, 5, 837-848.

Chorley, R. J., Beckinsdale, R. P., and Dunn, A. J. 1973. *The History of the Study of Landforms or the Development of Geomorphology: Volume 2: The Life and Work of William Morris Davis*. Routledge, New York, 874.

Cooper, C.L. 2001. *"Using Geographic Information Systems (GIS) to Investigate the Paleo-Drainage of the Lower Smoky Hill River, Central Kansas."* Masters' Thesis, Emporia State University, 69.

Crandell, D.R. 1958. *Geology of the Pierre area, South Dakota*. United States Geological Survey Professional Paper 307, 83. https://doi.org/10.3133/pp307.

Davis, W.M. 1889a. "A River Pirate." *Science*, 13, 108–9. https://doi.org/10.1126/science.ns-13.314.108.

Davis, W.M. 1889b. "The rivers and valleys of Pennsylvania." *National Geographic Magazine*, 1, 183–253.

Denson, N.M. and Gill, J. R. 1965. *Uranium-bearing lignite and carbonaceous shale in the southwestern part of the Williston Basin–a regional study.* United States Geological Survey Professional Paper 463. 75. http://dx.doi.org/10.3133/pp463

Ellis, A.J. and Meinzer, O. E. 1924. *Ground water in Musselshell and Golden Valley Counties, Montana.* United States Geological Survey Water Supply Paper 518, 92.

Fenneman, N.M. 1931. *Physiography of the Western United States.* McGraw-Hill Book Company, New York, 534.

Flint, R.F. 1955. *Pleistocene geology of eastern South Dakota.* United States Geological Survey Professional Paper 262, 173. https://doi.org/10.3133/pp262.

Gill, J. R., 1962, Tertiary landslides, northwestern South Dakota and southeast Montana: *Geological Society of America Bulletin,* 73, 725-735. http://dx.doi.org/10.1130/0016-7606(1962)73[725:tlnsda]2.0.co;2

Hayes, C. W. and Campbell, M. R. 1894. "The geomorphology of the southern Appalachians." *National Geographic Magazine,* 6, 63–126.

Hennen, R.V. and Reger, D.B. 1914. *Preston County.* West Virginia Geological Survey, 684.

Hunt, C.B. 1956. *Cenozoic Geology of the Colorado Plateau.* United States Geological Survey Professional Paper 279: 99. https://doi.org/10.3133/pp279.

Jackson, L. 2018. "The Paleo-Bell River: North America's vanished Amazon." *Earth,* 63 (7 and 8), 74–81.

Johnson, D.W. 1905. "The Tertiary history of the Tennessee River." *Journal of Geology,* 13 (3), 194–231. https://doi.org/10.1086/621220.

Johnson, D.W. 1931. *Stream sculpture on the Atlantic Slope.* Columbia University Press. 142.

Kehew, A.E. 1979. Evidence for Late Wisconsin catastrophic flooding in the Souris River area, north central North Dakota. *Proceeding, North Dakota Academy of Science,* 33, 32.

Kucera, R.E. (1962) *Geology of the Yampa District, northwest Colorado.* PhD dissertation, University of Colorado, Boulder, 675.

Kuhn, T. S. 1970. *The Structure of Scientific Revolutions; Second Edition, Enlarged.* The University of Chicago Press, 210.

Lee, J. 2013. "A survey of transverse drainages in the Susquehanna River basin, Pennsylvania." *Geomorphology,* 186, 50–67. https://doi.org/10.1016/j.geomorph.2012.12.022.

Lemke, R.W. 1960, *Geology of the Souris River area, North Dakota.* United States Geological Survey Professional Paper 325. Washington, DC, 138. http://dx.doi.org/10.3133/pp325

Leonard, A.G. 1912. *Bismarck Folio, North Dakota.* United States Geologic Atlas of the United States, 8.

Lillegraven, J.A. 1970. Stratigraphy, structure, and vertebrate fossils of the Oligocene Brule Formation, Slim Buttes, northwestern South Dakota. *Geological Society of America Bulletin*, 81, 831-850. http://dx.doi.org/10.1130/0016-7606(1970)81[831:ssavfo]2.0.co;2

Love, J.D. 1970. *Cenozoic Geology of the Granite Mountains Area, Central Wyoming.* United States Geological Survey Professional Paper 495-C, 154. https://doi.org/10.3133/pp495C.

Malhotra, C.L. and Teglund, E.R. 1959, A new Tertiary formation in Harding County, South Dakota. *South Dakota Academy of Sciences Proceedings*, 38, 263-274.

Odom, W.E. and Granger, D.E. 2022. "The Pliocene-to-Present Course of the Tennessee River." *Journal of Geology*, 130 (4), 325–333. https://doi.org/10.1086/719951.

Osterkamp, W.R. and Higgins, C.G. 1990. "Seepage-induced cliff recession and regional denudation." In *Groundwater geomorphology: The role of subsurface water in Earth-surface processes and landforms* edited by C. G. Higgins and D. B Coates. Geological Society of America Special Paper 252: 291–308. https://doi.org/10.1130/SPE252-p291

Pelletier, J.D. 2009. "The impact of snowmelt on the late Cenozoic landscape of the southern Rocky Mountains, USA." *GSA Today*, 19 (7), 4–11. https://doi.org/10.1130/GSATG44A.1.

Rapp, J.R., Visher, F. N. and Littleton, R. T. 1957. "Geology and Water Resources of Goshen County Wyoming." United States Geological Survey Water Supply Paper No. 1377, 17–18.

Russell, W.L. 1929. "Drainage alignment in the western Great Plains." *Journal of Geology*, 37, 249–255. https://doi.org/10.1086/623618.

Sears, J.W. 2013. "Late Oligocene-early Miocene Grand Canyon: A Canadian connection?" *GSA Today*, 23, 4–10. https://doi.org/10.1130/GSATG178A.1

Sears, J. W. and Beranek, L. P. 2022. "The great preglacial 'Bell River' of North America: detrital zircon evidence for Oligocene-Miocene fluvial connections between the Colorado Plateau and Labrador Sea." *Geoscience Canada*, 49 (1), 29–42. https://doi.org/10.12789/geocanj.2022.49.184.

Staisch, L.M., O'Connor, J. E., Cannon, C. H., Holm-Denoma, C., Link, P. K., Lasher, J., and Alexander, J. A. 2022. "Major reorganization of the Snake River modulated by passage of the Yellowstone Hotspot." *Geological Society of America Bulletin*, 134 (7/8), 1834–1844. https://doi.org/10.1130/B36174.1.

Stamm, J.F., Hendricks, R. R., Sawyer, J. F., Mahan, S. A., Zaprowski, B. J., Geibel, N. M., and Azzolimi, D. C. 2013. "Late Quaternary stream piracy and strath terrace formation along the Belle Fourche and lower Cheyenne Rivers, South Dakota and Wyoming." *Geomorphology*, 197, 10–20. https://doi.org/10.1016/j.geomorph.2013.03.028.

Steidtmann, J.R., Middleton, L.T. and Shuster, M. W. 1989. "Post-Laramide (Oligocene) Uplift in the Wind River Range, Wyoming." *Geology*, 17, 38–41. https://doi.org/10.1130/0091-7613(1989)017<0038:PLOUIT>2.3.CO;2

Stone, R.W. 1905. *Waynesburg folio, Pennsylvania*. Geological Atlas of the United States Folio, United States Geological Survey, GF-121.

Strahler, A.N. 1945. "Hypotheses of stream development in the folded Appalachians of Pennsylvania." *Geological Society of America Bulletin*, 56, 45–88. https://doi.org/10.1130/0016-7606(1945)56[45:hosdit2.0.co;2

Strahler, A.N. 1952. "Dynamic basis of geomorphology." *Bulletin of the Geological Society of America*, 63, 923–938. https://doi.org/10.1130/0016-7606(1952)63[923:dbog]2.0.co;2.

Sugden, D.E. 1976. "A case against deep erosion of shields by continental ice sheets." *Geology*, 4, 580–582. https://doi.org/10.1130/0091-7613(1976)4<580:ACADEO>2.0.CO;2 .

Suneson, N.H. 2020. *Roadside Geology of Oklahoma*. Mountain Press Publishing Company, Missoula, Montana, 385.

Thornbury, W.D. 1965. *Regional Geomorphology of the United States*. John Wiley and Sons, 609.

Thornbury, W.D. 1969. *Principles of Geomorphology, second edition*. John Wiley and Sons, 594.

Tight, W.G. 1903. *Drainage modifications in southeastern Ohio and adjacent parts of West Virginia and Kentucky*. United State Geological Survey Professional Paper 13, 111. https://doi.org/10.3133/pp13.

Toepelman, W.C. 1925. *The geology of a portion of the Slim Buttes region of northwestern South Dakota, with special; reference to unusual structural features due to slumping*. Unpublished PhD dissertation, University of Chicago.

Ward, R.D. 1892. Another River Pirate. *Science*, 19, 7-9. https://doi.org/10.1126/science.ns-19.465.7

White, W. A. 1972. "Deep erosion by continental ice sheets." *Geological Society America Bulletin*, 83, 1037–1056. https://doi.org/10.1130/0016-7606(1972)83[1037:DEBCIS]2.0.CO;2.

Publications Pertinent to the Author's Search for a Topographic Map Mystery Solution

The following is a complete list of the author's published papers and abstracts pertinent to his efforts to solve the topographic map mystery and then to promote the solution (unrelated publications and abstracts are not included). Links to open-access papers are provided. [In addition, more than 650 research notes in a blog format, which were written when developing the new paradigm can be accessed at the time of this book's publication at https://geomorphologyresearch.com and at https://phillylandforms.info]

Clausen, E., 1980, Origin of the Missouri Escarpment: *Proceedings of the North Dakota Academy of Science*, 34, 37.

Clausen, E., 1981a, Evolution of western North Dakota's regional slope and drainage network: *Proceedings of the North Dakota Academy of Science*, 35, 9.

Clausen, E., 1981b, Deep glacial erosion in the northern plains region of North America (abstract): *Program of the 1981 Annual Meeting of the American Association for the Advancement of Science.*

Clausen, E., 1981c, Deep glacial erosion in the northern Great Plains (abstract): *Abstracts with Programs, Geological Society of America, Rocky Mountain Section,* 193.

Clausen, E, 1982, Evidence for glaciation in southwestern North Dakota and northwestern South Dakota: *Proceedings of the North Dakota Academy of Science*, 36, 16.

Clausen, E., 1983, Jokullhlaups on the Great Plains: A study in deductive reasoning: *Proceedings of the North Dakota Academy of Science*, 37, 62.

Clausen, E., 1985, Significance of free-standing glacial erratics south and west of the Missouri River, North and South Dakota. *Proceedings of the North Dakota Academy of Science*, 39, 46.

Clausen, E., 1986a, Geomorphic history of southwest North Dakota: *Proceedings of the North Dakota Academy of Science*, 40, 16.

Clausen, E., 1986b, Origin of basal conglomerate in Chadron Formation, Southwestern North Dakota (abstract): *Program of the 1986 Annual Meeting of the American Association for the Advancement of Science.*

Clausen, E.,1986c, Origin of quartz latite porphyry cobbles found at base of White River Group Sediments in southwest North Dakota: in *Tertiary and Upper Cretaceous of South-Central and Western North Dakota:* 1986 Field Trip, North Dakota Geological Society, eds, Clausen, E., and Kihm, A., 41-45.

Clausen, E., 1986d, Free-standing glacial erratics and Quaternary and upper Tertiary sediments, undivided in southwest North Dakota: in *Tertiary and Upper Cretaceous of South-Central and Western North Dakota:* 1986 Field Trip, North Dakota Geological Society, eds, Clausen, E., and Kihm, A., 46-47.

Clausen, E., 1986e, Physiography of the Souris River Lowland: Origin of the Souris River Lowland: *Bulletin of the Association of North Dakota Geographers,* 36 (2), 51-58.

Clausen, E., 1987a, The case for Yellowstone River diversions across the Dakotas: *Proceedings of the North Dakota Academy of Science,* 41, 63.

Clausen, E., 1987b, Evidence for possible abandoned Yellowstone River channels in North and South Dakota (abstract): *Abstracts with Programs, 21st Annual Meeting, North-Central Section, Geological Society of America,* 193.

Clausen, E., 1987c, Late Cenozoic erosion of Williston Basin sediments: in Carlson, C.G. and Christopher, eds, *Fifth International Williston Basin Symposium:* Saskatchewan Geological Society, Special Publication Number 9, Regina, 190-195.

Clausen, E., 1987d, Record of possible diversions of the Yellowstone River across the Dakotas, North America (abstract): *XII International Congress, International Union for Quaternary Research, Programme with Abstracts,* 145.

Clausen, E., 1987e, Catastrophic flood model for deep Pleistocene erosion of northern Great Plains, North America (abstract): *Abstracts with Programs, 1987 Annual Meeting (Phoenix), Geological Society of America,* 620-621.

Clausen, E., 1988a, Age of White River Group, Southwest North Dakota, determined by Yellowstone River incision rates: *Proceedings of the North Dakota Academy of Science,* 42, 31.

Clausen, E., 1988b, Topographic map evidence for catastrophic flooding: Missouri River Basin, Montana and North Dakota: *Proceedings of the North Dakota Academy of Science,* 42, 33.

Clausen, E., 1988c, Catastrophic flood origin for eastern Montana landforms: *Abstracts with Programs, 41st Annual Meeting, Rocky Mountain Section, The Geological Society of America, 410.*

Clausen, E., 1989a, Meltwater flood origin for Great Plains drainage network: *Proceedings of the North Dakota Academy of Science,* 43, 40.

Clausen, E., 1989b, Origin of the Killdeer Mountain Lake basin, Dunn County, North Dakota: *Proceedings of the North Dakota Academy of Science,* 43, 41.

Clausen, E., 1989c, Presence of rounded boulders and large cobbles at base of White River Group (Oligocene) strata in southwest North Dakota and northwest South Dakota: *Contributions to Geology, University of Wyoming,* 27(1), 1-6.

Clausen, E., 1990, Northern Great Plains geomorphic history as determined from asymmetric drainage divides: *Proceedings of the North Dakota Academy of Science,* 44, 55.

Clausen, E., 1992, Topographic map analysis of landforms east of the Black Hills, South Dakota: *Proceedings of the North Dakota Academy of Science*, 46, 82.

Clausen, E., 1993, Evolution of drainage networks: western United States: *Proceedings of the North Dakota Academy of Science*, 47, 51.

Clausen, E., 1994a, North American landforms explained by multiple-step deglaciation: *North Dakota Academy of Science Proceedings*, 48, 79.

Clausen, E., 1994b, Meltwater origin for North Dakota's most recent ice sheets: *North Dakota Academy of Science Proceedings*, 48, 82.

Clausen, E., 1994c, North American glacial history as determined by use of topographic map and drainage network interpretation: abstract of a poster paper presented at the American Quaternary Association national meeting.

Clausen, E., 1996, Physiographic Provinces of North America's Central Region: *Proceedings of the North Dakota Academy of Science*, 50, 37.

Clausen, E., 1997a, Origin and age of southeast Alberta, southwest Saskatchewan, and Northeast Montana high-level alluvial deposits: *Proceedings of the North Dakota Academy of Science*, 51, 186.

Clausen, E. 1997b, Origin and age of eastern Montana and western North Dakota high-level alluvium: *Proceedings of the North Dakota Academy of Science*, 51, 187.

Clausen, E., 1998a, Evolution of southwest North Dakota's drainage network: *Proceedings of the North Dakota Academy of Science*, 52, 38.

Clausen, E., 1998b, North Dakota and other "glacial" lakes explained as slack water lakes: *Proceedings of the North Dakota Academy of Science*, 52, 39.

Clausen, E., 2012, Evidence of tectonic activity associated with continental ice sheets and meltwater erosion: *New Concepts in Global Tectonics Newsletter*, 63, 87-93.

Clausen, E., 2013, Origin of Allegheny, Genesee, and Susquehanna River drainage basins, poster paper abstract published in the Pennsylvania Geographical Society 2013 Annual Meeting Program.

Clausen, E., 2015a, Unraveling the Chester Valley drainage history, abstract of a presentation published in the Pennsylvania Geographical Society 2015 Annual Meeting Program.

Clausen, E., 2015b, Exploring the Geography of William Morris Davis' Pennsylvania roots: *The Pennsylvania Geographer*, 53 (1), 44-65.

Clausen, E. 2016a. "Origin of three north oriented Montgomery County water gaps." *The Pennsylvania Geographer*, 54 (2), 42–61.

Clausen, E. 2016b. "Using topographic map interpretation methods to determine Tookany (Tacony) Creek erosion history upstream from Philadelphia, PA, USA." *Journal of Geography and Geology*, 8 (4), 30–45. https://doi.org/10.5539/jgg.v8n4p30.

Clausen, E. 2017a. "Erosional history of Pennypack Creek drainage basin determined by topographic map interpretation techniques, Bucks, Montgomery, and Philadelphia Counties, PA, USA." *Journal of Geography and Geology*, 9 (1), 37–52. https://doi.org/10.5539/jgg.v9n1p37.

Clausen, E. 2017b. "Wissahickon Creek drainage basin origin as determined by topographic map interpretation." *Middle States Geographer*, 49, 33–42. https://middlestates.wpenginepowered.com/wp-content/uploads/2017/08/5-Clausen-MSG492016F.pdf.

Clausen, E. 2017c. Origin of erosional landforms along and near the Schuylkill River-East Branch Brandywine Creek drainage divide segment of the Schuylkill River-Delaware River drainage divide, Chester County, PA. in Bosbyshell, H., editor, The Piedmont: Old Rocks, New Understandings. *2017 Conference Proceedings for the 34th Annual Meeting of the Geological Association of New Jersey*, 2–15.

Clausen, E. 2017d. "Solving a perplexing Scenic and Sage Creek Basin drainage history problem, Pennington County, South Dakota, USA." *Journal of Geography and Geology*, 9 (2), 1–10. http://www.ccsenet.org/journal/index.php/jgg/article/view/68264.

Clausen, E. 2017e. "Using map interpretation techniques for relative dating to determine a western North Dakota and South Dakota drainage basin formation sequence, Missouri River drainage basin USA." *Journal of Geography and Geology*, 9 (4), 1–18. http://www.ccsenet.org/journal/index.php/jgg/article/view/70833.

Clausen, E. 2017f. "Origin of Little Missouri River-South Fork Grand River and nearby drainage divides in Harding County, South Dakota and adjacent Eastern Montana, USA." *Open Journal of Geology*, 7, 1063–1077. https://file.scirp.org/pdf/OJG_2017080415164872.pdf.

Clausen, E. 2017g. "Origin of mountain passes across Continental Divide segments surrounding the southwest Montana Big Hole and Beaverhead River drainage basins, USA." *Open Journal of Geology*, 7, 1362-1385. https://file.scirp.org/pdf/OJG_2017091815475553.pdf.

Clausen, E. 2017h. "Analysis of mountain passes along the east-west Continental Divide and other drainage divides surrounding the Boulder River drainage basin, Jefferson County, Montana, USA." *Open Journal of Geology*, 7, 1603–1624. https://file.scirp.org/pdf/OJG_2017112211024000.pdf.

Clausen, E. 2017i. "Understanding lower Neshaminy Creek direction change and barbed tributary evidence, Bucks County, Pennsylvania, USA." *Journal of Geography and Earth Science*, 5 (2), 1–15. http://jgesnet.com/journals/jges/Vol_5_No_2_December_2017/1.pdf.

Clausen, E. 2018a. "Topographic map analysis of high elevation Black Hills through valleys linking Spearfish and Rapid Creek headwaters valleys, Lawrence County, South Dakota, USA." *Journal of Geography and Geology*, 10 (1), 8–21. http://www.ccsenet.org/journal/index.php/jgg/article/view/72098.

Clausen, E. 2018b. "Topographic map analysis of Laramie Range bedrock-walled canyon complex and the Goshen Hole escarpment-surrounded basin, Albany and Platte Counties, southeast Wyoming, USA." *Open Journal of Geology*, 8 (1), 33–55. https://file.scirp.org/pdf/OJG_2018011514451172.pdf.

Clausen, E. 2018c "Belle Fourche River-Cheyenne River drainage divide area in the Wyoming Powder River Basin analyzed by topographic map interpretation methods, USA." *Journal of Geography and Geology*, 10 (2), 1–16. http://www.ccsenet.org/journal/index.php/jgg/article/view/73048.

Clausen, E. 2018d. "Probable deep erosion by continental ice sheet melt water floods: Chalk Buttes area of Carter County, Montana, USA." *International Journal of Geography and Geology, Consientia Beam*, 7 (1), 14–26. http://www.conscientiabeam.com/pdf-files/ene/10/IJGG-2018-7(1)-14-26.pdf.

Clausen, E. 2018e. "Topographic map interpretation of the Neshaminy-Perkiomen Creek drainage divide segment of the Delaware-Schuylkill River drainage divide, Bucks County, Pennsylvania. *The Pennsylvania Geographer*, 56 (1), 15–29.

Clausen, E. 2018f "Interpreting topographic map evidence related to northeast Nebraska barbed tributaries and drainage routes, USA." *Journal of Geography and Geology*, 10 (2), 66–79. http://www.ccsenet.org/journal/index.php/jgg/article/view/75258.

Clausen, E. 2018g. "Deep erosion by continental ice sheets: a northern Missouri River drainage basin perspective: North America." *Current Research in Geoscience*, 8, 27–38. https://thescipub.com/pdf/10.3844/ajgsp.2018.27.38.

Clausen, E. 2018h. "Geomorphic history of the Beaver Creek drainage basin as determined from topographic map evidence: eastern Montana and western North Dakota, USA." *Journal of Geography and Geology*, 10 (3), 79–91. http://www.ccsenet.org/journal/index.php/jgg/article/view/76842.

Clausen, E. 2019a. "Origin of the Redwater River drainage basin determined by topographic map interpretation: eastern Montana, USA." *Journal of Geography and Geology*, 11 (1), 42–54. http://www.ccsenet.org/journal/index.php/jgg/article/view/0/38586.

Clausen, E. 2019b. "Upper Sun River drainage basin origin determined by topographic map interpretation techniques, Lewis and Clark and Teton Counties, Montana, USA." *Open Journal of Geology*, 9 (5), 257–277. https://www.scirp.org/journal/paperinformation.aspx?paperid=92358.

Clausen, E. 2019c. "Use of Wyoming southern Bighorn Mountains topographic map evidence to test a recently proposed regional geomorphology paradigm." *Journal of Geography and Geology*, 11 (3), 1–14. http://www.ccsenet.org/journal/index.php/jgg/article/view/0/40923.

Clausen, E. 2019d. "Use of topographic map evidence to test a recently proposed regional geomorphology paradigm: Wind River-Sweetwater River drainage divide area, central Wyoming, USA." *Open Journal of Geology*, 9 (8), 404–423. https://www.scirp.org/journal/paperinformatio-n.aspx?paperid=94332.

Clausen, E. 2019e. "Topographic map interpretation of Bighorn River-Wind River drainage divide located east of Wyoming's Wind River Canyon, USA." *Universal Journal of Geoscience*, 7 (2), 56–67. http://www.hrpub.org/download/20190630/UJG2-13913277.pdf.

Clausen, E. 2019f. "How a fundamentally different and new glacial history paradigm explains North America's glaciated prairie region erosional escarpments and drainage patterns." *Earth Science Research*, 8 (2), 23–34. http://www.ccsenet.org/journal/index.php/esr/article/view/0/40147.

Clausen, E. 2019g. "Use of stream and dismembered stream valleys now crossing Wyoming's northern Laramie Mountains to test a recently proposed regional geomorphology paradigm, USA." *Open Journal of Geology*, 11, 731–751. https://www.scirp.org/journal/paperinformation.aspx?paperid=95527

Clausen, E. 2020a. "Use of detailed topographic map evidence of southeast Wyoming Gangplank area to compare two fundamentally different geomorphology paradigms, USA." *Open Journal of Geology*, 10 (4), 261–279. https://www.scirp.org/journal/paperinformation.aspx?paperid=99330.

Clausen, E. 2020b. "Topographic map analysis of mountain passes crossing the continental divide between Colorado River headwaters and North and South Platte River headwaters to test a new geomorphology paradigm, Colorado, USA." *Journal of Geography and Geology*, 12 (1), 50–64. http://www.ccsenet.org/journal/index.php/jgg/article/view/0/42663.

Clausen, E. 2020c. "Use of topographic map evidence from drainage divides surrounding Wyoming's Great Divide Basin to compare two fundamentally different regional geomorphology paradigms." *Earth Science Research*, 9 (1), 45–57. http://www.ccsenet.org/journal/index.php/esr/article/view/0/41802.

Clausen, E. 2020d. "Analysis of Medicine Bow-Laramie River drainage divide using topographic map interpretation techniques, southeastern Wyoming, USA." *Open Journal of Geology*, 10, 741–759. https://www.scirp.org/journal/paperinformation.aspx?paperid=101766.

Clausen, E. 2020e. "North Platte River-South Platte River confluence area drainage system history as determined by topographic map interpretation: western Nebraska, USA." *Journal of Geography and Geology*, 12 (2), 28–39. http://www.ccsenet.org/journal/index.php/jgg/article/view/0/43638.

Clausen, E. 2020f. "Analyzing anomalous topographic map drainage system and landform evidence as a glacial history paradigm problem: a literature review." *Open Journal of Geology*, 10 (11): 1072–1090. https://www.scirp.org/pdf/ojg_2020112614183110.pdf.

Clausen, E. (2021a) Topographic map analysis of the North Platte River-South Platte River drainage divide area, western Larimer County, Colorado, USA. *Earth Science Research*, 10 (1), 49–60. **DOI:** 10.5539/esr.v10n1p49

Clausen, E. 2021b. "How two different Cenozoic geologic and glacial history paradigms explain the southcentral Montana Musselshell-Yellowstone River drainage divide origin, USA. *Earth Science Research*, 10 (2), 42–53. **DOI:** 10.5539/esr.v10n2p42

Clausen, E. 2021c. "Yampa River-Colorado River drainage divide origin determined from topographic map evidence, southern Routt County, Colorado, US." *Open Journal of Geology*, 11, 319–339. https://www.scirp.org/journal/paperinformation.aspx?paperid=111183.

Clausen, E. 2021d. "How a new geology and glacial paradigm explains Colorado South Platte-Arkansas River drainage divide topographic map evidence, USA." *Open Journal of Geology*, 11, 573–595. https://www.scirp.org/pdf/ojg_2021110913574134.pdf.

Clausen, E. 2021e. "How a new paradigm explains topographic map drainage system and erosional landform evidence in the Fremont County Royal Gorge area, Colorado, USA." *Journal of Geography and Geology*, 13 (2), 32–46. https://ccsenet.org/journal/index.php/jgg/article/view/0/46407.

Clausen, E. 2021f. "Topographic map interpretation techniques used to determine Casselman River drainage basin history, Maryland and Pennsylvania: a new paradigm demonstration paper." *The Pennsylvania Geographer*, 59 (1), 33–56.

Clausen, E. 2021g. "What caused the geology discipline's channeled scablands controversy?" *Academia Letters*, Article 3465. https://doi.org/qo.20935/AL3465.

Clausen, E. 2022a. "Use of topographic map evidence to locate a new Cenozoic glacial history paradigm's deep 'hole' rim in northeast New Mexico and Southern Colorado, USA." *Journal of Geography and Geology*, 14 (1), 28–42. https://doi.org/10.5539/jgg.v14n1p28

Clausen, E. 2022b. "How a new Cenozoic geology and glacial history paradigm explains Arkansas-Red River drainage divide area topographic map evidence in and near Pontotoc County, Oklahoma, USA." *Open Journal of Geology*, 12, 313–332. https://doi.org/10.4236/ojg.2022.124017.

Clausen, E. 2022c. "How a new Cenozoic geology and glacial history paradigm explains anomalous Monongahela River drainage basin topographic map evidence, PA, WV and MD, USA." *Earth Science Research*, 11 (1), 47–63. https://doi.org/10.5539/esr.v11n1p47.

Clausen, E. 2022d. "How a new Cenozoic geology and glacial history paradigm explains topographic map drainage system and erosional landform evidence: Elbert and Lincoln Counties, Colorado, USA." *Open Journal of Geology*, 12, 663–684. https://doi.org/10.4236/org.2022.129031.

Clausen, E. 2022e. "How a new glacial history paradigm explains northeast Alabama's Tennessee River-Gulf of Mexico drainage divide area topographic map evidence." *Journal of Geography and Geology*, 14 (2): 38–51. https://doi.org/10.5539/jgg.v14n2p38.

Clausen, E., 2023a, Using a new Cenozoic geology and glacial history paradigm to explain Saline-Smoky Hill River drainage divide area topographic map evidence. *Earth Science Research*, 12, 1-15. https://ccsenet.org/journal/index.php/esr

Clausen, E., 2023b, William Morris Davis, father of geomorphology or father of geology's unrecognized paradigm problem. *Open Journal of Geology*, 13, 579-597. https://doi.org/10.4236/ojg.2023.136025

Clausen, E., 2023c, Use of French Broad River drainage basin topographic map evidence upstream from Asheville, North Carolina to test a new geology and glacial history paradigm, USA. *Journal of Geology and Geology*, 15 (2), 1-15. https://doi.org/10.5539/jgg.v15n2p1

Clausen, E., 2023d, Use of the 1893 Cranberry, North Carolina topographic map to determine Blue Ridge Escarpment area drainage system and erosional landform origins, USA. *Open Journal of Geology*, 13 (11), 1220-1239. https://doi.org/10.4236/ojg.2023.1311052

Clausen, E., 2024a, Eastern Continental Divide origin in the Blacksburg, Virginia area determined by topographic map interpretation, USA. *Journal of Geography and Geology,* 16 (1), 1-15. https//doi.org/10.5539/jgg.v16n1p1

Clausen, E. 2024b. Yellowstone region drainage history as determined from the 1955 Ashton, Idaho, Montana, and Wyoming 1:250,000 scale topographic map. *Open Journal of Geology,* 14 (3), 317-338. 10.4236/ojg.2024.143017

Clausen, E, 2024c. Geomorphic history determined by a new glacial history paradigm and topographic map interpretation, Towanda Creek drainage basin, PA (USA). *Journal of Geography and Geology,* 16 (2), 1-15. https://doi.org/10.5539/jgg.v16n2p1

Clausen, E., 2024d. Using a new glacial history paradigm and Bald Eagle through valley topographic map evidence to determine central Pennsylvania geomorphic history, USA. *Open Journal of Geology,* 14, 880-899. https://doi.org10.4236/ojg.2024.149038

INDEX

U

V

W

Y